ALPHA BRAVO DELTA
GUIDE TO
THE U.S. AIR FORCE

BARRETT TILLMAN

SERIES EDITOR
WALTER J. BOYNE, USAF (RET.)

ALPHA

A member of Penguin Group (USA) Inc.

This book is dedicated to John and Matt Anderson, the sons and grandsons of Air Force officers.

CONTENTS

FOREWORD

Looking for a great summary of nearly a century of U.S. Air Force history and heritage? If so, grab a cup of coffee and settle into an easy chair with the *Alpha Bravo Delta Guide to the U.S. Air Force*.

The book is packed with vignettes of Air Force people and aircraft. Interspersed are tales of daring feats that pushed the state of the art from the Wright Brothers first feeble efforts on Kill Devil Hill through the hypersonic flights of the X-15. The Guide chronicles how the Air Force has built upon such successes—and upon our share of deadly, hard-earned lessons—to produce today's formidable aerospace forces that can bring swift-and-decisive war to our nation's enemies anywhere on the face of the earth.

The author skillfully blends in statistics among the stories of aerial adventure. You, too, may find the account disconcerting in that the nation bought combat aircraft by the tens of thousands during World War II, and now we buy some highly advanced—and extremely expensive—models in the tens, or the low hundreds at best. You may be haunted by tales of deadly days when we lost airplanes by the scores and airmen by the hundreds. You'll learn that in the spring and summer of 1944, the Army Air Force was losing 1,000 to 1,500 aircraft per month in the war against Germany.

Alpha Bravo Delta Guide to the U.S. Air Force includes stories of brave men you'll recognize as being memorialized in the names of Air Force bases throughout the country. The author selected interesting tidbits to include in the many descriptions of the aircraft upon which the U.S. Air Force built the heritage proudly shared by those of us who served and by those on active duty today.

This well-researched book has a flavor of stories exchanged among airmen on long overwater flights or sitting alert or in bull sessions at a stag bar. I've always enjoyed first-person accounts. Some stories provide incredible insights from those who were out at the tip of the sword.

Air Force ace and legend General Robin Olds—who flew against more than his share of surface-to-air missiles—said, "The truth is you never do get used to the SAMs. I had about 250 shot at me and the last one was as inspiring as the first."

In just a few words, an unnamed SR-71 pilot gave me a new perspective about flying at the edge of space: "You've never been lost until you've been lost at Mach 3!"

Among the revelations that caused me to laugh out loud was the report of a sign posted at an officer's club bar in England during World War II: "Lieutenant colonels under 21 must be accompanied by a parent or guardian."

Alpha Bravo Delta Guide to the U.S. Air Force is a book for military professionals and for those who remember pressing against fences as kids to watch aircraft thunder from the runways beyond. I found the book to be a great refresher. Even with 28 years as a USAF Academy cadet and career officer, I learned any number of fascinating facts and details.

Colonel Jimmie Butler, USAF (Ret.), and author of *A Certain Brotherhood*

INTRODUCTION

Neatly lettered above ready-room doors or scrawled in officer's club bars, the unofficial motto has been the same: "The mission of the United States Air Force is to fly and fight. And don't you forget it."

The sentiment might seem obvious: If the Air Force has another mission, what would it be? However, there is much, much more to military aviation than flying and fighting. After all, wars and rumors of wars have been with us for millennia, as testified in Scripture. But the actual work of the U.S. Air Force is perennial, unending. That mission is to be prepared to fight anywhere on the planet, often on short notice. That means maintaining a constant supply of well-trained aircrews and maintenance personnel at such a state of readiness that a potential aggressor will think twice (or thrice) before launching an attack. It hasn't always worked that way—witness Pearl Harbor and the wars in Iraq and Afghanistan. Military readiness is one thing; political willpower is another.

However, wars are best won by deterrence, and no better example exists than the half-century Cold War, enforced in large part by the bombers and missiles of the Strategic Air Command. The third leg of the "nuclear triad" was the U.S. Navy's missile-carrying submarines. Among them, they kept a brittle, often uneasy peace to manageable levels while avoiding a global catastrophe. In the meantime, a succession of lesser "conflicts" occupied two generations of Air Force officers and enlisted personnel.

If this brief history of the U.S. Air Force accomplishes one thing, I hope that it will demonstrate that airmen are vastly more important than airplanes. Aviation—especially military aviation—is the most glamorous part of the national defense establishment. It is the most visible, the most reported, and the most responsive. The hardware is enchanting: fabulous machines that grasp the imagination and keep recruiting officers occupied. But for every pilot or navigator there are dozens of support personnel: mechanics, technicians, meteorologists, planners, cooks, and truck drivers. It's their Air Force, too.

And dear reader, it is yours as well.

ACKNOWLEDGMENTS

Thanks to Marty Greenberg (again) for getting me involved in another interesting project. Dipping my oar in strange waters (for a life member of the Tailhook Association) was made easier by Dr. Richard Hallion and Dr. Wayne Thompson; and Major John Beaulieu of the Air Force History Office. Others who lent aid were Terry Aitken of the Air Force Museum, USAF Academy archivist Duane Reed, and Robert F. Dorr.

First-person assistance came from several colleagues, including Major Bill Allen and Colonels Bud Anderson and Walter Boyne. Lieutenant Colonel Dick Jonas of Erosonic contributed lyrics from his days as a poor but honest Phantom pilot.

Eric Caubarreaux provided Internet research assistance, and John Tillman answered every question put to him, from cruise missile technology to the German language.

CHAPTER 1

MEET THE U.S. AIR FORCE

The vision statement of the U.S. Air Force (USAF) is succinct: "Global vigilance, reach, and power." The mission statement is not much longer: "To defend the United States and protect its interests through aerospace power."

In the year 2000, the vision was met and the mission was performed by 355,654 active-duty personnel plus 244,500 in the Guard and Reserve in addition to 161,000 civilian employees. The Air Force owned some 6,200 aircraft of all types: supersonic fighters, stealth bombers, attack aircraft, air tankers, transports, command and control aircraft, helicopters, trainers, and liaison and observation planes. As of 2000, there were some 65 Air Force bases in 37 states plus 15 more in 8 foreign countries. Air National Guard and Air Force Reserve units account for many other USAF facilities, in addition to "tenant" rights at foreign air bases.

As the millennium turned over, the Air Force was composed of nine major organizations: Air Combat Command, Air Mobility Command, Special Operations Command, Pacific Air Force, Air Forces Europe, Education and Training Command, Materiel Command, Reserve Command, and Space Command. During the Cold War, what became Air Combat Command was composed of the Strategic Air Command and Tactical Air Command, the former with long-range bombers, the latter with fighters and attack aircraft.

"That's good sport, but for the army the airplane is of no use."
—French General Ferdinand Foch, 1910

The Department of the Air Force is run by a civilian secretary, a political appointee who reports to the Secretary of Defense, a presidential Cabinet member. The service's senior uniformed officer is a four-star general, the Air Force chief of staff, who presides over the Air Staff, which guides personnel, plans and programs, air and space operations, logistics, etc. There are also separate offices in the chain of command including those responsible for intelligence and scientific programs.

To produce a continuing supply of professional officers, the Air Force Academy (AFA) at Colorado Springs graduated its first class in 1959. Previously, Air Force officers were products of Reserve Officers Training Courses (ROTC) at civilian colleges or interservice transfers from the Army or Navy. Today, recruiting and training is conducted by Air Education and Training Command (AETC) headquartered at Randolph Air Force Base, Texas.

"THE FIRST COMMAND"

AETC rightly considers itself "The First Command," noting that future aerospace dominance begins with the raw human material for officers and enlisted personnel. Toward that end, the command has 62,000 military and civilian men and women plus about 1,600 aircraft. Some 1,400 recruiters work throughout the United States, Puerto Rico, Japan, and Guam to acquire an average of about 36,000 recruits per year.

Flight training begins with civilian instructors who guide prospective Air Force pilots through a 50-hour course ending with a private pilot's license. Depending upon the needs of the service, those who complete the initial course then progress to joint jet pilot training or special undergraduate training, flying a variety of aircraft. Since the end of the Cold War, military flight training has tended toward multiservice, multination programs to enhance efficiency and reduce costs. Thus, an Air Force officer may fly with a foreign instructor at a U.S. Army or Navy base such as Ft. Rucker, Alabama, or Pensacola, Florida. The usual training planes are the Cessna T-37 "Tweet," the supersonic Northrop T-38 Talon, the Navy's turboprop Beech T-34 Mentor, and the newer Raytheon-Beech T-6 Texan II.

Navigator training is conducted at Randolph AFB and NAS (Naval Air Station), Pensacola, Florida, with instruction in T-43 trainers leading to assignments in C-130s, KC-135s, or other transport or refueling aircraft.

Continuing education is a hallmark of an Air Force career. Professional development is provided at such facilities as the Air University at Maxwell AFB, Alabama; the Air Command and Staff College (majors slated for squadron command and higher); and the Air War College, which stresses joint operations with other U.S. and friendly services. There are also courses for noncommissioned officers and technical specialists.

GUARD AND RESERVE

The Air National Guard traces its history to the 1920s, as Army National Guardsmen flew border patrols and searched out forest fires after World War I. When the Air Force became a separate service in 1947, the Guard and Reserve continued providing experienced fliers and support personnel as "citizen airmen."

The Air Force Reserve consists of officers and enlisted personnel who have completed their obligatory service but want to participate on a part-time basis. They remain current in the same types of aircraft that the Regular Air Force flies and report for active duty as needed. The Reserve accounts for about 10 percent of total Air Force manpower but typically conducts 30 percent of the missions required, with some 300 flying and support units organized into 36 wings.

Air National Guard units are controlled by the individual states, but, like the Reserves, they maintain designated levels of training and staffing. Like the Army National Guard, the Air Guard serves three roles: supporting national security; protecting life and property; and contributing to local, state, and national programs. Air Guard units generally own their aircraft, whereas the Reserve units often use Regular Air Force planes on weekends. Both the Guard and Reserve have proven highly capable organizations, usually with greater levels of experience than the Regulars. Both programs offer continuing training, education, and retirement benefits.

Whether Regular, Guard, or Reserve, the basic Air Force tactical unit is the squadron, typically organized around a specific aircraft or function. Each wing (fighter, bomber, transport, etc.) is composed of two or more squadrons, although composite wings with a variety of aircraft are organized for specific missions, usually in a particular part of the world. The echelons above wings are administrative rather than operational, including air divisions and numbered or named air forces (7th Air Force or Pacific Air Forces). Squadrons normally are commanded by lieutenant colonels, wings by colonels.

> "The airplane lends dignity to what would otherwise be a vulgar brawl."
> —Anonymous

PULLING RANK: AIR FORCE PAY GRADES

Air Force officers use the same ranks as the U.S. Army with the same emblems. The logic in assigning silver higher ranks than gold (lieutenant colonel and first lieutenant) appears symptomatic of "the military mind." Theoretically, the grade of O-11 is possible, but the Air Force position of five-star general has only been granted to Henry H. Arnold.

OFFICERS

General (O-10): four stars

Lieutenant general (O-9): three stars

Major general (O-8): two stars

Brigadier general (O-7): one star

Colonel (O-6): eagle

Lieutenant colonel (O-5): silver oak leaf

Major (O-4): gold oak leaf

Captain (O-3): two silver bars

First lieutenant (O-2): one silver bar

Second lieutenant (O-1): one gold bar

Noncommissioned Officers and Enlisted Personnel

Chief master sergeant of the Air Force (E-9): as standard E-9 with wreath

Chief master sergeant (E-9): eight stripes (five descending, three rising)

Senior master sergeant (E-8): seven stripes (five descending, two rising)

Master sergeant (E-7): six stripes (five descending, one rising)

Technical sergeant (E-6): five stripes descending

Staff sergeant (E-5): four stripes descending

Senior airman (E-4): three stripes descending

Airman first class (E-3): two stripes descending

Airman second class (E-2): one stripe descending

Airman recruit (E-1): no stripe

Each grade above technical sergeant (one or more rising chevrons) is eligible for the first sergeant position or equivalent. The first sergeant is the senior noncommissioned officer (noncom) in the command (usually from squadron up) and is identified by a diamond between the upper and lower stripes. Thus, a master, senior master, or chief master sergeant can be the first sergeant of his organization. There is also a command chief master sergeant (star in place of diamond) for more senior positions. The highest E-9 grade, chief master sergeant of the Air Force, is held by only one noncom at a time.

CIVIL AIR PATROL: FLYING MINUTEMEN

The Civil Air Patrol (CAP), a civilian organization founded during World War II, operates as an auxiliary of the Air Force. It was the idea of aviation writer and poet Gill Rob Wilson, who, with the support of General Hap Arnold, established the organization one week before the attack on Pearl Harbor. The CAP provided private aircraft to perform search duties, especially coastal patrols for enemy submarines. During the war, CAP fliers were credited with sinking two U-boats in American waters. Logging half a million miles, the "flying minutemen" also conducted search and rescue missions, courier flights, and the dangerous, thankless job of towing aerial targets.

In 1948, Congress chartered the CAP as the Air Force's official auxiliary, making the organization eligible for financial and material assistance. The law simultaneously expanded the organization's responsibilities to include aerospace education and training, cadet programs, and civilian flight instruction. Since 1951, the CAP has held workshops at colleges and universities, explaining to educators the advantages and requirements of an Air Force career or other work in the aerospace field. The CAP also sponsors the National Congress on Aviation and Space Education, keeping qualified instructors updated with information, materials, and teaching techniques.

(Photo courtesy of the USAF via Robert F. Dorr)

Two of the great men of the early U.S. Air Force: General Henry H. "Hap" Arnold, right, and Lieutenant General James Doolittle, left.

The cadet program includes young people from the sixth grade to age 20, beyond which individuals are eligible for the adult program. Most states have a CAP wing responsible for activities within that jurisdiction, including recruiting and periodic encampments. Nationwide there are more than 1,700 units, with more than half containing both cadets and adults. Total enrollment tops 50,000, including 34,000 seniors. The CAP itself maintains some 530 light aircraft, while individual members own about 4,700 more. The planes are widely used for instruction and emergency work. The CAP is heavily involved in search and rescue work throughout the country, accounting for at least 80 percent of such operations within the borders of the United States.

Additionally, the CAP owns nearly 1,000 vehicles suitable for emergency relief or search and rescue functions. Communications also feature prominently in the Patrol's capabilities, with thousands of land, air, and mobile stations used by trained operators.

A PRETTY GOOD SCHOOL

Some cynics (and a few graduates) characterize the Air Force Academy as "a pretty good engineering school with a funny dress code." However, the stunningly beautiful campus near Colorado Springs (18,500 acres hard upon the Rocky Mountains) has a full-time mission: to train professional airmen for leadership in time of war. In short: In time of peace, prepare for war. Recall the words of Lieutenant General Hubert R. Harmon, the first superintendent: "The mission of the academy is to train generals, not second lieutenants."

Toward that end, as of 2000 the Academy had produced some 280 general officers and 31 astronauts. Additionally, AFA alumni have been awarded one Medal of Honor and 16 Air Force Crosses.

Like the other service academies, entrance to Colorado Springs is largely based on competitive examination. Members of the U.S. House of Representatives typically nominate qualified youngsters, aged 17 to 22, from their congressional districts. If successful, they are eligible to enter the academy as freshman cadets, or "doolies." (An official publication defines a doolie as "that insignificant whose rank is measured in negative units; one whose potential for learning is unlimited; one who will graduate in some time approaching infinity.")

Demographics for the class of 2006 show 81 percent males among the 1,209 cadets. High academic standards have become the norm, with two thirds of the cadets finishing in the top 10 percent of their high school classes. The 225 rated as minorities included 11 foreign students, for 18.75 percent of the total entering class.

Naturally, there is an aviation focus. Freshmen are introduced to jet simulators, some classroom work, and a visit to an operational base. Sophomores begin flying in sailplanes, with most reaching the solo stage. Juniors are eligible for parachuting and navigation courses in addition to instructor certification as part of their leadership development. Medically qualified seniors learn to fly the Cessna T-41 (Model 172) and, if successful, are able to apply for military flight training after graduation. Other seniors are required to take additional instruction in applied navigation.

The AFA academic curriculum is varied, with 30 majors and minors available including aeronautical or astronautical engineering, behavioral sciences, computer science, economics, foreign languages, mathematics, meteorology, philosophy, political science, physics, and military operations and strategy. Qualified individuals are eligible for multiple majors, and exchange programs include the Chilean, French, and German air academies. All AFA instructors hold Master's degrees and half have Ph.Ds.

Cadets participate in intercollegiate sports plus intramural competition. The Falcons have done extremely well against their service academy competitors: Through the 1998 football season, Air Force was 23–12–1 against Army and 21–10 versus Navy. As of 2000, the Falcons had produced some 850 All-American athletes.

Special-interest clubs include arts and drama, chorus, skiing, flying, honor guard, drum and bugle corps, campus radio, yearbooks, scuba, shooting teams, and chess.

Another popular activity is falconry. In 1955, the first cadets chose the falcon as the AFA mascot for its speed, aggressiveness, and the grace of seemingly effortless flight. In reference to the speed of sound, it was named Mach I. A dozen cadets supervised by the academy veterinarian manage 12 to 15 falcons of various types at a time, training them for demonstrations at AFA functions and sporting events.

Like any military organization and most universities, the AFA has various traditions. They come in two flavors: those more or less mandated and the informal (and more enjoyable) variety. Examples of the former include acceptance or recognition parades, selection of the class color and ring, and ultimately the graduation hat toss. Procedural traditions involve the ritualized passing of hot plates at mess tables with inevitable comparisons to "landing" on arrival.

"Hell Week" may be regarded as a tradition, although not a wholly enjoyable one for the fourth classmen (freshmen). Physically demanding, it also can be frivolous, including tasks such as retrieving the class rock from a site north of the AFA grounds. An athletic tradition requires performing a suitable number of pushups for each point scored in a football game.

A tradition that mysteriously comes and goes is "Bedcheck Charlie." Over the years, the ghostly apparition has appeared at sporting events, parades, and even atop the futuristic chapel. Charlie invariably is dressed as a World War I aviator with leather helmet, jacket, and boots, plus a silk scarf and goggles to conceal his features. He was depicted in Milton Caniff's *Steve Canyon* comic strip as a helpful prankster who showed up at convenient times to aid unfortunate doolies enduring the unwelcome attentions of humorless upperclassmen. Charlie's various true identities over the years remain a closely guarded secret.

THE AIR FORCE UNIFORM

Until 1947, when the Air Force became an independent branch of the armed forces, airmen wore the standard Army uniforms, usually khaki with distinguishing Army Air Force pins and patches. The most popular World War II uniform was known as "pinks and greens," a combination of tan trousers and an olive green blouse that was considered attractive to females. As of September 1947, the newest military service adopted its own blue uniforms for normal wear and formal occasions. The working uniform has typically been practical green "battle dress utilities" (BDUs) for flight line wear, but camouflage patterns for desert or woodland areas are common.

Leather flight jackets came back in vogue during the late 1980s, part of the Air Force's heritage program recalling the glory days of open cockpit flying. Only personnel on flight status are eligible to wear the classic A-2 jacket, which is decorative rather than functional. Most aircrew wear fire-resistant Nomex flight suits, jackets, and gloves.

In the 1990s, the Air Force chief of staff decided to change decades of tradition by adopting naval-style rank emblems for officers. Silver instead of gold braid was applied to the sleeves of normal and dress uniforms: a full cuff stripe for second lieutenants, one and a half for first lieutenants, two full stripes for captains, two and a half for majors, etc. The result was widespread confusion and even ridicule. Civilians familiar with naval ranks said they could not tell if the Air Force officer was a member of the Coast Guard or an airline pilot. The fad ended when the succeeding chief of staff reverted to the usual shoulder or collar insignia of bars, oak leaves, and eagles.

The customary uniform for administrative and many nonflying personnel is a light blue shirt, dark blue trousers, and shined black shoes. Women may wear skirts or a pantsuit. Officers wear their rank insignia on epaulets, while noncommissioned and enlisted personnel wear stripes on their sleeves. The fore and aft "flight cap" is typically worn, although the dress blue uniform involves a visored hat with the "blouse" similar to a suit coat.

"Mess dress" for formal occasions is the Air Force equivalent of a tuxedo with bow tie and dinner jacket for men, full-length skirt for women.

THE AIR FORCE MUSEUM

Perhaps more than any other branch except the Marine Corps, the Air Force has long understood the value of an active history and museums program. Partly the attitude is pragmatic, as public support (which translates into funding) is enhanced by visible links to the Air Force's past, dating from its secondary status in the Army Signal Corps before World War I.

The Air Force Museum is located on Wright-Patterson AFB six miles northeast of Dayton, Ohio. The location itself is appropriate, as Dayton was the home of the Wright Brothers. "USAFM" is a large facility with some 200 aircraft and missiles plus an annex that includes several former presidential aircraft. Among others, the historic airplanes at "Wright Pat" include the B-29 *Bock's Car*, which dropped an atomic bomb on Nagasaki, Japan, in 1945. A rare surviving Medal of Honor aircraft is the Douglas A-1 Skyraider flown by Major Bernard Fisher in a dramatic rescue of a fellow flier in Vietnam.

Visitors can enhance their knowledge and appreciation of the exhibits via items in the gift shop, bookstore, model shop, and poster shop. The museum's layout and displays permit a self-guided tour without reliance on formal presentations. A café, picnic tables, and wheelchairs are provided for the convenience of the 1.2 million visitors per year. Most visitors spend several hours looking at exhibits, asking questions, and perusing the museum's shops.

The museum, including an IMAX theater, is open seven days a week except Thanksgiving, Christmas, and New Year's Day. Admission and parking are free. For serious historians, a research facility is also open most weekdays, but requires prior contact for access.

A FEW WORDS ABOUT MEDALS

One year at the Williams AFB airshow near Phoenix, a former Army Air Forces pilot was taking in the displays, appreciating the enormous changes in aircraft from what he had flown. Some of the exhibits were attended by enlisted personnel in full uniform. Eventually, the old timer grew visibly restless, and finally he approached a female airman second class. "Excuse me, miss," he began. "I'd like to ask a question about your ribbons."

"Yes, sir," she replied.

"Well, you see, I was a fighter pilot in World War II. I shot down six enemy aircraft and at the end of the war I had two rows of ribbons including the Silver Star, DFC, and the Air Medal. I see that you also have two rows of ribbons and I just wonder what they're for."

Obviously embarrassed, the two-striper looked down at her ribbons. "Gosh, sir, I don't really know. They just give them to us from time to time."

Stalking away, the veteran muttered, "I guess the Air Force gives medals for perfect attendance these days."

Following is a partial list of the 20 or more decorations awarded to Air Force personnel, in order of precedence. Note that some noncombat "gongs" are superior to combat decorations. The full list is too long and too dull to repeat here.

- **Medal of Honor:** "For conspicuous gallantry and intrepidity at the risk of life, above and beyond the call of duty, in action involving actual conflict with an opposing armed force." The Air Force, Army, and Navy (including the Marine Corps) award separate versions of the Medal of Honor, but airmen received the Army medal through the Korean War. The Air Force version was not presented until 1966. As of 2001, airmen have received 59 Medals of Honor, including 5 for actions on the ground: 4 in World War I, 38 in World War II, 4 in Korea, and 13 in Vietnam. Nearly half of all USAF Medals of Honor (including the Army awards) were made posthumously.

- **Air Force Cross:** "For extraordinary heroism in connection with military operations against an opposing armed force." First awarded in 1962, as of 2000 about 185 AFCs had been presented, including 20 to enlisted men. Very few duplicate awards have ever been made; in the Vietnam War, Colonel James H. Kasler, an F-105 pilot, received three Air Force Crosses while two fliers each received a second AFC. The Army equivalent is the Distinguished Service Cross, presented to airmen in both world wars and Korea. At least three fliers each received three DSCs in World War II and in Korea.

- **Distinguished Service Medal:** "For exceptionally meritorious service to the government in a duty of great responsibility." The DSM has also been called "the senior officer's good conduct medal."

- **Silver Star:** "For gallantry in action against an opposing armed force." The Air Force record probably is four awards to Brigadier Generals Robin Olds, a World War II and Vietnam fighter leader; and Richard S. Ritchie, the service's only fighter ace in Vietnam.

- **Legion of Merit:** "For exceptionally meritorious conduct in the performance of outstanding service."

- **Distinguished Flying Cross:** "For heroism or extraordinary achievement in aerial flight." Usually awarded for a specific event, the DFC also has been presented for a cumulative record. The record is 13 awarded to Colonel Francis S. Gabreski, a World War II and Korean War fighter leader.

- **Airman's Medal:** "For heroism that involves the voluntary risk of life under conditions other than those of conflict with an opposing armed force."

- **Bronze Star:** "For heroic or meritorious achievement of service, not involving aerial flight in connection with operations against an opposing armed force." A bronze "V" device indicates valor.

- **Purple Heart:** "For wounds or death as a result of an act of any opposing armed force, as a result of an intentional terrorist attack, or as a result of military operations while serving as part of a peacekeeping force."

- **Air Medal:** "For meritorious achievement while participating in aerial flight." A bronze "V" device indicates valor. In wartime the Air Medal frequently is awarded on a "strike-flight" basis, depending on an arbitrary number of missions or flights. However, the Air Medal also recognizes single events. Colonel Clyde B. East received 42 Air Medals as a reconnaissance pilot in World War II and Korea.

- **Aerial Achievement Medal:** "For sustained meritorious achievement while participating in aerial flight."

- **Air Force Commendation Medal:** "For outstanding achievement, meritorious service, or acts of courage."

THE AIR FORCE CHIEFS OF STAFF

Carl A. Spaatz	1947–1948
Hoyt S. Vandenberg	1948–1953
Nathan F. Twining	1953–1957
Thomas D. White	1957–1961
Curtis E. LeMay	1961–1965
John P. McConnell	1965–1969
John D. Ryan	1969–1973
George S. Brown	1973–1974
David C. Jones	1974–1978
Lew Allen Jr.	1978–1982
Charles A. Gabriel	1982–1986
Larry D. Welch	1986–1990
Michael J. Dugan	1990
Merrill McPeak	1990–1994
Ronald F. Fogelman	1994–1997
Michael E. Ryan	1997–2001
John P. Jumper	2001–

Nine of the chiefs mainly came from fighters, five from bombers, and one from observation. The others had mixed careers.

CHAPTER 2

THE WRIGHT BROTHERS MEET THE U.S. ARMY

In December 1903, two bicycle mechanics from Dayton, Ohio, solved the riddle of the ages and gave humanity the gift of wings. Orville and Wilbur Wright probably were not geniuses, but they had something better than genius: persistence. They not only taught themselves everything they needed to know (aerodynamics, structures, propulsion, and control), but they questioned the conventional scientific wisdom of their era and found it wanting. Undaunted, they proceeded methodically, patiently, and skillfully. Lacking a suitable lightweight engine, they built one. Lacking a wind tunnel, they devised their own. Lacking knowledge of flying, they taught themselves on homebuilt gliders. In an astonishingly short time, they succeeded, launching the Wright Flyer from Kill Devil Hill near Kitty Hawk, North Carolina.

They changed the world forever.

In fact, they surprised themselves. In 1908, Wilbur, addressing an aeronautical meeting in France, confessed that as late as 1901 he felt that powered flight was 50 years off. Happily, his pessimism was misplaced.

At first the sensible, buttoned-down bachelors from Dayton gave little thought to the military application of their flying machine. They later said that they hoped the airplane would render war less likely by its ability to see beyond the far side of the hill. Presumably, advance knowledge of a potential enemy's capabilities would serve as a deterrent to both contenders. In the end, they got it half right. Observation would become one of military aviation's most important missions from the Great War onward, from almost ground level to more than 80,000 feet. But wars continued—even accelerated—with perfection of the flying machine.

Today the Wright Flyer looks antediluvian: the pilot lying prone on the bottom wing, manipulating the primitive controls partly by body english with the elevator out in front instead of behind. The Wrights developed their flying machine from a series of homebuilt gliders, and then applied a homebuilt engine. Even then, the Flyer was too underpowered to take off unassisted, requiring a runway track and a catapult. The first flight from Kill Devil Hill in December 1903 measured just 120 feet. Only 66 years later, men walked on the moon. Orville and Wilbur put the nascent U.S. Air Force in business and launched men toward the stars. The Wright Model A spanned 36 feet, 4 inches, weighed 740 pounds empty, and eventually achieved a top speed of 44 mph.

Initially the Wrights found a numbing lack of interest or even belief in their mechanical marvel. Among others, prestigious journals such as *Scientific American* magazine and *The New York Herald* newspaper insisted that the Kitty Hawk achievement was a hoax. Scientific and technical "experts" attested that controlled, heavier-than-air flying was impossible, while others reportedly opined that manned flight might be achieved in the next 100,000 years.

Undoubtedly miffed but certainly not dissuaded, the brothers offered their services to the U.S. government, which declined twice in 1905, so Wilbur and Orville took themselves to Europe. There they found success, acclaim, and interested customers, but the potential for military use lagged behind civilian outlets.

"When my brother and I built the first man-carrying flying machine we thought that we were introducing into the world an invention which would make further wars practically impossible."
—Orville Wright, 1917

Nevertheless, four years after the Wrights' success at Kill Devil Hill, the Army issued specifications for a flying machine: endurance of one hour with two men aboard, attaining a speed of 40 miles per hour. Forty or more proposals were received but only three seemed likely to achieve the desired performance. Initially, the Wright bid (deliverable in 200 days for $20,000) was deemed excessive and not considered. When the "winners" failed to deliver, the Army dragged itself back to the bicycle boys from Dayton.

The Army Aeronautical Board conceived a series of tests to determine the Wright Flyer's capabilities, which began in August 1908. Because Wilbur was demonstrating their product in Europe, Orville fetched himself to Fort Meyer, Virginia, the early home of military aviation. There he began what a later generation would call "proof of concept" demonstrations, circling the field for 57 minutes almost immediately. It was an impressive performance: The previous record was only 38 minutes. Soon thereafter, Orville was remaining aloft for more than an hour, easily checking that box in the Army's requirements.

On September 17, Wright offered a ride to Lieutenant Thomas Selfridge, one of the Army board members. They had made four full orbits of the field at 150 feet when one propeller flexed excessively, striking a bracing wire. Wilbur descended to about 75 feet before the Flyer dropped to the earth. Both men were critically injured; Selfridge died in the hospital, the first person killed in an airplane. Wilbur was laid up for nearly two months. However, the Flyer was rebuilt and returned to Fort Meyer in June 1909.

Two months later (a full year after tests began), the U.S. Army purchased the Wright Type A for $25,000 plus a $5,000 bonus for exceeding specifications. The Wrights began formal instruction of Lieutenants Frederick E. Humphreys, an engineer officer, and Frank P. Lahm of the cavalry. Both soloed on October 26, 1909, becoming military aviators numbers one and two. They were followed by Lieutenant Benjamin D. Foulois, originally an infantryman but possessing dirigible experience. All three survived to become generals.

BRIGADIER GENERAL FREDERICK E. HUMPHREYS
(1883–1941)

The U.S. Army's first certified pilot was a graduate of West Point, where he stood eighth of 78 in the class of 1906. He was commissioned in the engineers, serving most of his career in that capacity. As one of the Wright brothers' original students, he soloed on October 26, 1909, minutes ahead of Frank Lahm.

Completing mandatory service, Humphreys resigned his commission to join his family's homeopathic medicine business but remained affiliated with the New York National Guard. Humphreys's unit was activated for Mexican border patrol in 1916 and subsequently became part of the 27th Division destined for France. While training his regiment in South Carolina, Humphreys was returned to aviation and, following recertification, he applied his considerable engineering talents. His wartime service included study at Massachusetts Institute of Technology and hands-on work at McCook Field, the Air Service's test site near Dayton, Ohio.

Honorably discharged in 1919, Humphreys returned to civilian life and became commanding officer of the 102nd Engineers in the New York National Guard. Failing health forced his retirement in 1939, but he was promoted to brigadier general on the retired list.

Because of the relatively frail nature of the Wrights' machine, other facilities had to be found, especially during winter. Consequently, the Army's expanding aeroplane operation was moved to College Park, Maryland, and alternated in climes such as San Antonio, Texas; Augusta, Georgia; and San Diego, California. There was also a period of activity in the Philippine Islands from 1912 to 1915, originally with Frank Lahm at the controls. He instructed other aspirants at Fort William McKinley, including Corporal Vernon L. Burge, who became the Army's first noncommissioned pilot. However, owing to the moist climate, flying was considered impractical for seven months each year, and Lahm temporarily returned to the Seventh Cavalry. Eventually flights were made from "the rock" of Corregidor, in the entrance to Manila Bay, anticipating events three decades hence.

Flying was considered far more a sport than a profession in those days. After all, mortality could be high among the inattentive or unlucky, especially in the period before aerodynamics and control were fully understood. The most lethal evolution was the stall-spin, in which the normal airflow over the wing is disturbed to the point that lift is lost. Typically, a stall occurs when airspeed is allowed to bleed off, resulting in an uneven airflow over the wing. Too steep an angle in a climb or turn is the historic pattern, although today jet fighters can accelerate going straight up. However, when the stall, or "departure from controlled flight" occurs, the machine needs a certain amount of altitude to nose down, regain airspeed, and recover level flight. Because many stalls occur on takeoff or landing, the earth frequently interrupts the process with predictable results. An early byword among aeroplane pilots was, "Never stretch a glide." In event of engine failure, it was always preferable to make a forced landing straight ahead rather than risk stalling in a slow-speed turn. Such knowledge came at a price.

Through 1915, the Army acquired a hodgepodge of aircraft types, 59 in all: a dozen Wrights (1909–1913), 23 Curtisses (1911–1915), 11 Burgess models (1912–1915), and 13 Martins (1914–1915). The breakthrough Wright design clearly was a technological dead end, as major advances had been made in airframe design and control. A bitter patent feud between the Wrights and Glenn Curtiss dragged on for years, but the Army paid relatively little attention. Something approaching standardization emerged with Curtiss's JN-2 in 1915, which still left much to be desired, but it led to the famous JN-4 "Jenny," about which you'll read more later.

BRIGADIER GENERAL FRANK P. LAHM (1877–1963)

Frank P. Lahm was "Mr. Ballooning" in the Army Air Service. A notable balloonist with his father (a friend of the Wrights), Lahm graduated from West Point in 1902 as a cavalry officer. Three years later, he was sent to Europe to study aeronautics in France, Belgium, and Germany. His career path was typical of prewar airmen, with alternating aviation and line assignments. He was a Gordon Bennett Free Balloon Cup winner, became the second Army pilot in 1909, and established a flight school in the Philippines in 1912. One month after American entry into the war, he became Commanding Officer (CO) of the Army Balloon School and later established the American Expeditionary Force (AEF) Balloon Service school and a center for equipment and personnel. He finished the war as a colonel and later commanded flight training facilities in San Antonio. Lahm was promoted to brigadier general in 1930, serving in staff and administrative positions until retirement in November 1941.

FATAL NUMBERS

It is said that figures lie and liars figure. At any rate, statistics can definitely be misleading. For instance, in 1909, when the first Army pilots learned to fly, the personnel strength of the aviation service had doubled over the previous year—from 13 to 27. More dramatic was the growth from 1910 to 1917, with a 1,200 percent increase—from 11 to 1,210. In 1910, the service also had an airship and three balloons, as Army LTA (lighter than aircraft) remained into the 1930s.

Another statistic of the era was the mortality rate. Although the percentages appear daunting today, in truth they were relatively small. For instance, in 1911 the Army lost 1 pilot of the 9 on duty, representing an 11 percent fatality rate. But the 33 passengers also exposed to risk reduced the figure to barely two percent. Overall, the Signal Corps logged 65 flying hours per casualty that year with 372 flights per casualty. In the early days, flights were inevitably brief, in this case barely 10 minutes per "hop."

Two years later, the Army lost 5 pilots and 2 passengers: a mortality rate of 12.8 percent. Among the early airmen, median air time at death was 22 hours in 60 flights with a high of 87 hours in 469 flights and low of 12 hours in 52 hops. Even by 1913, pilots were rarely airborne 20 minutes between takeoff and landing.

Still, there was progress amid the danger. In June 1911, Lieutenant H. H. Arnold set an altitude record of 6,540 feet in a Burgess-Wright, but military applications of aviation evolved at the same time, including the origin of U.S. Air Force bombing, which appears comical in retrospect. At the Los Angeles Flying Meet in January 1910, Signal Corps Lieutenant Paul Beck flew aboard Louis Paulhan's French-built Farman biplane with a lap full of two-pound sandbags. Beck's object was to hit a ground target, and although it resembled more of a carnival stunt than a serious effort, it represented the first experiment with aerial bombing. Nine decades later, his feat was still being reproduced in airshows across the country.

Apparently, the first test of a weapon fired from an American aircraft occurred in August of that year when Glenn Curtiss took Lieutenant Jacob E. Fickel aloft with a rifle at a New York race track. The Army man aimed at a three-by-five-foot target and reported satisfactory results. The next month a semiautomatic pistol was used with uncertain effect, but tests continued. Perhaps the most notable occurred in June 1912 when Lieutenant Thomas D. Milling flew a Wright Model B at College Park, Maryland, while his passenger, Captain Charles D. Chandler, fired a prototype Lewis Gun at a ground target. The machine gun had been mated to the aeroplane. By then, airplanes had flown in conflicts as far afield as Mexico and Tripoli (Libya) with crude hand-dropped bombs first being used.

Meanwhile, the 1st Aero Squadron was organized at San Diego in December 1913, boasting 16 officers, 77 men, and 6 flying machines. A larger force structure emerged 7 months later when, on July 8, 1914, the Aviation Section of the Signal Corps was authorized with 60 officers and 260 enlisted men. The European war erupted the next month, but America largely squandered the ensuing three years of potential preparation.

MAJOR GENERAL BENJAMIN D. FOULOIS
(1879–1967)

The Army's third pilot, Benjamin Foulois, began his military career as a private during the Spanish-American War. During service in the Philippines, he was commissioned in 1901 and saw extensive combat against Moro insurgents. Subsequently, he conducted mapping expeditions in the islands.

Upon return to the United States, Foulois graduated from the Signal School, leading to his affiliation with the fledgling Aeronautical Division. He followed Frederick Humphreys and Frank Lahm as students of the Wright brothers.

Foulois was the only pilot on flight status from late 1909 to early 1911, setting records for speed, altitude, and endurance. He led the 1st Aero Squadron in the Mexican expedition of 1916 and, as a brigadier general, became the 39-year-old chief of the Air Service, AEF, in November 1917. Foulois efficiently managed this huge assignment with a staff of only 20 officers. His main concerns were training and supply, which required coordination with French and British aviation facilities and aircraft. Upon relief by Mason M. Patrick, Foulois took over training for squadrons preparing for operations in France and in August 1918 piloted one of the first American-built DH-4s in France. He returned to the United States in 1919 but later served as an air attaché in Europe.

Foulois became chief of the Air Corps in 1931, the first pilot to hold the position. He retired in 1935 after 37 years of service. In 1955, he became president of the Air Force Historical Foundation—appropriate for an airman who made so much history.

Aerial reconnaissance was deemed potentially useful, and a field trial occurred in Mexico. On March 9, 1916, some 400 guerrillas under bandit chieftain Pancho Villa attacked civilian and military facilities near Columbus, New Mexico, in reprisal for Mexican deaths in El Paso, Texas. Nearly 20 Americans were killed, prompting a U.S. Army punitive expedition under Brigadier General John "Black Jack" Pershing, who a year later commanded the American Expeditionary Force in Europe. However, in five months of operations between March and August 1916, the 1st Aero Squadron lost or wrote off six of its eight airplanes. The surviving two were withdrawn from service as inadequate.

Numerous problems arose, most attributable to inadequate preparation. Some pilots had never flown at night, and navigation was problematic. The machines had been tested at sea level, but never at elevations of 5,000 feet or more; in Mexico, the foothills of the Sierra Nevadas surpassed the aircraft ceiling. There were all kinds of problems: weather, darkness, and balky engines. Captain Foulois even ended up in the Chihuahua City jail due to a brief misunderstanding. Nevertheless, the rickety Curtiss biplanes demonstrated the potential of aircraft in tracking friendly forces while carrying mail and dispatches between units or outposts 300 miles apart.

Concluded Captain Foulois, "Aviation is indispensable to military operations," while earnestly requesting future types "should tend to greater speed, dependability, and weight-carrying capacity."

Following the Mexican misadventure, the squadron received Lewis machine guns, light bombs, and cameras to test capabilities. The 1st Aero Squadron arrived in France in September 1917, this time flying far better equipment.

By then, other American airmen already had been in combat, as future leaders of the fledgling U.S. Army Air Service had literally jumped the gun and entered the European war. In April 1916, seven U.S. citizens in France founded the *Escadrille Americaine* to fight Germany, ignoring American neutrality. Officially the unit was Escadrille N.124, indicating its Nieuport scouts. Other pilots followed, eventually totaling 38 Americans who served under French officers. The squadron drew considerable press, especially their mascots, lion cubs named Whiskey and Soda. Not unreasonably, the German government protested, prompting a name change to the *Escadrille de Lafayette*, honoring the French officer who supported

American independence. By February 1918, the Lafayette Escadrille was a valuable asset for the Allies, with 22 months of combat and nearly 40 official victories against 9 pilots killed. Absorbed into the U.S. Air Service as the 103rd Aero Squadron, the men of the Lafayette provided badly needed experience and continuity. Meanwhile, more than 200 other American airmen served in other French units, generically known as the Lafayette Flying Corps. When America finally entered the war, the pool of seasoned fliers was of immense value, however tenuous the legality of their prior service.

CHAPTER 3

THE WAR TO END ALL WARS

In June 1917, the U.S. Army's Aviation Section became the Airplane Division of the Signal Corps. It seems a small enough distinction now, but at the time it boded well for expansion of the embryonic air arm—the scratch-built sandlot team that soon would be thrown into the European big leagues, where the home team across the river (the Rhine) played a tough brand of full-contact ball. As the Yanks would discover, the big boys in the pros gave very little slack to the visiting amateurs.

There was no option but to grow as quickly as possible to professional size and standards. From 1917 to 1918, the Army's air branch absorbed a staggering 193,800 personnel for a total of 195,000. The latter figure would remain unmatched until 1942.

BACKGROUND TO CONFLICT

When war erupted among the great powers in Europe in August 1914, America was geographically and emotionally removed. The murder of Austro-Hungarian Archduke Franz Ferdinand by a Serbian nationalist set in motion a series of alliances that eventually set Britain, France, Italy, and Russia against Germany, Austro-Hungary, and Turkey. Democrat Woodrow Wilson, a nominal pacifist, had been elected president in 1912, and what was called "some damned thing in the Balkans" was of only passing interest to

Americans. Some Americans regarded the war as a gigantic family spat involving grandchildren of Queen Victoria, who occupied the thrones of Britain, Russia, and Germany.

Despite a sizeable influx of immigrants from Germany, America's historic connection with England and regard for France eventually influenced public sentiment. Hundreds of Americans joined the British and French armed forces, including those who flew with the Royal Flying Corps, the Royal Naval Air Service, or the *Aviation Militaire*.

Germany's High Seas Fleet, unable to challenge the Royal Navy in warships, resorted to submarine warfare and came close to choking off the vital sea lanes that kept Britain supplied. Despite a legal right to intercept shipping entering the war zone, U-boats gained poor press in a series of highly publicized sinkings. The most famous was the liner *Lusitania*, sunk in Irish waters in May 1915, resulting in 128 American and more than 1,000 other deaths. The fact that she was carrying U.S.-produced munitions in no way mollified American outrage (perhaps because it was concealed at the time).

Nevertheless, nearly two years elapsed before the United States declared war on Germany. The final straw was the "Zimmermann note," a secret communication from the German foreign minister to his ambassador in Mexico offering return of large tracts of the Southwest to Mexican control in exchange for military pressure against the United States. British intelligence decoded the message and leaked it to American newspapers, setting in motion the results desired by London. Years later Winston Churchill stated that without American entry into the war, the exhausted European powers likely would have arranged a cease-fire in 1917.

In a final irony, Woodrow Wilson asked for a declaration of war against the Kaiser less than a year after being re-elected as "the man who kept us out of the war."

Of 4,735,000 Americans in uniform during the Great War, 116,500 died of all causes and 204,000 were wounded. More than 600 Air Service personnel were killed, wounded, or missing.

A KID IN A CRATE

More bunk and hokum has been penned about the Great War than any other era of aviation history. The adage "It's a crime to send a kid up in a crate like that" has become "camp" in some circles, but the "chewing gum and bailing wire" image remains. Nine decades after World War I, there are still references to "canvas-covered wings" when, in fact, canvas was too heavy for the airframes and engines of the era. Great War airplanes were wooden structures covered with cotton or linen, heavily doped to conform to the airframe and "rib-stitched" for strength.

Likewise, the extreme youth of many World War I airmen has been overstated. Yes, there were 18-year-old airmen, but most were of college age; many were Ivy Leaguers from Harvard, Princeton, and Yale. The chivalric image conjured by the hackneyed phrase "knights of the air" is mostly pure Hollywood. On rare occasions the victor might stand the vanquished to a drink in the squadron bistro, but neither side refrained from shooting an unwary opponent in the back. Done properly, an aerial kill was an execution rather than a combat. Said one ace, "If it's a fair fight, you've screwed up." Accounts of disengaging because the enemy's guns jammed are extremely rare; true reports rarer yet. After all, the enemy you let off today might kill you tomorrow—or somebody who owes you money.

SYNCHRONIZED MACHINE GUNS

When the war erupted in 1914, airplanes on both sides were lightly armed. That was partly due to the observation and reconnaissance missions of military aircraft, and partly because no air-to-air weapon had emerged other than rifles and pistols. Free-swiveling machine guns were then mounted in the observer's cockpit of two-seat airplanes, but the front propeller severely limited the field of fire. Some "pusher" designs were employed, which allowed a forward-firing machine gun with the engine behind the pilot or crew. However, the configuration was considered structurally unsatisfactory.

In 1915, French airman Roland Garros affixed deflector plates to the propeller of his Morane Saulier monoplane and made an immediate impression, as he could point his airplane directly at the enemy. With his forward-mounted Hotchkiss, he shot down three German planes and forced two or three more to land. However, he was soon forced down and captured.

Anthony Fokker, a Dutch designer with prewar ties to Germany, investigated Garros's aircraft. Fokker soon found a better solution, which he claimed he invented, although a Swiss engineer had patented a mechanism in 1912, as had two Britons in 1914. In any case, Fokker's cam-linked synchronizer permitted a Maxim gun to fire between the spinning propeller blades with complete safety. Fitted to Fokker Eindecker monoplanes, the system proved extremely effective, leading to Germany's first period of air superiority. Once the Allies perfected similar systems, fighter combat accelerated tremendously. As late as 1945, some World War II fighters were still using the synchronizer to fire automatic weapons through the propeller arc, a system that finally fell into disuse in the jet age.

Apart from getting shot at, Great War airmen faced hazards that seem quaintly precarious today. The frailty of World War I aircraft has been overstated, but structural failure was not unheard of, and Allied pilots were not issued parachutes. Engines often were cranky, and because the prevailing wind in France was from the west, AEF fliers could not always stretch a glide to safety. Although much progress had been made in the science of flight, most new pilots still were woefully undertrained; many entered combat with fewer than 100 hours in their logbooks.

While fighter or "pursuit" pilots always received the majority of the ink, the fact is that aviation's primary roles in World War I were observation and reconnaissance. Pursuit squadrons existed to deny the enemy access to "our" airspace and to protect friendly observation and bombing formations. For every ace, there were dozens of two-seater crews who accomplished unglamorous, decidedly dangerous missions such as photography and artillery spotting.

Apart from bombing, an increasingly important aviation role was direct air support. Only the Germans specially equipped and trained squadrons for such work, but the Allies employed fighter and two-seater units to attack enemy troops, positions, and transport. As a result of Great War experience, the U.S. Air Service later developed "attack" aircraft and deployed them in squadrons dedicated to that task.

The World War II role missing from the Great War was transportation. By 1918, aviation technology had produced large, multi-engine aircraft with unusual range and significant bomb loads, but cargo capacity remained insignificant. However, had the war lasted into 1919, dedicated night-bombing units would have emerged in far greater numbers.

Not all airmen went aloft in airplanes. The lowly balloon, tethered perhaps 3,000 feet in the air, provided a splendid observation platform enabling friendly artillery batteries to fire "blind" by telephoned instructions. Armed with binoculars and a telephone, one sharp-eyed observer swinging in his wicker basket could do more to win the war than any fighter squadron. The Army's Balloon Section was capably led by Colonel Charles Chandler, whose troops enjoyed almost none of the "luxurious" benefits accorded aviators at prepared airfields. Of necessity the balloon companies operated close behind the lines, sometimes living more like infantry than airmen. Although 21 AEF balloons were lost to enemy action, only one observer was killed. However, several aeronauts made multiple emergency jumps, the record being five. It was a mighty hard way to make "ace."

(Photo courtesy of the USAF via Robert F. Dorr)

One of the first American fighter pilots, Lieutenant Alan Winslow, poses next to his first victim in April 1918.

PLAYING CATCH-UP

In 1914, the United States ranked seventh in "frontline" aircraft with 55, just behind Austro-Hungary but ahead of tiny Belgium. Russia and Germany both had well over 200, Italy 150, France nearly 140, and Britain about 110. Uncle Sam had a long, long trail a'winding through the airy halls of clouds.

However, despite having to play catch-up in the European big leagues, the Yanks made a valiant effort. They never came close to the goal they set themselves (nor the goals of their allies), but the U.S. Army's tiny air arm made impressive strides in organization, training, and doctrine. The biggest lapse was in equipment, as the Army produced no indigenous combat aircraft. (The Navy did, but not in significant numbers.) In 19 months of combatant status between April 1917 and November 1918, AEF relied wholly on foreign-built and -designed airplanes while earning the respect of allies as well as enemies.

CURTISS JN-4 "JENNY"

American aviation grew to maturity on the wings of the Curtiss Jenny, which evolved from the company's J and N designs of 1914. The 1916 biplane trainer, clanking along at 70 miles per hour (mph) behind its 90-horsepower Curtiss OX-5 engine, was undoubtedly the most common U.S.-built aircraft to the mid-1920s. Barnstormers, flying circuses, and other air-minded people took up flying in the available, economical Jenny. Charles Lindbergh made a poor but honest living with one, absorbing the lessons that would propel him to unprecedented fame in 1927. Lesser lights hopped from one Jenny to another (with and without parachutes), hung by their knees from the axle, and did the Charleston in flight. Others flew into barns, performed car-to-plane transfers, looped the loop, stalled and spun, and had a peachy good time. It was said "Jenny was no lady," but she lifted her skirts (and America) into the air.

The JN-4D spanned 43 feet, 7 inches, tipping the scales at 1,580 pounds empty, and was clocked at 75 miles per hour with an 8,000-foot service ceiling.

In April 1917, the Aviation Section of the Signal Corps boasted one squadron with an assortment of obsolete aircraft, 65 officers (fewer than 50 trained pilots), and 1,055 other personnel. The tiny Army air arm's only institutional experience had been gained in the fruitless pursuit of Mexican bandit chief Pancho Villa. There was no operating doctrine for a major war, even if there had been adequate equipment.

Yet America's greatest aviation ally, France, dreamt great things—impossible things. Premier Alexander Ribot requested that America deliver 4,500 aircraft to France by the summer of 1918, with 5,000 pilots and more than 10 times as many support personnel. Toward that end, the good premier suggested a monthly production of 2,000 aircraft and 4,000 engines. It was a cosmic leap of faith, considering that the eventual total exceeded what France herself produced.

Ground schools were established at eight American universities; airfields were constructed almost overnight. Pilot, aircrew, and technical training courses were provided in the United States and Canada while overseas facilities were arranged in Britain, France, and Italy. The U.S. government arranged to purchase frontline aircraft and observation balloons from those same allies.

In short, there was a universal shortage of everything and precious little time in which to produce it. Amid such urgency, an efficient leadership and administrative scheme had to be established for planning, coordination, and production. The men who built the fledgling U.S. Army aviation branch remain largely unknown to history nine decades later, but they included Major General Mason M. Patrick, 55, who succeeded Foulois as chief of AEF aviation in May 1918.

MAJOR GENERAL MASON M. PATRICK (1863–1942)

A West Point classmate of "Black Jack" Pershing, Patrick graduated second in the class of 1886 and became a well-regarded engineer. Although a nonflier, he oversaw reorganization of Air Service structure, including addition of a night-bombing program in conjunction with Britain. Anticipating continuation of the war into 1919, Patrick forecast the need for 202 American squadrons by June of that year. When the plan was submitted in August 1918, there were 24 U.S. squadrons in Europe; the addition of 178 more in only 10 months was problematical at best.

After the war Patrick remained in aviation and became chief of the Air Service in 1921, having learned to fly at age 60. In 1923 he said, "The next war will be decided in the air." He supported the global navigation of the Douglas World Cruisers and the goodwill flights to Latin America, remaining long enough for the Army Air Corps to be established in 1926. Patrick retired the next year but lived to see his service grow to maturity before his death during World War II.

THE MAJOR FRONTS

The Army Air Service (AAS) was almost wholly committed to France, operating in conjunction with French and British forces. From the spring of 1918—roughly a year after Washington declared war on Berlin—U.S. Army squadrons began combat operations in central and southern France. Although U.S. Navy aircraft patrolled the English Channel and a few

Marine Corps squadrons operated in northern France and Belgium, the huge proportion of American aviation was the Army pursuit, bombardment, and observation wings in the sector around Verdun. The first major campaign was defense of the Château-Thierry sector northeast of Paris from May to July 1918. American air power's offensive debut occurred in the St. Mihiel operation south of Verdun in September, quickly followed by the Meuse-Argonne attack.

To a much lesser extent, Army airmen also served in Italy. The first contingent arrived in September 1917 and began training for combat missions with Italian squadrons. The Yanks were assigned to Caproni bomber units, helping to blunt a major Austrian offensive in June 1918. Flying day and night missions, the Americans suffered extraordinarily light casualties (two killed, one captured) throughout the Italian campaign.

OVER THERE IN THE AIR

In May 1918, the Aeronautics Division became the AEF Air Service (AEFAS), indicating greater autonomy for the aviation branch. However, the airmen were administratively if not literally lashed to the ground forces, performing a variety of missions in support of infantry and artillery. Observation and bombing squadrons flew three types of aircraft: the well-regarded Breguet Type 14 and Salmson Type 2 from France and the British-designed DeHavilland 4, with American-built models arriving late in the war. Upon receiving their wings, the crews of such aircraft were necessarily cross-trained in artillery observation, photography, cartography, communications, and gunnery. By later standards, training was incredibly simple; some recently graduated pilots were made instructors with fewer than 50 hours of total flight time.

Nevertheless, the first-generation airmen accomplished their mission, assuming they survived to learn the appropriate lessons. A DH-4 pilot recalled one of his first sorties, flying at 3,500 feet a few miles behind the American lines. Abruptly, a sharp-shooting German artillery battery put a shell below and behind the DeHavilland, shaking the crew and puncturing several holes in the tail. It was a lesson learned: Never again fly straight and level, except while taking photographs, anywhere near the lines.

Artillery observation was a crucial task. Normally, single planes were used to regulate artillery fire on different types of targets. While "spotting" for 155mm rifles, aircrews flew over the trajectory of the shells, but when directing 8-inch howitzers, they flew under the trajectory. When the gun was ready to fire, the pilot turned away from the target so that the observer would be looking over the tail to send a wireless message informing the battery of the estimated necessary correction.

The arrangement also had the observer, with two Lewis Guns, facing the direction from which German fighters would likely appear. "We would play cat and mouse with the fighters," recalled one veteran. "When they got too close, or tried to get behind us, we would open the throttle wide, put the nose below the horizon, and hotfoot for home! They were a little faster, but as long as we did not let them get a chance to make a dive, they wouldn't follow us very far over the lines; then we would go back to work."

One of the most important but underreported observation missions was the "contact patrol." During Allied offensives it was essential for division and corps headquarters to know how far friendly troops had advanced as of a given time and how enemy forces were responding. In the era before two-way aircraft radios, aerial observation was invaluable because phone lines were often cut by shellfire, leaving couriers and even carrier pigeons as the last resort. Low-flying two-seaters braved heavy gunfire and poor weather to identify the doughboys' leading elements in the 1918 attacks at St. Mihiel and the Argonne.

Chief among the factors leading to heavy U.S. infantry casualties was the impact of enemy air superiority. The situation was particularly notable in the Chateau-Thierry and Belleau Wood area in June, when German reconnaissance aircraft and observation balloons largely went unhindered. However, the cause was more one of inadequate Allied air cover rather than lack of effort or appreciation. As the AEF gained strength, its wings also grew stronger.

One example is the Meuse-Argonne operation, involving one of the legendary actions of the AEF. In early October, a battalion-size formation of the 77th Infantry Division was trapped in extremely rugged terrain, outflanked by German shock troops. Lieutenant Colonel Charles Whittlesey's "lost battalion" sustained itself for five perilous days, taking heavy casualties from both enemy gunfire and "friendly" artillery.

DH-4

During World War I, no American-designed aircraft logged even one hour over the front lines. However, the "Liberty DeHavilland" was a British type produced in the United States and built in greater numbers than any other Army aircraft for years to come. Powered by an American-designed 420-horsepower engine, the U.S. DH-4 served in the observation and bomber role during the last months of the Great War.

The first example was built in February 1918, with some 4,800 produced by 1919 and another 5,100 cancelled after the armistice. The Liberty DH saw considerable combat from August to November, equipping a dozen squadrons of the American Air Service.

Despite its overall success, the Liberty DH was not beloved by many crews. The 2nd Day Bombardment Group concluded, "For a bombing plane it carries to any altitude an inferior quantity of bombs. The fuel tank between the pilot and observer is the target of every pursuit plane that attacks it. The fuel tank is unsupported, works by pressure, and explodes when shot up. When the plane crashes, the tank leaves its bedding, having nothing to keep it there, and crushes the pilot against the motor."

As important as it was in France, the DH-4 proved perhaps more significant afterward. In the lean years following the war, new aircraft were scarce, and a generation of airmen grew up with the old war horse. It did nearly every conceivable job, from flying the early airmail to forest fire patrol.

The "Liberty" was a large airplane for its day: a wingspan of 42 feet, 5 inches, weighing 2,732 pounds empty. Its top speed was rated (perhaps optimistically) at 124 miles per hour with a service ceiling of not quite 16,000 feet.

Despite low ceilings and heavy automatic weapons fire, DH-4s of the 50th Aero Squadron searched for Whittlesey's beleaguered force and finally found it. There ensued probably the first sustained aerial resupply mission in history as food, medicine, and ammunition were dropped by the lumbering DeHavillands. However, poor visibility in the tangled Argonne Forest resulted in many drops falling wide of the mark. On October 6, the crew of Lieutenants Harold E. Goettler and observer Erwin B. Bleckley made two trips into the cauldron, the first resulting in severe damage to their aircraft. They returned to base, climbed aboard another DH and set off again. Flying lower than ever to make an accurate drop, their plane was shredded by close-range gunfire—some from rocky crags above them!

Goettler turned the dying DeHavilland for friendly lines but crashed short of base. Both fliers died in their heroic, selfless effort and after the war received posthumous Medals of Honor.

PURSUIT PILOTS AND BALLOON BUSTERS

The 1st Pursuit Group was organized with four squadrons in early 1918, short on everything but enthusiasm. Originally equipped with Nieuport 28s—racy biplanes with rotary engines—some of the first patrols were unarmed because insufficient guns had arrived. Another shortage was leadership. Although American veterans of the French and British air arms were often selected for command positions, there was a good deal of bickering as to whether French or Royal Flying Corps (RFC) doctrine and methods should pertain. By far, the best-known squadron commander was the 94th's Major Raoul Lufbery, ace of the *Lafayette*, but he was killed in May. Lufbery represented an institutional dilemma because the combat veterans possessed knowledge essential to performing the mission but most had no command experience. Worse yet, few of them understood the workings of the U.S. Army, requiring a mixture of old hands and professional officers.

The 94th and 95th Aero Squadrons began operations in March, the 27th in June. Lufbery's Hat in the Ring outfit claimed the AEF's first victories during an extremely short "scramble" on April 13, downing two German fighters near Gengoult Aerdrome at Toul. The Yanks were on their way.

However, the game was about to change. AEF pursuit squadrons frequently faced second-line German *Jagdstaffeln* that spring, but summer brought the varsity to play. Two of the Kaiser's elite "flying circuses" moved to the American front, with dramatic results. Hermann Goering's *Geschwader No. 1 "Richthofen"* (named for its first commander, killed in April) and Captain Bruno Loerzer's *Geschwader No. III* made their presence known amid a riot of colored Fokkers and glowing tracer bullets. The eight squadrons of these two wings, plus other "*Jastas*," gave the Yanks a series of hard-fought combats as Goering and Loerzer's aces fattened their scores at the expense of Nieuports and SPADs.

SPAD XIII

The French-built SPAD was *the* American "pursuit" aircraft of World War I. Although U.S. squadrons also flew Nieuports and British types, the majority of AEF fighter pilots made their records on the sturdy, boxy design from the *Société Anonyme pour l'Aviation et ses Dérivés.* At war's end, most U.S. fighter squadrons flew SPADs, with almost 900 purchased from France. In comparison, the flying Yanks obtained 300 Nieuport 28s and about 180 British Sopwith Camels or SE-5s.

First flown in 1917, the SPAD XIII was a formidable contender. With two machine guns, a robust airframe, and a 220-horsepower Hispano-Suiza engine, it made 130 miles per hour at 6,500 feet, a very respectable speed in World War I. The type became best known as the mount of Eddie Rickenbacker and Frank Luke, as well as most of the ranking French aces.

After the armistice, 435 SPADs were shipped to America, where they remained in service for several years. A wartime plan to build 3,000 in the United States fell through owing to insufficient engines.

The SPAD's wingspan was 26 feet, 11 inches; and it weighed 1,255 pounds empty. Typically, it could reach 10,000 feet in nine minutes.

Meanwhile, beginning in July, two other pursuit units fought farther north in the British sector. The 17th and 148th Squadrons, equipped with Sopwith Camels, were American-manned and gave a good account of themselves. After the war their work was ably described by Elliott White Springs, a colorful Carolinian who wrote a popular book and numerous magazine articles. Springs finished the war as the AEF's third-ranking ace with 13 victories.

Other Army fliers gained combat experience in regular French and British units. Although wearing American uniforms, such Yanks were fully integrated into the Allied squadrons. Whatever their units, by November 11, U.S. Air Service (USAS) pilots and gunners were credited with some 624 enemy airplanes and 60 balloons, although not all were "hard" kills as in the French and German services. The policy has been expressed as "every kill was a victory but not every victory was a kill."

ACES HIGH

By custom more than regulation, a fighter pilot credited with downing five or more enemy aircraft is considered an ace. The tradition dates from

France in 1915, and by 1918 the leading European fighter pilots claimed scores of kills. The war's ace of aces was Germany's Baron Manfred von Richthofen, the Red Baron (80), while French Lieutenant René Fonck (75) topped the Allied list. With far less combat time, and a more lenient victory credit system, the USAS was led by Captain Edward V. Rickenbacker (26), followed by Lieutenant Frank Luke (18), who was killed in September 1918. However, Americans also flew with the French and British, the latter including Lieutenant Frederick Gillet (20) who flew Sopwith Dolphins. In all, some 100 American "pursuit" pilots were recognized as aces by November 1918.

Americans also flew with foreign services in World War II, most notably with the British Royal Air Force and with the Chinese in the American Volunteer Group. The nation's two top guns were 5th Air Force P-38 pilots: Majors Richard I. Bong (40) and Thomas B. McGuire (38). Both died in 1945, McGuire in combat and Bong in an accident. The top surviving aces of the Army Air Forces (AAF) were Lieutenant Colonel Francis S. Gabreski (28), and Colonel Charles H. MacDonald and Captain Robert S. Johnson (27 each). Gabreski and Johnson flew P-47s from Britain in the 8th Air Force; MacDonald commanded a Pacific P-38 group. All told, some 800 AAF pilots rated as aces in the Second World War.

Many World War II veterans experienced jet combat in MiG Alley during the Korean War. They were led by a former navigator, Captain Joseph M. McConnell (16), closely followed by Major James Jabara (15) and Captain Manuel J. Fernandez (14.5). The Air Force produced 38 aces in Korea, of whom six (including Gabreski) had "made ace" during World War II.

Only one Air Force fighter pilot achieved acedom during the long Vietnam War: Captain Richard S. Ritchie, who downed five Communist MiG-21s in 1972. One of his Phantom radar operators, Captain Charles B. DeBellevue, participated in six MiG kills while another "GIB" (guy in back), Captain Jeffrey S. Feinstein, was involved in five. Colonel Robin Olds, also a World War II ace, held the lead for five years with four MiGs.

The top post-Vietnam scores were recorded by four F-15 or F-16 pilots, with three each. It is entirely possible that no more American aces will be "crowned" when wars tend to be rare, short, and expensive.

THE TOP AIR FORCE ACES

Major Richard I. Bong, 40, WW II, KIFA 1945

Major Thomas B. McGuire, 38, WW II, KIA 1945

Colonel Francis S. Gabreski, 34.5, WW II, Korea, 28 in WW II

Major Robert S. Johnson, 27, WW II

Colonel Charles H. MacDonald, 27, WW II

Major George E. Preddy, 26.83, WW II, KIA 1944

Colonel John C. Meyer, 26, WW II, Korea, 24 in WW II

Colonel Walker M. Mahurin, 24.25, WW II, Korea, 20.75 in WW II

Major Raymond S. Wetmore, 22.6, WW II, KIFA 1951

Colonel David C. Schilling, 22.5, WW II

Colonel Gerald R. Johnson, 22, WW II, KIFA 1945

Colonel Neel E. Kearby, 22, WW II, KIA 1944

Major Jay T. Robbins, 22, WW II

Captain Dominic S. Gentile, 21.83, WW II, including 2 in RAF, KIFA 1951

Captain Frederick J. Christensen, 21, WW II

Major George C. Davis, 21, WW II, Korea, KIA 1952

Captain John J. Voll, 21, WW II

Major William T. Whisner, 21, WW II, Korea, 15.5 in WW II

Lieutenant Colonel Glenn T. Eagleston, 20.5, WW II, Korea, 18.5 in WW II

Lieutenant Colonel Thomas J. Lynch, 20, WW II, KIA 1944

Lieutenant Colonel Robert B. Westbrook, 20, WW II, KIA 1944

Ranks are highest attained in combat.
KIA: Killed in action
KIFA: Killed in flying accident

Publishers seldom lost an opportunity to sell papers to a public eager for details of Our Boys flying Over There. Much of what was printed was sensationalized or inaccurate, but a few pilots lived up to the tabloid image. Certainly one was Lieutenant Frank Luke, a headstrong youngster who actually made a measurable contribution to the war. The 21-year-old Arizonan impressed many of his squadronmates as a brash egotist when he arrived at the 27th Aero and made some unconfirmed claims. Subsequently, however, he found his legs and began a spectacular spree in conjunction with the St. Mihiel offensive. During 18 days in September, Luke was credited with 14 balloons and 4 airplanes, becoming the AEF's ace of aces and using up 5 SPADs in the process. Luke and his partners conducted an unrelenting assault on the German balloon line, reducing the effectiveness of enemy artillery during the offensive. However, he lost two friends in the process and brooded on their deaths. Typically in hot water with his CO, on September 29 he defied orders (probably with a wink from the sympathetic group commander) and took off to drop a note asking American observers to watch German *Drachen* along the River Meuse. He burned three gasbags in a matter of minutes and then force-landed behind enemy lines, where he died in a Tombstone-style gunfight. It was a Medal of Honor action.

Luke's mantle as the leading pursuit flier was assumed by a very different type of fighter pilot. At 27, Lieutenant Edward V. Rickenbacker was older and wiser than Luke, and possessed leadership talent besides. The 94th "Hat in the Ring" Squadron had played second fiddle to the 27th during Luke's scoring spree, but the former race driver turned the 94th into the most successful pursuit outfit in the AEF.

Rickenbacker's success was not achieved without effort—and luck. In May 1918, he survived an encounter with the enemy and with fate. Although separated from his wingman, Rickenbacker attacked three German planes and shot down one, diving at high speed to escape the others. In an abrupt pullout, the top right wing of his Nieuport 28 buckled. Structural failure was an occupational hazard in those days, and Allied pilots had no parachutes. To Rickenbacker, the snapping, wrenching noise "sounded like the crack of doom." The fabric covering the top of the wing was torn off in the slipstream, lurching the little Nieuport on its right side. The tail reared up and the nose lurched downward, forcing the fighter into a "tailspin."

Two of Rickenbacker's squadronmates had experienced leading edge failure of their top wings and survived—one as a prisoner. "Rick" knew that he had to act quickly. At 3,000 feet he could see German troops watching his fall, but he noted that the speed of the spin had stabilized. There was a chance.

"With a vicious disregard for the consequences I pulled open the throttle," he said. (French throttles operated the reverse of U.S. and British planes.) It worked: The nose came up and Rickenbacker stopped the spin. Pointed toward the French lines, Rickenbacker endured a spate of German anti-aircraft fire. His antipathy toward the Nieuport turned to love: He talked to his crippled mount, promising "a good rubdown when we reached the stable." He managed a high-speed landing, safe at last, spared to fly and fight again—and again.

By Armistice Day, "Captain Eddie" claimed 26 victories. After much political maneuvering, he also received the Medal of Honor, although not until 1930.

> "Fighting in the air is not sport. It is scientific murder."
> —Eddie Rickenbacker, 1918

WINNERS AND LOSERS

At the end of the shooting match, the American team comprised 45 squadrons, including 20 pursuit outfits. The fighters were organized into four groups with two more groups forming at the time of the armistice. Eighteen squadrons in six observation groups supported the First and Second Armies and their respective corps. Only the 1st Bombardment Group's three squadrons saw combat, as the 2nd Group was warming its engines for takeoff on the morning of November 11.

The Allies won a clear victory over the Central Powers, but only at enormous cost. From a global total of 65 million men under arms, the victors (including Russia, which opted out in 1917) lost more than 5 million dead, while the losers buried 3 million. Another 20 million or more were wounded; millions of others (mostly civilians) died of famine or disease.

Because the war ended in an armistice rather than a genuine surrender, lingering resentment in Germany prompted the "stab in the back" theory, claiming that the Kaiser's armed forces were not truly defeated. Combined with the onerous reparations required under the Treaty of Versailles, a slow fuse was set smoldering in 1918; it would explode with even more dire consequences 21 years later.

Germany's *Luftstreikrafte* held its own through most of the war. Blessed with strong leadership, innovative designs, and superior organization, the German Air Service and its naval counterpart consistently outperformed the Allies. In the end, however, entente numbers made the difference, and American airmen rode the high tide of victory, buoyed by friendly wings from France and Britain.

The Army's air arm proved itself in Europe, drawing considerable attention from the nation at home. The exploits of the aces captured the public imagination, but of far more consequence was the establishment of an organizational structure and professional competence that was worlds removed from America's laughable aviation force at the beginning of 1917.

Among airmen, the greatest winner in the war was aviation itself. Scientific and technical knowledge had advanced enormously in 4 years—progress that might have taken 20 years or more in peacetime. Louis Bleriot had flown the English Channel in 1911; five years later it was an unremarkable flight. Engines were vastly improved by 1918, more powerful and more reliable. Structures also had come a long way, as all-metal monoplanes were beginning to appear. The layman's yardstick of aviation progress—speed—had leapt from a typical 70 to 120 miles per hour, but more important, altitude, range, and payloads grew with large, multi-engine aircraft pointing to the future.

At the end of the war, America ranked about fifth overall in air strength, although of course Russia was no longer a factor, being riven by civil war. France fielded 4,500 combat aircraft, Britain 3,300, Germany nearly 2,400, and Italy 1,200. However, the 740 planes available to the AEF represented not only a 1,400 percent increase over 4 years previously, but the variety and capabilities were vastly improved.

THE DOLDRUMS: 1919–1929

Even before the end of World War I, U.S. Army fliers were looking to the future. The war had accelerated technical progress enormously, setting the stage for more advances. In September 1918, Major Rudolph "Shorty" Schroeder set an altitude record of 28,899 feet at Dayton, Ohio. A year and a half later, he took a turbo-supercharged Packard-LePere to 33,113 feet. Then, in June 1921, Lieutenant Harold Harris tested a pressurized cabin in a modified DH-9A.

In June 1920, the Air Service was established at 1,516 officers and 16,000 men—a force structure that ensured that the fliers largely knew one another. The next year the first Army Air National Guard units were formed, adding additional manpower potential in time of crisis.

"New weapons operating in an element hitherto unavailable to mankind will not necessarily change the ultimate character of war. The next war may well start in the air but in all probability it will wind up, as did the last war, in the mud."
—Board to Study Development of Aircraft for the National Defense, 1925

The Army aviation branch entered the 1920s with most of the same aircraft it had used during the war. New planes were hard to come by, as evidenced by President Calvin Coolidge's alleged suggestion to "buy one aeroplane and let the aviators take turns flying it." The first U.S.-designed fighter to appear after the war was the Orenco D in early 1919, but only four were procured. The most significant type was the Thomas-Morse MB-3, with 200 delivered in 1922. It remained the largest pursuit contract until 1937. The mainstay pursuit aircraft was the long-lived Curtiss series, beginning in 1923. The P-1, progenitor of the new designation system, appeared in 1925. A milestone was passed in 1931 when the Curtiss XP-22/P-6E became the first American combat aircraft capable of 200 miles per hour in level flight.

The Air Corps Act of 1926 not only changed the name of the Air Service but recognized the increasing need for modernization. Appropriations tripled from 1925 to 1931, calling for 1,800 modern aircraft, but left aviation under the control of the "ground pounders" on the General Staff. However, the force structure still suffered by European standards as the Army Air Corps (AAC) remained a defensive organization. At the end of 1928, the AAC possessed only 60 bombers among 825 combat aircraft. There was no better illustration of the Air Corps's established role than the fact that 506 planes were observation types, directly supporting the ground forces.

In 1920, the Army ordered 20 Martin MB-2s, lumbering 98-mph biplanes with 2 Liberty engines and a 74-foot wingspan. One of the most ponderous designations ever was tagged to Barling's XNBL-1, for experimental night bombardment long distance. Weighing nearly 14 tons empty, the huge (120-foot span) machine had multiples of everything: 3 wings, 4 rudders, 6 engines, and 10 wheels. Historian Ray Wagner described it as "more likely to antagonize the air than to pass through it." Flown in 1923, it was termed "Mitchell's Folly" and proved a dead end. The twin-engine Martin-Curtiss NBS-1 biplane remained the standard heavy bomber until the similar Keystone series of the late 1920s.

REAL MEN DON'T USE PARACHUTES

Apart from the obvious benefits in combat, parachutes were a means of saving lives in flight tests and routine operations. The advantages presumably were obvious, but in the USAS only balloonists had routinely been equipped with "umbrellas" throughout the Great War.

Incredibly, many officials and even some pilots still scorned lifesaving chutes. Said one officer, "Pilots had been trained to expect danger and disregard risks that were beyond their control. Anyone wearing a parachute was evidently really afraid to fly!" An Army major wrote, "We think that if pilots are encouraged to use them, it will lead to many crashes that could have been perfectly safe landings and will encourage faint-heartedness." This after it was noted that one third of the aviation deaths in 1920 through 1921 might have been averted by parachutes.

Finally, reason ruled. In March 1922, the very well-regarded Lieutenant Frederick W. Niedermeyer was killed in a Fokker V-40 with control failure; he definitely could have survived with a parachute. Despite the uncomfortable bulk and inevitable razzing, more men began wearing chutes. Seven months later, Lieutenant Harold Harris (of the pressurized cabin test) again earned a place in history when he jumped from a crippled Loening PW-2A, an awkward-looking parasol monoplane—and became the first American pilot to save his life by parachute. When Lieutenant Frank B. Tyndall jumped in November, the evidence seemed conclusive. In January 1923, the chief of the Air Corps issued an order requiring use of "jump sacks" (a) when available, and (b) when they fit in the aircraft.

Aviation medicine also made significant advances in the two decades following the Great War. Aircraft with greater altitude capabilities required more knowledge of the physiological effects of oxygen deprivation and prolonged cruising above 18,000 feet (the altitude at which the atmosphere is half the density at sea level). Air Corps flight surgeons conducted extensive tests in altitude chambers, which permitted close study of aircrew at simulated heights by reducing the atmospheric pressure within the chambers. The gravitational effect of high-"G" dive recoveries also was systematically examined, eventually leading to G-suits that partly negated the loss of blood to the brain.

> ## WHAT'S IN A NAME?
>
> Today's Air Force has continually grown from its fledgling origin as a tiny part of the Army Signal Corps. The growing importance of the service is reflected in the evolution of its title:
>
> Aeronautical Division, Army Signal Corps, August 1, 1907
>
> Aviation Section, Army Signal Corps, July 18, 1914
>
> Airplane Division, Army Signal Corps, June 1917
>
> Air Service, American Expeditionary Force, April 24, 1918
>
> Army Air Service, June 4, 1920
>
> Army Air Corps, July 2, 1926
>
> Army Air Forces, June 20, 1941
>
> U.S. Air Force, September 18, 1947

RACERS AND RECORDS

In the decade following the Great War, Army fliers repeatedly made headlines with speed, distance, endurance, and altitude records. Apart from technical or scientific achievement, the flights caught the public's imagination, building awareness and goodwill for military aviation. In the process, the knowledge of flight was extended considerably.

Despite poor funding, the 1920s became a progressive era for Army aviation. Long-range flights demonstrated increasing competence, developing techniques that would pay dividends well into the future. One was the May 1923 cross-country record by Lieutenants Oakley Kelly and John Macready, who completed the first nonstop transcontinental crossing by flying from New York to San Diego in 27 hours. The next month at Rockwell Field, San Diego, Lieutenants Lowell Smith and John Richter conducted the first in-flight refueling in DH-4s. They extended their string to a record 37 hours in August, pioneering what became a crucial aspect of jet operations decades downstream. A year later, Macready was again in the news when he reached 35,239 feet in a LePere.

THE IRREPRESSIBLE BILLY MITCHELL (1879–1936)

French-born "Billy" Mitchell served as an infantryman in the Spanish-American War before receiving a commission. He joined the Aviation Section of the Signal Corps in 1915 and was one of five observers sent to France for a look at the European air war. Colonel Mitchell became Air Commander in the Zone of Advance, selecting airdrome and depot sites while building an operational structure. As aviation commander in the 1st Army Corps, he led nearly 1,500 French and American planes (including 25 U.S. squadrons) in the successful Meuse-Argonne offensive of 1918. Consequently, he was briefly promoted to brigadier general but reverted to colonel after the war and served as assistant chief of the Air Service.

Mitchell's postwar public pronouncements demonstrated that he had lost none of his ardor for aviation as the dominant military arm. Influenced by the writings of Italian air theorist Guilio Douhet, Mitchell agitated for an independent air force and a bigger part of the shrinking defense appropriations. Again promoted to general, his dramatic bombing tests against captured German warships off the Virginia Capes in July 1921 demonstrated that aircraft could sink battleships (although the tests were rigged), confounding the Navy and Army hierarchies. Little reported is the fact that naval aircraft played a larger role in the tests than Mitchell's composite squadron. Nevertheless, two years later Mitchell again made news by establishing a world speed record, an unprecedented achievement for a general officer.

Eventually Mitchell lost the support of his wartime commander, General John J. Pershing, and was exiled to Texas in a nonflying position. Following avoidable air disasters, such as loss of the airship *Shenandoah* in 1925, he accused the military leaders of incompetence, criminal negligence, and "almost treasonable administration of the national defense," thus ensuring his court-martial. The court, chaired by General Douglas MacArthur, found him guilty of gross insubordination and sentenced him to five years separation from the service. Mitchell resigned his commission and continued his campaign for air power but died in 1936, on the eve of World War II.

In his memoir, *Reminiscences,* MacArthur revealed that he was the only member of the court who voted to acquit Mitchell. "That he was wrong in the violence of his language is self-evident; that he was right in his thesis is equally true and incontrovertible," MacArthur wrote.

In 1946, Congress voted Mitchell a gold medal in tribute to his dedication and sacrifice of his professional career. Contrary to legend, he was not awarded the Medal of Honor, but he was promoted to major general.

More than 70 years after the court-martial, Mitchell remains one of a handful of American general officers who have ever relinquished their careers for their cause.

The most easily grasped records for John Q. Taxpayer were speed runs, especially in organized races. Recognizing the benefits, the Air Service supported a variety of efforts that otherwise might have been passed up. Two Curtiss R-6s swept Detroit's 1922 Pulitzer Race as Lieutenants Russell Maughan and Lester Maitland finished one-two. Newspaper accounts seemingly resorted to hyperbole by stating that the 206 mph winning speed was so great that Maughan lost consciousness. Actually, he experienced brief blackout in high-speed, 80-degree banked turns around the pylons. Engineers computed that he pulled upward of seven Gs in the corners—a respectable figure in the jet age, let alone in the 1920s. General Patrick, the nonflying chief of the Air Service, was thrilled with his two racers' performance. Observers noted that the old gentleman was so flustered that he patted Maughan's head instead of shaking his hand.

An attempt on the outright speed record shortly followed, with Maughan getting the nod. However, as the October date neared, the speedster declined the offer in favor of his wife's pregnancy. Although generals seldom claimed speed records, Billy Mitchell himself accepted the challenge. Alternately flying both Curtisses at Selfridge Field (his record runs were his initial checkout), the air-power advocate set a world 1-kilometer speed record of 224 miles per hour. It was only the second time that America owned the outright speed record; the first occasion was in 1909.

Subsequently, the Army bought a Curtiss R3C-1 from the Navy for $1 and, retaining the naval designation, it took Lieutenant Cyrus Bettis to victory in the 1925 Pulitzer. The same machine, fitted with floats, was flown to victory by Lieutenant Jimmy Doolittle in the Schneider Race that same year, and then set a world seaplane record of 245 miles per hour. These records were notable achievements, gained over the best that Europe could field. The successes not only demonstrated that U.S. Army airmen could hold their own internationally, but that U.S. manufacturers were keeping pace with foreign designers. Although postwar budgets were predictably miserly, at least American air power was retaining its human and technological strength.

"It is probable that future war will be conducted by a special class, the air force, as it was by the armored knights of the Middle Ages."
—Billy Mitchell, 1924

Army aviators began testing the potential global reach of aircraft with an around-the-world flight in 1924. Four Douglas World Cruisers (DWCs) set off in April that year, christened *Seattle*, *Chicago*, *Boston*, and *New Orleans*. Although partly sold to Congress as a means of demonstrating the "routine" competence of Army aviation, only bachelors were accepted for the world flight: 27,553 miles westward around the globe.

The expedition leader, Major Frederick L. Martin, brushed an Alaskan hilltop in thick clouds; *Seattle* came to grief, but Martin spent 10 days walking out with his mechanic. The six other crewmen experienced wild extremes: sweltering Indian heat (where a stowaway reporter was discovered) to a landing amid icebergs in the frigid North Atlantic.

Everywhere they alit, the Army fliers were feted, although nowhere as much as France. Three planes reached Paris, where the six men were noted asleep in their seats at the Folies Bergeres, prompting speculation about the virility of American males. Lieutenant Leigh Wade, pilot of *Boston*, recalled, "After the performance we were asked, 'If the Folies can't keep you awake, what will?'" Another of the world-circling fliers mumbled something about drowsiness from the tropics.

DOUGLAS WORLD CRUISER

It is ironic that the U.S. Army's first significant international flight was made with an aircraft that began as a Navy torpedo plane. Based on the Douglas DT of 1921, the Army's World Cruiser was a large (50-foot span) single-engine biplane weighing more than 2 tons empty. It first took wing in 1923 with a 420hp Liberty engine, yielding a cruising speed of 80 miles per hour. Five DWCs were built, of which four began the great adventure from Seattle in April 1924. Led by Major Frederick Martin, two of the DWCs were lost en route—without loss of life—but the others completed the historic mission in September, taking six months to cover 27,500 miles on wheels and floats. The flight required vision, planning, and considerable logistics as spare parts were prepositioned around the globe. Nonetheless, the DWCs hinted at what might yet be achieved.

Two World Cruisers are preserved in the Air Force Museum and the National Air and Space Museum.

Ultimately, only Lieutenant Lowell Smith's *Chicago* and Lieutenant Erik Nelson's *New Orleans* completed the six-month evolution. Although much of the trip was accomplished with floats attached, the DWC crews demonstrated that Army aviation was populated with forward-looking individuals willing to probe the boundaries of their equipment and operating techniques.

At the end of 1927, the Army Air Service completed its first five-year expansion program. There were nearly 30 regular bases and depots, plus 16 National Guard or Reserve bases from Washington, D.C., to the Philippines. It was the year the Jenny disappeared from the inventory, with 269 on hand at the time. Some 300 DH-4s soldiered on, and they lasted longer. But big changes were in the wind.

In May 1927, the world was irrevocably changed by a former Air Service pilot with a reserve commission. He was Charles Lindbergh, a lanky, handsome 25-year-old who seized glory's golden ring by flying solo from New York to Paris in 33½ hours. "Lindy" was promoted to colonel, awarded the Medal of Honor (in violation of the Army warrant requiring combat), and became the most famous human on the planet. He focused aviation in the public mind as no one before or since, and inspired a generation of youngsters to seek their future in the air. Fifteen years later, the seeds that he planted would sprout full-grown in the battle skies of Europe and Asia.

Meanwhile, Army fliers were making their own headlines. Barely a month after Lindbergh's astonishing achievement, Lieutenants Albert F. Hegenberger and Lester J. Maitland flew a Fokker C-2 from Oakland to Honolulu in less than 26 hours. Although not a truly transpacific flight, it was nearly 2,100 miles over water, demonstrating aviation's growing capability.

Hegenberger was back in the headlines in May 1932 when he made the first blind flight by an active duty Army pilot. Completely "on the gauges" from takeoff to landing, Hegenberger made a full circuit of Wright Field near Dayton, Ohio. His contemporary, Jimmy Doolittle, had pioneered the technique while "on loan" to Sperry Gyroscope Company in 1929. The implications for future operations were enormous.

GENERAL CARL A. SPAATZ (1891–1974)

He was born Carl Andrew Spatz; at age 45 he changed the spelling to Spaatz, but to his friends he was "Tooey." The nickname was acquired at West Point, where he graduated in 1914. Two years later, Lieutenant Spaatz won his wings and subsequently became director of training at the huge U.S. base at Issoudon, France. Itching for combat, Captain Spaatz was granted three weeks flying SPADs with the 13th Aero Squadron and was credited with downing three German planes.

Between the wars Spaatz enjoyed a varied career, usually in the cockpit. He made headlines with the crew of the Fokker *Question Mark* during its 1929 endurance flight and commanded both fighter and bomber units. Spaatz was chosen to observe the European air war in 1940 and subsequently was promoted to brigadier general and chief of staff under Hap Arnold in July 1941. The next year he began planning AAF operations from Britain but he returned to the United States to establish the 8th Air Force. Subsequent assignments took Spaatz to ever greater responsibility in the Mediterranean theater, where he commanded the 12th Air Force through most of 1943. For the rest of the war he oversaw AAF strategic operations in Europe and then in the Pacific.

In March 1946, Spaatz succeeded Arnold as AAF chief of staff, remaining as the first chief of the independent Air Force. He retired in July 1948, serving as chairman of the Civil Air Patrol and contributing to various publications.

(Photo courtesy of the USAF via Robert F. Dorr)

General Carl "Tooey" Spaatz, the first Air Force chief of staff.

Further development of in-flight refueling led to headlines in 1929, six years after the original experiments. On New Year's Day 1929, the Fokker C-2A *Question Mark* took off from Mines Field, Los Angeles, attempting to establish an endurance record. The plane's name reflected the uncertainty, as nobody knew how long the Fokker could remain airborne. Nevertheless, it had a star-studded crew: Major Carl A. Spaatz, Captain Ira C. Eaker, Lieutenants Elwood P. Quesada, and Harry Halvorsen (all significant leaders in World War II), plus Sergeant Ray Hooe. They stayed airborne for the next five days, receiving 5,600 gallons of fuel, 250 gallons of oil, and about a ton of food and supplies. All transfers in flight came from Douglas C-1C "tankers." When an engine problem forced the *Question Mark* to land, the 5 fliers had logged 11,000 miles nonstop.

AIR FORCE WORLD SPEED RECORDS

These are absolute world speed records certified by the *Federation Aeronautique Internationale* in France. Air Force pilots and planes also established dozens of other records over specified distances in addition to altitude and endurance flights.

- 1922, Brigadier General W. Mitchell, Curtiss R-6, 223 mph
- 1923, Lieutenant R. L. Maughan, Curtiss R-6, 236 mph
- 1947, Colonel A. Boyd, Lockheed XP-80R, 625 mph
- 1948, Major R. L. Johnson, North American F-86A, 670 mph
- 1952, Captain J. S. Nash, North American F-86D, 698 mph
- 1953, Lieutenant Colonel W. F. Barnes, North American F-86D, 715 mph
- 1953, Lieutenant Colonel F. K. Everest, North American YF-100A, 755 mph
- 1955, Colonel H. A. Hanes, North American F-100C, 822 mph
- 1957, Major A. E. Drew, McDonnell F-101A, 1,207 mph
- 1958, Captain W. W. Irwin, Lockheed YF-104A, 1,404 mph
- 1959, Major J. W. Rogers, Convair F-106A, 1,525 mph
- 1965, Colonel R. L. Stephens and Lieutenant Colonel D. Andre, Lockheed YF-12A, 2,070 mph
- 1976, Captain E. W. Joersz and G. T. Morgan, Lockheed SR-71A, 2,193 mph

LIGHTER THAN AIR

Record flights were not limited to airplanes. The Air Service experimented with lighter than air (LTA) craft for almost 20 years, expanding scientific knowledge but contributing very little to operational development.

A Balloon and Airship School was established at Brooks Field, Texas, in 1919 with emphasis on hydrogen-filled airships. The Army purchased the Italian airship *Roma*, intending to explore rigid LTA designs at a time when the Navy was investing heavily in them. However, *Roma* never made it to Brooks, being lost with most of its crew in a New York crash in February 1922.

That same year the LTA school moved to Scott Field, Illinois, where free ballooning became the focus. Some exciting developments occurred, especially in March 1927 when Captain Hawthorne A. Grey set an altitude record of 25,500 feet. Grey made another record attempt eight months later but died in the process. Although he succumbed to oxygen failure, his barograph recorded a height well over 30,000 feet.

A Berliner Joyce YP-16 fighter, circa 1930.

(Photo courtesy of the USAF via Robert F. Dorr)

Despite such setbacks, the LTA program continued. On November 11, 1935, Captains A. W. Stevens and O. A. Anderson launched in *Explorer II*, a huge balloon sponsored partly by the National Geographic Society. They reached 72,395 feet, recording atmospheric and physiological data decades ahead of fixed-wing aircraft.

However, in 1937 the Army Air Corps determined that the practical utility of balloons and airships had reached an end. The program was terminated after 18 years, and the future clearly belonged to airplanes.

AIRCRAFT DESIGNATIONS

Before 1925, military aircraft mostly were known by their factory designations. For instance, the famous "Jenny" trainer was called by its Curtiss
identification, JN-4. The British-designed DeHavilland Model 4 was just
DH-4, etc. Thereafter, the Army adopted a system using alphanumeric
designations: A for attack aircraft, B for bombers, C for cargo, O for observation, P for pursuit (fighters). The first such fighter type was the P-1; the
second bomber was called the B-2, and so on. The system proceeded
logically and sequentially for more than half a century.

Prefixes indicated the status of an aircraft in its development: X for experimental and Y for service test. Thus, the Martin XB-10 was a prototype
bomber; the YB-10 was a preproduction model for evaluation.

When the Air Force became an independent branch in 1947, a few changes
occurred. The most notable involved fighters, which switched from P to F
(as in Lockheed P-80 to F-80). Ironically, the previous designation for reconnaissance planes was F, which subsequently received the R prefix, as in
the RF-80 version of the Shooting Star.

In 1963, the Department of Defense decided to merge designations for Air
Force and Navy types. Some planes were given new labels: the McDonnell
Phantom II, just entering Air Force service, was briefly called F-110 before
becoming the F-4. Originally it was a Navy design called the F4H (fighter,
fourth type from McDonnell). The biggest change involved the Navy and
Marine Corps, which had used a seemingly complex but logical system
since the 1930s. For instance, the Douglas A4D Skyhawk became the A-4,
etc. With a "unisex" designation system in place, fighters continued up to
the Navy F-14 Tomcat, the Air Force F-15 Eagle and F-16 Falcon, and beyond.

Things settled down until the 1980s when the old Air Force system dating
from the mid-1920s had progressed to the North American XB-70 Valkyrie
and General Dynamics F-111 "Aardvark." Then, for no apparent reason,
the clock turned back. Northrop's futuristic B-2 stealth bomber, which first
flew in 1989, had the same designation as the lumbering Curtiss biplane of
1927. After more than 70 years, the system had come full circle.

CHAPTER 4

THE GOOD WAR

Some historians contend that there were not two world wars but one, separated by 21 years while the combatants prepared for round two. Whatever the facts, the Second World War has come to be known as "the Good War," because in retrospect the issues appear so vivid, the options so well defined. At the time they were not always so: Many Americans felt the nation had no interest in another European feud, and Congress could not even manage a unanimous declaration of war against Japan after Pearl Harbor.

Nevertheless, the Air Corps slowly—glacially—began preparing for the next conflict. It was no easy task, especially in the depression years with millions of people out of work and far greater priorities in the national consciousness. Both technological and organizational progress was made, however, most visibly in the form of new equipment. The aircraft themselves were notable in that monoplanes began replacing the familiar biplanes of the past 30 years.

A landmark aircraft entered service in 1934 with Martin's twin-engine B-10, the Army's first monoplane bomber. Although procured in small numbers with limited service life, the Martin was proof of the advancing capability of military aircraft. The B-10's best-known endeavor was the 10-plane flight from Washington, D.C., to Alaska, led by Lieutenant Colonel Hap Arnold in 1934.

The 7,400-mile round trip was accomplished safely amid tremendous press coverage, gaining favorable publicity for the depression-strapped service. Like the Douglas World Cruiser flight 10 years previously, the Alaska venture required stashes of spare parts and supplies along the route—an unrealistic option for wartime. Nevertheless, the successful completion of the ambitious undertaking demonstrated the Air Corps's growing reach.

BOEING P-26

America's first significant monoplane fighter began as a private venture, the Boeing Model 248. Although an all-metal airplane, it still needed bracing wires for the top and bottom of the 28-foot wing. Weighing 2,200 pounds empty, the stubby little "pursuit" first flew in 1932, powered by a Pratt and Whitney 550-horsepower radial engine at 234 miles per hour. The Army ordered 136 "pea shooters" while a few export models went to Spain and China. The Philippine Air Force operated the type briefly in 1941, but by then the P-26 was far out of date; its armament of two .30-caliber guns was a holdover from World War I.

Nevertheless, the '26 provided some of "the greatest generation" of airmen with their first operational experience, and the little Boeing would be fondly remembered by pilots who only hung up their helmets after flying supersonic jets three decades later.

In February 1934, the Air Corps was suddenly called upon to take over the nation's airmail routes. Although the Army had inaugurated service from Washington, D.C., in 1918, private contractors soon took over the job and established the forebearers of most major airlines. However, President Franklin Roosevelt accused the previous Hoover administration of favoritism in granting airmail contracts, leading to cancellation of most carriers until a review could be completed. He directed General Foulois to assume the task, and the Air Corps chief assured the president that the Army was up to the task.

It was good practice for war: a no-notice, "come as you are" event. Unfortunately, the Army Air Corps (AAC) failed the test. Poorly trained and equipped for flying at night in bad weather (many planes had no landing lights), the Army suffered serious losses: Three pilots were lost in training for the operation. During the first week of actual mail flights, two pilots were killed, six injured, and eight aircraft wiped out. The AAC halted operations for a week to assess the situation, then plunged onward with new aircraft such as the Martin B-10. Flying at night in miserable winter weather, the Army fliers incurred further losses. In all, a dozen fliers were killed and 66 planes destroyed or damaged during the 78-day fiasco. The cost of flying airmail quadrupled to an astounding $2.21 per mile, forcing the Roosevelt administration to recant and resume commercial flights on May 8.

MARTIN B-10

Although widely forgotten today, Martin's B-10 and B-12 series (with twin 775-horsepower (hp) Wright and 700hp Pratt and Whitney engines, respectively) were an important step on the road to American air-power superiority. As the first "modern" bomber in the U.S. inventory, it marked a departure from the traditional fabric-covered biplanes, featuring all-metal construction, retractable landing gear, and enclosed cockpits and turret. Although weighing nearly 5 tons empty, the B-10B delivered in 1935 showed an impressive top speed of 210 miles per hour—equal to many fighters of the era. Although Depression budgets permitted the U.S. Army to obtain only 150 B-10s or B-12s, foreign orders from Holland, Argentina, and Turkey more than doubled that figure.

The up side of the equation was that the airmail scandal forced Congress to provide better aircraft, equipment, and training for the AAC. The latter included Link Trainers to give pilots badly needed instrument flying familiarization.

Despite the Great Depression, during the decade of the 1930s AAC personnel nearly doubled, from 12,000 to 23,000. The grim year of 1934 was gloomy for another reason: Merely 115 Army aircraft were ordered, by far the lowest annual number in an era when 300 to 400 were typical. The order for 88 Martin bombers took up the lion's share of the total. It was still a tiny force, but planning was underway to absorb the immense numbers necessary to gear up for a major war. Personnel more than doubled again in 1940 (51,000), and tripled in 1941 (152,000). In the year following Pearl Harbor, the Army Air Forces (AAF) began to reach its potential, absorbing nearly 610,000 new people. However, in 1943, even that figure was eclipsed with 1,433,000 additional officers, men, and cadets. For the rest of the war, strength hovered around 2,200,000.

BACKGROUND TO CONFLICT

When the Allies triumphed in 1918, the peace terms dictated to Germany in the Treaty of Versailles almost guaranteed that political and economic factors would result in another war. Beset by internal conflict and staggering inflation, Germany sought a unity of purpose and found it in an unlikely figure. Adolf Hitler, a lance corporal in the Kaiser's army, became chancellor and head of state in 1933, and his power base, the National Socialist (Nazi) Party, imposed a dictatorial reign of awesome proportions. Combined with like-minded regimes in Italy and Japan, Germany embarked upon an expansionist foreign policy based on a resurgent military. The three members of the 1940 Tripartite Pact sought domination of Europe, Africa, and Asia, while Germany had stunned the world in 1939 by concluding a non-aggression pact with its ideological enemy, Soviet Russia. As in 1917, most Americans were sympathetic to Britain but wanted no part of another European war.

In September 1939, Germany invaded Poland from the west and Russia split the spoils from the east. By the end of 1940, Germany and Italy dominated most of Europe and held major portions of North Africa. Japan had expanded its empire in China and Manchuria and was casting covetous eyes southward to the oil-rich Dutch East Indies. President Franklin Roosevelt, a devoted Anglophile determined to avoid the Neutrality Act passed by Congress, authorized clandestine operations against Germany and Japan. He ordered U.S. Navy destroyers to escort British convoys in the North Atlantic, approved establishment of the American Volunteer Group to fly in China and Burma, and allowed American pilots to join the Royal Air Force (RAF).

Meanwhile, Germany turned against Russia in June 1941, and in December, Japan struck American and British bases in the Pacific and Asia. Literally overnight, American isolation evaporated. The U.S. AAF had been building toward a war footing since 1938 but, as in World War I, had a long way to go. Ultimate victory was seized in an awesome display of aviation mated to physics that took air power to undreamed-of heights in only four years. The world would remain irrevocably changed.

Some 16 million Americans entered the armed forces in World War II (more than three times as many as in 1917 and 1918), with 291,500 battle deaths and 113,800 dead from other causes. It was the first war in which combat accounted for more deaths than disease and accident. More than 670,000 were wounded, bringing total casualties to more than 1 million Americans. The AAF lost 52,173 airmen in combat (1,160 per month) and more than 13,000 in stateside training and operations (288 per month).

REAL BOMBERS

Billy Mitchell was long gone by the time his dream of a genuine strategic bomber took wing, but the Boeing B-17 appeared in 1935, a year before the prophet's death, and the reality was breathtaking in concept and form. A large (103-foot span) 4-engine machine with graceful tail and gleaming aluminum skin, the B-17 came to define its era as no other aircraft.

(Photo courtesy of the USAF via Robert F. Dorr)

Three B-17G Flying Fortresses en route to Germany in 1944. This photo was taken by actor Clark Gable, who served in the USAF and rose to the rank of major.

The classic bomber began life as the Boeing 299, and flew at Seattle in July 1935. The timing was fortuitous, as Hitler had abrogated the Versailles Treaty in March. Propelled by four powerful radials, the gleaming giant boasted five gun turrets and was hailed as a Flying Fortress—hence its wartime name. The "X job" could deliver 2,500 pounds of bombs nearly 1,000 miles at 200 miles per hour.

The prototype was lost in October 1935, but the program was too important to delay. After some budget crunching (the Boeing cost twice as much as its Douglas and Martin competitors), the Army ordered 65 with deliveries commencing in 1937. Airmen were thrilled with the B-17's potential, but purchases remained low until the "arsenal of democracy" kicked into second gear in 1939 and 1940. Meanwhile, long-range flights to Latin America and a 750-mile interception of a fast ocean liner demonstrated the Boeing's capabilities. More than 12,000 were manufactured during the coming war.

B-17 FLYING FORTRESS

Britain had the Spitfire; Germany had the Stuka; Japan had the Zero. America's "poster plane" was the Boeing B-17. First flown in 1938, the Flying Fortress was the first heavy bomber with turbo-supercharged engines: Four Wright radials that pushed production models took it to 300 miles per hour. Blessed with heavy armament, good looks, and operational success, the B-17 was the embodiment of American air power and the doctrine of daylight precision bombing. Although empty weight grew from the prototype's 12 tons to 18 tons in the G model, all Fortresses had a 103-foot, 9-inch wingspan.

B-17s were flown in every theater of war, but the Fortress became identified with the strategic bombing campaign against Germany. Forts based in Britain and Italy conducted a three-year war against the Nazi *Reich,* often facing *Luftwaffe* fighters without a friendly escort. Heavy losses called into question the concept of the "self-escorting bomber," but by late 1943 long-range P-51s were available, and the course of the air war was established.

With a crew of 10 men including 5 gunners, the Fortress typically carried 3 tons of bombs to Berlin and beyond. Its use in the Pacific largely ended in 1943 in favor of the longer-ranged B-24, but more than 12,700 B-17s came to represent American aviation in World War II. To this day, the Flying Fortress accounts for more Medals of Honor—and more movies—than any aircraft in history.

Recognizing the likely need for more heavy bombers, the Air Corps ordered Consolidated's B-24 into production in 1939 with deliveries beginning the next year. Often overshadowed by the Flying Fortress, the Liberator would become the most produced aircraft in American history with an eventual total of 18,000. Between them, the 17 and the 24 would carry the strategic bombing load for the AAF in Europe and the Mediterranean from 1942 to 1945.

Other projects anticipated even bigger airplanes, although only one of each was produced. The Boeing XB-15, with 4 radial engines and 149-foot span, was first flown October 1937—a "proof of concept" project in later terminology. Despite so-so performance, it demonstrated adequate range to fly from Guam to Tokyo and back—exactly the mission profile of B-29s seven years later.

The Douglas XB-19 was an even greater aerial behemoth. With an incredible 212-foot span and 42-ton empty weight, it was the largest American aircraft ever built, spanning 100 feet more than the Hughes "Spruce Goose." The factory did not want to complete the project, but the Air Corps Materiel Division needed flight data for future projects. The gigantic bomber first flew in June 1941 with the same Wright engines that would power the '29. The Douglas possessed a phenomenal 7,000-mile range with 3 tons of bombs and a crew of 11 to 18, depending on the mission. Heirs to the B-19 (scrapped in 1949) would be the Boeing B-29 and the Consolidated B-36. Clearly, the AAC was increasingly serious about long-range bombardment.

Development of the aforementioned bombers from the mid-1930s to early 1940s went hand in glove with the way the AAC expected to fight the upcoming war. It became an article of faith among bombardment advocates that "the bomber would always get through." Heavy defensive firepower and decent speed were the keys to penetrating enemy airspace, even without fighter escort. In fact, the latter raised some bitter internecine squabbling between what would later be called the "bomber mafia" and the "fighter mafia." A disgruntled fighter pilot, Major Claire Chennault, brought professional ruin upon himself with a 1935 paper titled "The Role of Pursuit Aviation." The "self-escorting bomber" had been called into question, and the high priests of bombardment would brook no heresy. Chennault took himself to China to sell his theories there (more on that later).

There also emerged a heady belief in the capability of the Norden bomb sight. Developed by the Navy but embraced by the AAC, the Norden's reputed "pickle-barrel" accuracy from 10,000 feet was one of the legs upon which bombardment aviation rested. That was the good news. The bad news was yet to come: Flying predictable courses at 10,000 feet amid Germany's scientifically layered flak was suicide; 12,000 became the minimum for medium bombers. Heavy-bomber altitudes were raised to 25,000 feet, and far from hitting the proverbial pickle barrel, combat proved that usually no more than half the bombs dropped (often far less) would strike within 1,000 feet of the aimpoint.

Meanwhile, the "peashooters" were not entirely discounted. Between 1939 and 1941 fast, capable interceptors were developed such as Lockheed's futuristic P-38 Lightning and Republic's big P-47 Thunderbolt. With turbo supercharged engines and heavy armament, they were expected to knock down enemy bombers at high altitude. In retrospect, it was an institutional contradiction because the AAF believed its own bombers would brush aside hostile fighters. However, highly motivated young National Socialists in Messerschmitts and Focke-Wulfs had other ideas.

The AAC turned an important corner in 1940 with an astonishing 3,150 aircraft ordered (an otherwise respectable 621 were acquired in fiscal year 1939). The 1940 buy was enormous: It exceeded the combined total of the previous seven years. The new figure included 744 pursuits and 722 bombers or attack aircraft but barely 100 observation types—a sure sign that the AAC was outgrowing its traditional direct support mission for the ground forces. In order to help provide pilots and crews for all those combat planes, 1,000 new trainers were acquired as well.

FORCE STRUCTURE

From 1941 to 1942 alone, USAAF training aircraft acquisitions doubled, fighters increased two and a half times, bombers eightfold, and transports six times. Perhaps most amazing of all, the humble liaison "bird dogs" multiplied by a factor of nearly 12. The expanded ground force structure eventually assigned 10 or more L-4s and '5s to each infantry and armored division, requiring thousands of additional planes and pilots. The "grasshoppers" (so named because they flew so low) proved invaluable in spotting for division artillery batteries.

In round numbers, the AAF expanded procurement from 15,600 planes in 1941 to 41,000 the following year. Still, the accumulation of materiel was useless without trained personnel. In 1941, the AAF had 151 bases in the United States; that figure grew to 670 by VJ-Day, including outlying fields. Throughout the war years, the AAF graduated 193,000 pilots, 56,000 navigators, and 28,000 bombardiers, plus tens of thousands of aircrew and maintenance men. The trickle of 1941 became a flood thereafter: from 7,244 pilots in 1941 to some 24,000 a year later; from a miserly 137 navigators and 206 bombardiers in 1941 to nearly 4,000 each in the 12 months after Pearl Harbor.

More was on the way, but not soon enough.

PLANNING FOR WAR

In August 1941, General Hap Arnold knew that war was coming to America. In his three years as chief of the Air Corps (redesignated the Army Air Forces in June 1941), he had overseen significant growth in men, bases, and aircraft. But it wasn't enough. He also needed a plan for waging a truly global war against the Axis powers, especially Germany. Therefore, he turned to former instructors at the Air Corps Tactical School at Maxwell Field, Alabama, and appointed four officers of the brand new Air War Plans Division to synthesize how the AAF should prosecute a modern war.

That wasn't all. Arnold needed the document almost immediately for discussion at the Anglo-American conference at Placentia Bay, Newfoundland. President Franklin Roosevelt and Prime Minister Winston Churchill would discuss details of the Grand Alliance with their senior military and naval representatives, and Arnold was included.

MR. AIR FORCE: GENERAL HENRY H. ARNOLD
(1886–1950)

Known as Harley to his family, the cheerful, optimistic Henry H. Arnold was "Hap" to two generations of American airmen. He learned to fly from the Wright brothers and 30 years later he commanded the greatest air force in history—past, present, or future.

Graduating from West Point in 1903, Arnold became a pilot eight years later and alternated between "line" and aviation assignments. Although bitterly disappointed at not reaching France until October 1918, Arnold played an important role in America's first air war, holding numerous administrative offices, including director of military aeronautics. He emphasized the vital relationship between the air arm and American industry, with an almost intuitive appreciation of the importance of scientific research. In 1920, he reverted to his permanent rank of captain, but the foundation was laid for his vital part in leading the AAF to victory in "the next war."

As a disciple of Billy Mitchell, Arnold promoted air power in every way possible, including writing a series of boys' books and leading a notable formation flight to Alaska. Promoted to brigadier general in 1935, he became assistant chief of the Air Corps in 1936; two years later he "shook the stick" and set about planning for the global war that would soon absorb his life. As a lieutenant general in December 1941, he oversaw the worldwide growth and combat of the USAAF, leading to victory over Germany and Japan in 1945. During most of the war he was a member of the Combined Chiefs of Staff responsible for overall Allied strategy. Intensely interested in scientific progress, he was an early supporter of rocket research.

In November 1944, Arnold was elevated to five-star rank as a general of the Army, a recognition of the importance of the AAF. Subsequently the title was changed to general of the Air Force when the service achieved independence. Although Arnold was retired by then, the distinction remains; he is the only individual ever to hold the title.

With increasing heart problems, Arnold retired in 1946 after 43 years of active duty. He settled in California, where he died in 1950.

The Tactical School brain trust came through with a landmark document. AWPD-1 anticipated nearly everything the AAF would need to defeat a modern, industrialized enemy. The plan was necessarily modified as events unfolded, becoming AWPD-42, but Hap Arnold could tell the Combined Chiefs of Staff how he intended to train, equip, deploy, sustain, and operate a greatly expanded AAF. More remarkably, the document was written in just nine days, long before personal computers were available for the task. The priority targets were electrical production, transportation, petroleum, and enemy morale. As things developed, electricity was dropped from first to thirteenth place by other planners, including civilian analysts who doubted that Germany's electrical grid could be disrupted. Postwar analysis confirmed the judgment of AWPD-1's authors.

The airmen who produced AWPD-1 more than earned their pay that sultry summer. Lieutenant Colonels Harold L. George and Kenneth N. Walker, along with Majors Haywood S. Hansell and Laurence S. Kuter, all became generals during the war. Each made their marks over the next four years: George led Air Transport Command; Hansell commanded B-29s in the Pacific; Kuter held commands in Europe, North Africa, and the Pacific. Ken Walker received a posthumous Medal of Honor for leading the V Bomber Command in early 1943.

SHAKE THE STICK

In two-seat, tandem aircraft, one pilot silently transfers control to the other by shaking the stick to announce "You've got it." The new pilot in command briefly shakes in response, tacitly saying, "I have it."

The aviation slang also is applied to transfer to command of a unit, be it a squadron, wing, or air force. Thus, a retiring general might say, "I shook the stick for old Bob."

MAJOR FRONTS

World War II was truly a global conflict for the AAF. Fifteen numbered air forces were established, and eleven of them were deployed overseas. The strategic 20th Air Force, with B-29s, was administered from Headquarters AAF in Washington, D.C. (There were no 16th through 19th Air Forces.) Smaller organizations such as the North African Tactical Air Force and the China Air Task Force grew in size and importance, becoming the 12th and 14th Air Forces, respectively.

- **United States and Latin America:** Primarily training and defense organizations, the 1st through 4th Air Forces were based in "ConUS" or the continental United States. Regionally they occupied the Northeast (1st), Northwest (2nd), Southeast (3rd), and Southwest (4th). The little known 6th Air Force served in the Panama Canal Zone and Caribbean.

- **Northern Europe:** The 8th and 9th Air Forces, based in Britain before D-Day, were strategic and tactical organizations, respectively. After D-Day most of the 9th Air Force and elements of the 8th moved to France and followed the Allied ground forces into Germany.

- **The Mediterranean, including North Africa:** The original 9th Air Force was joined by the 12th in North Africa during 1942 and 1943. Subsequently, with the occupation of Italy, the 15th (strategic) Air Force was established, with the 12th remaining the tactical arm.

- **Pacific Ocean areas:** Several numbered air forces were assigned to various Pacific Ocean war zones. The 5th was "MacArthur's Air Force" in the Southwest Pacific theater, notably New Guinea and the Philippines. The 7th, originally based in Hawaii, eventually extended across the Central Pacific to include Iwo Jima. The 13th was heavily engaged in the Solomon Islands and points west. In Alaska and the Aleutians, the small 11th Air Force flew through some of the worst weather on the planet. Meanwhile, XXI Bomber Command began flying from the Marianas in late 1944.

- **Asia:** On the Asian mainland, the 10th (India) and 14th (China) Air Forces opposed the Japanese at the end of one of the war's longest supply lines. The 10th began combat operations in April 1942; the 14th grew out of Chennault's China Air Task Force. The semi-independent XX Bomber Command originally operated B-29s from China before moving to the Marianas.

PEARL HARBOR

On December 7, 1941, six Japanese aircraft carriers launched two waves of dive bombers, torpedo planes, and horizontal bombers—escorted by fast, agile fighters—against the U.S. Pacific Fleet. In barely 2 hours, at a cost of 29 carrier planes and 5 midget submarines, the Imperial Navy had sunk or damaged 7 American battleships, 6 other combatants, and destroyed 188 aircraft. Fifty-five Japanese and 2,403 Americans were killed. The attackers escaped without scraping the gray paint on any of their ships.

Few American planes got airborne during the attack, but two P-40 pilots gave an excellent account of themselves. Lieutenants George Welch and Ken Taylor of the 47th Pursuit Squadron had spent Saturday night (and early Sunday morning) in pursuit of a good time. After gambling and partying, they finally got to bed barely in time to be roused by Japanese bombs and gunfire. Without bothering to change into uniform, they raced to their dispersal field and immediately took off. Between them they shot down seven Japanese aircraft in four sorties, Taylor being wounded in the process. They received the Distinguished Service Cross, although legend holds that they were nominated for the Medal of Honor, which was denied because they took off without orders.

P-40 SERIES

The long-lived Curtiss P-40 served not only the USAAF but several Allied nations including Britain, Canada, South Africa, Australia, New Zealand, China, and Russia. When 524 Curtiss fighters were ordered in April 1939, the $12,872,000 contract was the largest ever let by the Air Corps. Eventually some 13,700 P-40s were produced from 1940 to 1944, but the type's greatest fame was gained with the mercenary organization called the American Volunteer Group—world famous as the Flying Tigers. Colonel Claire Chennault's cast-off export models were put to good use in China and Burma, and the shark-mouth paint jobs (a British innovation) inspired generations of modelers.

Eventually, all U.S. P-40s were called Warhawks, while the British Commonwealth used the titles Tomahawk for A to C models and Kittyhawks for D to F versions. Most of the series used the reliable Allison V-12, although some mid-war models had Packard Merlins. The last production model, the P-40N, was optimistically rated at 375 miles per hour at 10,500 feet but the type's range, altitude performance, and rate of climb were second rate by 1944.

P-40s scrambled from Hawaiian airfields on December 7, 1941 and scored their first kills against Japan. Almost four years later only one AAF fighter group still flew the type, but the Curtiss design had left its stamp on history.

The American survivors logged the full spectrum of what a later generation called post-traumatic stress syndrome. Some were benumbed, others tremulous, and all were livid with rage. An AAF sergeant at Hickham Field looked at the remains of the base beer garden and shook his fist at the withdrawing enemy planes: "You dirty SOBs! You've bombed the most important building on this post!"

Unquestionably one of history's most stunning successes, Pearl Harbor and subsequent operations gave a small island nation an opportunity to neutralize Western military and naval power in the region while seizing vital oil sources. It was a roll of the geopolitical dice, and for six months Tokyo rolled sevens.

A dreadful dirge of defeat sounded across one quarter of the earth's surface: Wake Island, Guam, Singapore, Malaya, the Philippines, Shanghai, the East Indies, and more. The Anglo-American alliance, a de facto pact for months, was violently welded into reality by the shared misery of Japanese triumphs. Perhaps the lowest point was the British surrender of Hong Kong on Christmas Day. Meanwhile, Germany and Italy had declared war on America on December 11.

However, President Franklin Roosevelt and Prime Minister Winston Churchill already agreed that Nazi Germany represented the more serious threat, and Berlin would remain the priority target. Adolf Hitler did nothing to ameliorate the situation when he declared war on America four days after Pearl Harbor. In truth, it mattered relatively little—U.S. ships and German submarines had been waging a secretive war in the North Atlantic for months.

Still, the rage and confusion attending the Pearl Harbor debacle forced attention to the Pacific rather than the Atlantic. Army Air Force bombers began searching the California and Mexican coastlines for a reported invasion fleet. Marine Corps fighters flew "combat air patrols" over Point Loma near San Diego. And following a grim Christmas season but before rationing took effect, other wartime concessions were made. Out of fear of Japanese attack, the fortieth-anniversary Rose Bowl game was "transplanted" from California to North Carolina (Oregon State over Duke, 20–16).

PHILIPPINES DEBACLE

The news that holiday season could hardly have been worse. Besides the disaster in Hawaii, things were dismal in the Philippines, where war began on Monday, December 8. General Douglas MacArthur managed to lose most of his air force on its fields more than 8 hours after Pearl Harbor: 17 of 35 B-17s and some 80 other types were written off, including 58 P-35 and P-40 "pursuit" craft. In Hawaii, Admiral Husband Kimmel and Lieutenant General Walter Short were made responsible for the disaster; in the Philippines, MacArthur eventually took a boat ride and received the Medal of Honor.

Despite the appalling situation, there were small benefits. Said Lieutenant Joseph H. Moore of the 20th Pursuit Squadron (later commanding the 7th Air Force in Vietnam), "Finally we could take off our damn neckties and throw them away."

Wandering among the rubble at Clark Field was a temporarily unemployed bomber pilot, Lieutenant Ed Jacquet. Looking into a bomb crater, he noticed fragments in the bottom of the hole and decided to grab some souvenirs. He picked up a jagged piece of steel and saw some English lettering; it was stamped "Singer Sewing Machine Company." Years later, Jacquet said, "I guess it's true, you shouldn't sell anything that somebody can shoot back at you."

In the Philippines a legend quickly grew around a B-17 pilot of the 19th Bomb Group. Captain P. Colin Kelly Jr. attacked a Japanese invasion force off Aparri on Luzon's north coast on December 10, bombing from 22,000 feet. However, en route home he was intercepted by Japanese fighters. The Zero pilots included Flight Petty Officer Saburo Sakai, who later wrote of his admiration for Kelly and other American fliers. Kelly's plane was a B-17C, lacking a tail gunner or self-sealing fuel tanks. With his Boeing badly damaged and one gunner dead, Kelly remained at the controls so that the other six crewmen could bail out. Within sight of Clark Field, he prepared to jump just as the plane exploded.

Based on misidentification of Japanese ships, Kelly was credited with bombing or even sinking the battleship *Haruna*, which was nowhere near. More likely Kelly attacked a cruiser, for which he allegedly was awarded the Medal of Honor. While he was nominated for the ultimate accolade, he received the Distinguished Service Cross, although later bomber pilots were presented the "Congressional" for similar sacrifice.

1942: A DISMAL NEW YEAR

MacArthur's boast that the Philippines could not be conquered proved laughably hollow. The Japanese landed at Lingayan Gulf and barely a week later, on December 27, Manila had been declared an open city to prevent further bombing. The Philippines were clearly doomed, although some defenders held out until early May. American air power had little opportunity to demonstrate its capability in the Philippines.

Far to the southwest, on December 25, badly needed reinforcements arrived in the form of Curtiss P-40s to help defend Java. The Dutch were hard-pressed to fend off the inevitable Japanese invasion of the petroleum-rich East Indies, and losses would be serious before the Allies were forced to withdraw.

Meanwhile, America was scrambling to play catch-up in the bottom of the first. With the Japanese scoring repeatedly, and committing precious few errors, the U.S. armed forces were fully extended merely to keep abreast of events. However, the nation was blessed with visionary leaders, men who had spent their entire professional lives preparing for this time, if not specifically this circumstance. One indicator of faith in the future occurred in Savannah, Georgia, on January 28 when the 8th Army Air Force was activated. Before the new year was over, the fledgling bomber force would stream its contrails over Nazi Occupied Europe.

Despite the "Germany First" policy in London and Washington, the fact remained that Japan was consistently defeating American and British forces throughout the Pacific and the Far East. On February 1, some of the handful of Curtiss P-40s still operational in the Philippines opposed an enemy landing at Quinauan Point. Flying low, picking their targets, the "pea shooters" strafed landing craft and troops already ashore but could not prevent the amphibious operation from gaining another hold in the islands. Cut off from outside reinforcement or resupply, the American squadrons fought a descending spiral of attrition: planes, pilots, mechanics, spares, ammunition, and fuel.

Southwest Pacific Theater

Well to the south, the new 5th Air Force launched strikes against Japanese forces in Java. The Dutch East Indies, rich in petroleum and rubber, were a prime candidate to join Tokyo's "Greater East Asia Co-Prosperity Sphere," and like the Philippines they were targeted for early conquest. American and Dutch airmen fought a losing battle, despite gallant efforts to keep hopes afloat.

Toward that end, on February 27 came a notable naval engagement, the Battle of Java Sea. Units of the 5th Air Force flew steadily in support of the American, British, and Dutch command, but exerted little effect on the battle. Five allied ships were sunk with little damage inflicted upon the Japanese Navy. An aircraft ferry, the USS *Langley*, was sunk with 32 badly needed P-40s for the Dutch East Indies.

On March 1, the Americans flew their last heavy bomber mission from Java. They evacuated the islands the next day, leaving a prize to Tokyo rich in strategic materials and, perhaps equally, immense prestige.

Things only got worse.

Singapore surrendered on February 15; the greatest British defeat in history. A week later, Roosevelt ordered General MacArthur out of the

Philippines. Although his overall conduct of the campaign left a great deal to be desired, the vainglorious commander had become a symbol of American resolve, and his status as a prewar army chief of staff precluded leaving him to be captured. He established new headquarters in Townsville, on Australia's eastern coast.

As if in welcome, on March 3 the Japanese bombed Broome, in Northern Australia. It seemed they could reach anywhere in the expanse of the Pacific.

Forced out of the Philippines and the East Indies, the AAF regrouped in Northern Australia. Heavy bombers flew frequent reconnaissance missions, while B-25s continued attacking the southern Philippines by staging through interim bases. However, American offensive air power was limited. Of necessity the emphasis turned to defense.

Defending Australia

The 49th Fighter Group had arrived in Australia in February, woefully undertrained: Only a dozen of the 102 pilots had flown a fighter before arrival. Of the two other fighter groups available, one had been decimated in Java and the other was still building. The "Forty-Niners" had to carry the load during the interim.

Darwin had been bombed on February 19 and the Royal Australian Air Force was stretched too thin to provide adequate defense. The 9th Fighter Squadron took up the slack, making interceptions from late March.

On April 4, Lieutenant Andy Reynolds, a Java survivor, led the interception. He recorded, "We sighted the enemy over Darwin, seven miles south of the township. There were bombers in extended V formation and 3 Zeros in V formation 500 feet above and behind as an escort. We delivered a head on, diving attack. The Zeros were completely surprised and attempted to climb. I shot down one bomber and one Zero. The escort along with these bombers never took any fighting positions due to the fact that they were caught unawares." The 9th Squadron lost two P-40s in the fight.

The group's three squadrons were reunited at Darwin later that month, leading to a major combat on April 25. The Americans reported 24 bombers with 9 escorting Zeros, and for once the defenders had the numbers. Fifty P-40s intercepted, and the Warhawks had a field day, claiming ten kills. Captain Bill Hennon, another Java veteran, droned the P-40 litany into his younger pilots: Avoid combat at higher altitude (where the unsuper-charged Allison engine was a disadvantage). Instead, use height to gain speed in a dive, pick a specific target, fire only when in range, and zoom climb back to "the perch."

The next day the 49th Group claimed three bombers but lost four P-40s. The rate of attrition only continued.

Meanwhile, the AAF provided what assets it could to the southwest Pacific. Among the units dispatched by sea was the 22nd Bomb Group, sent to Hawaii and then on to Australia. The first Martin Marauder group committed to combat, the 22nd would soon become known as the Red Raiders, making a growing reputation for the B-26 despite stateside allusion to "one a day in Tampa Bay" for units training at McDill Field.

A June 9 bombing mission against the Japanese port at Lae, New Guinea, went undocumented for decades. Lieutenant Commander Lyndon Johnson, a Texas congressman given a Navy commission prior to the 1942 elections, rode in a B-26 of the 22nd Group at Port Morseby. His tardiness in arriving at Morseby disrupted the mission schedule, resulting in the loss of two Marauders and one crew. Despite the fact that Johnson's aircraft aborted 80 miles south of Lae, he received a Silver Star from General Douglas MacArthur for "coolness under fire" and "returning with valuable information." Johnson wore the medal lapel pin for the rest of his life.

In late July, the Japanese landed more troops at Gona on the north coast of New Guinea's Papuan peninsula. The 5th Air Force launched everything available: B-24s, B-25s, B-26s, even Douglas A-24 Banshees as well as fighters. Although the AAF never achieved the success with dive bombers that the Navy and Marine Corps did with their version, known as the SBD, the A-24 had one irrefutable asset: It was available. But not indefinitely—on one notable mission seven took off and one returned.

The tenacious Japanese continued their advance, taking Buna and Kokoda and threatening Allied supply lines. The result was a prolonged slugfest with air power playing an increasingly important role.

About that same time, the 11th Bomb Group begin staging B-17s to Espiritu Santo in the New Hebrides. Air support for the upcoming Guadalcanal invasion required long-range reconnaissance as well as strategic reach to strike the enemy naval-air bastion at Rabaul, New Britain. Attention turned to the Navy-controlled Pacific Theater of Operations (PTO).

Pacific Theater

The Pacific theater was by far the largest on earth: The ocean covers one third of the planet. Consequently, in contrast to Europe the Pacific war was necessarily a joint-service operation on a daily basis. An interdependence arose among the services that was not fully duplicated elsewhere, although certainly interservice rivalry was never extinguished.

Arguably the most desolate portion of the theater was the Aleutian Islands, but in March, the 11th Air Force was established with the fighter command activated at Elmendorf Field, Alaska. In coming months, the 11th would not only fly but fight in possibly the world's worst aviation climate—the Aleutians weather factory.

Doolittle Do'ed It!

Lieutenant Colonel Jimmy Doolittle was called "the master of the calculated risk." His exceptional Army and civilian flying career in the 1920s and 1930s established his impeccable piloting, scientific, and organizational skills. Therefore, when AAF chief Hap Arnold asked him to investigate prospects for the First Special Aviation Project, Doolittle typically took charge. It would be America's response to Pearl Harbor.

Conceived by a naval officer, the plan called for B-25 Mitchell bombers to take off from the aircraft carrier, bomb Tokyo and other Japanese cities, and land at prepared fields in eastern China. The more Doolittle learned of the prospect, the more he liked it. So much, in fact, that he appointed himself to lead the mission.

GENERAL JAMES H. DOOLITTLE (1896–1993)

A superb pilot, scientific intellect, and exceptional commander, James Harold Doolittle has no peer for aviation accomplishment and leadership. Although denied combat in World War I, he embarked upon a stunning career between the wars. He was the first pilot to cross America in less than 24 hours, then in 12 hours. He practically invented instrument flying, earned the first aviation Ph.D., won nearly every race and honor possible, and even performed the first outside loop. Upon leaving active duty he midwifed high-octane fuel between the Army and Shell Oil, neither of which was inclined to pursue the matter unilaterally.

Recalled to service in 1941, Doolittle organized the First Special Aviation Project, leading 16 Mitchells from the aircraft carrier USS *Hornet* to bomb Japan in April 1942. He was jumped to brigadier general, leading the 12th Air Force in North Africa and, with a second star, organized the 15th. In January 1944, as a lieutenant general, he commanded the Mighty 8th in Britain where he remained for the last year and a half of the war. On VJ-Day he was aboard the battleship USS *Missouri,* having earned a place in the ranks of war-winning commanders. He received his fourth star well after retirement, by special act of Congress.

Quiet, competent, and modest, "General Jimmy" remains one of aviation's all-time superstars.

Doolittle assembled 16 Mitchells plus some spare crews that trained in secrecy in Florida during early 1942. The trick was safely launching a fully loaded bomber in as little as 450 feet of deck space, but tests proved it could be done. The B-25s then flew cross country and were hoisted aboard the *Hornet* at Alameda, California, Doolittle's hometown.

Escorted by the carrier *Enterprise* and other ships, the *Hornet* steamed across the Pacific, expecting to launch Doolittle's crews about 400 miles from Tokyo. However, on the morning of April 18 the task force was spotted by a Japanese picket ship, requiring takeoff some 200 miles sooner than planned. Doolittle nursed his bomber off the deck, circled to get his bearings, and headed west. The other B-25s followed over the next hour.

The attack went well. Surprise was achieved as Mitchells dropped explosive and incendiary bombs on Tokyo, Yokohama, and Nagoya. All bombers got away, but their schedule was badly askew. Arriving over the China coast in darkness, the crews crash-landed or bailed out, while one plane diverted to Soviet territory where it was interned.

Of the 80 fliers on the mission, three were killed and eight captured. Three of the latter were executed as "war criminals," but the others later served in other theaters of war. Doolittle returned home to universal acclaim and the Medal of Honor. Upon accepting the decoration he said, "I'll spend the rest of my life earning this honor."

The Doolittle Raid inflicted little physical damage but the strategic results were significant. Stung by the daring impudence of the mission, the Japanese navy increased its resolve to defeat the remainder of the U.S. Pacific Fleet and thus surged ahead into the Battle of Midway.

B-25 MITCHELL

If it had done nothing else, the twin-engine, twin-tailed North American bomber would have a place in history for the Doolittle Raid of April 1942. The 16 Mitchells that launched from the aircraft carrier *Hornet* (CV-8) represented America's first response to Pearl Harbor. But that was barely the beginning of the B-25's long war.

When the prototype took off in August 1940, the Battle of Britain was just peaking. The U.S. Army recognized the need for a medium bomber before long, and North American (which was also designing the Mustang) won a sizeable contract. Named for air-power advocate Billy Mitchell, the B-25 proved a versatile aircraft, especially in the Pacific and Mediterranean theaters. The Mitchell proved devastatingly effective against Japanese shipping with a combination of guns, bombs, and even 75mm cannon.

With two Wright engines and typically a five-man crew, the B-25 spanned 68 feet and was capable of 270 miles per hour. With considerable "stretch," the bomber's empty weight only increased from 17,800 to 19,500 pounds between the A and J models while gross weight jumped from 27,000 to 35,000 pounds. For most models the stated range was 1,350 miles.

Some 9,800 B-25s were built, including 700 naval versions (PBJs), largely for the Marine Corps. The type was also used by Britain, Russia, China, the Netherlands, and Brazil.

Midway

The Pacific war took an abrupt turn in early June: a turn for the better for the Americans, an irrecoverable disaster for Japan. Powerful naval units including four aircraft carriers descended on Midway Atoll, 1,100 miles northwest of Oahu, but their approach was known to American code breakers. Admiral Chester Nimitz committed almost his entire Pacific Fleet to the battle, mainly relying on his three available carriers. The 7th Air Force contributed what it could: Lieutenant Colonel Walter Sweeney's 17 B-17s of the 5th and 11th Bomb Groups, plus four B-26s under Captain William F. Collins. Midway was an all-or-nothing throw of the dice: The Americans felt they could not afford a Japanese base so close to Hawaii.

The Fortresses conducted long-range reconnaissance missions before the battle, augmenting Navy patrol planes. The AAF crews did well in their overwater searches, proving that they could locate the enemy fleet units and presumably validating Mitchell's philosophy about the superiority of land-based aviation. However, when the battle flared up on the morning of June 4, the high-level bombers were consistently frustrated. Bombing from 20,000 feet, they learned how difficult it was to hit a ship maneuvering in the open sea. By one reckoning, the B-17s dropped 322 bombs during the battle without a hit. One vivid strike photo shows three clusters of hits near the carrier *Hiryu*, from 600 to 1,600 feet wide.

Collins's Marauders got a much closer look at the enemy. In company with land-based Navy and Marine planes, the B-26s conducted an unescorted torpedo attack on the Japanese carriers. Swarmed by defending Zeros and faced with a sky full of flak, the Martins bored in low and fast. Only Collins and Lieutenant James Muri's planes survived. The shot-up Marauders returned with wounded aboard, claiming hits on the enemy flagship.

In truth, no land-based planes of any service inflicted damage on the Japanese carriers. However, Navy dive-bombers sank all four flattops as well as a cruiser.

Because the AAF planes returned to Oahu before the Navy aircraft, 7th Air Force had the PR advantage. In the appalling confusion of the attacks, the Army men believed they had done significant damage, which was duly reported. Naval aviators who arrived a few days later indulged in some serious "disagreements" that escalated into fisticuffs.

Whatever disputes arose in Hawaii, the Army, Navy, and Marines continued operating together against their mutual enemy, Imperial Japan. In August, the first American offensive of the war kicked off as Marines occupied Tulagi and Guadalcanal in the Solomon Islands, 10 degrees below the equator. The AAF provided fighters and bombers to the campaign, which lasted six months in a sweltering, hostile climate against a tenacious, skillful enemy.

Guadalcanal's code name was Cactus, and Henderson Field became "the cactus patch." The Army was represented by a variety of planes, most notably P-39s and the P-400 export model of the Bell Airacobra. Major Dale Brannon's pilots sardonically noted that a P-400 was "a P-40 with a Zero behind it," and generally kept out of the way of Imperial Navy fighters. However, the Bells flew repeated attacks against enemy ground forces and even tried their hand at ship attacks.

In November, the "Cactus Air Force" received a boost in the form of P-38s from the 347th Fighter Group. The Lightnings provided the much-needed high-altitude capability lacking in the anemic Airacobras. Although difficult to maintain in that tropical environment, the big Lockheeds proved their worth repeatedly.

China-Burma-India

With their glamorous reputation, splashy headlines, and undoubted success, the fighter pilots of the American Volunteer Group captured the public's imagination. Claire Chennault's Flying Tigers easily became stars of the China-Burma-India (CBI) theater in 1942, providing badly needed combat experience to new AAF pilots arriving to fight the Japanese. However, the major aviation contribution to the theater over the next three years was made not by fighters nor bombers. It went to the unglamorous, often unheralded transport crews who kept China's vital lifeline moving in often wretched conditions. The fliers called their route "the Hump."

India-based Hump flights began with C-47s in April 1942, ostensibly to stash supplies for Doolittle's raiders who were expected to land in eastern China. The aerial bridge over the Himalayas began as a trickle but eventually became a span that sustained China and kept millions of her men in the war. With closure of the Burma Road, the logistics deficit could only be made up by an air bridge leaping over Japanese controlled territory. It was unprecedented in its scope and ambition, and that it ultimately succeeded was a tribute to optimism, skill, courage, and persistence.

Meanwhile, early in March, Major General Lewis H. Brereton took over the 10th Air Force, supervising a move from the United States to India. Brereton had been MacArthur's newly arrived air commander when the war began but had been unable to accomplish anything, owing nearly as much to MacArthur's poorly structured staff as to Japanese efforts. In India he would make a new beginning, leading to a major command in Europe by D-Day.

In June, the theater's few B-17s and '24s were transferred to North Africa, leaving no heavy bombers in the CBI. The situation was slowly redressed, but American air power was largely defensive for several months.

MAJOR GENERAL CLAIRE L. CHENNAULT
(1890–1958)

Fighter pilot Claire Chennault rocked the Air Corps's boat by insisting on the primacy of pursuit aviation when bombardment ruled the roost. Retired officially because of deafness, he looked elsewhere to prove his theories, and offered his services to Chinese leader Chiang Kai-shek in 1937. Four years later Chennault formed the American Volunteer Group, a clandestine organization composed of Army, Navy, and Marine personnel to fight on behalf of China against Japan. The Flying Tigers received much favorable publicity, leading to Chennault's reinstatement as a U.S. Army brigadier general. Perennially short of everything, at the end of the world's longest supply line, he nevertheless led the 14th Air Force through most of the war. His hope of conducting offensive operations against the Japanese homeland was realized far beyond his early plans for B-25s. Subsequently, the 14th obtained heavy bombers, although the China B-29s in 1944 were "owned" by XX Bomber Command. Chennault retired in 1945, still devoted to his beloved China.

On the Fourth of July, the American Volunteer Group was disbanded and most of the personnel were left in limbo. Their treatment by the U.S. Army was, in a word, appalling—testimony to the bitter political hassles between Claire Chennault and the theater commander, Major General "Vinegar Joe" Stillwell. The combat-experienced Flying Tigers were told that if they declined to transfer to the AAF they could make their own way home, where their draft boards had already been notified.

Consequently, most Tigers were absorbed into the AAF as part of the China Air Task Force. The 23rd Fighter Group was established with a nucleus of Chennault's veterans, who provided much needed leadership for the untried Army pilots. Chennault chose a West Pointer to command the group: 34-year-old Colonel Robert L. Scott, a 5,000-hour fighter pilot who had already cadged a P-40E from "the old man" for a series of solo bombing and strafing missions. Eager and aggressive, Scott's ambition riled many fliers but even his detractors conceded his dedication to the group. "Put me on the board for every mission," he told his operations officer, "and I'll tell you when I'm ready to lead." Meanwhile, the former Tigers led in the air.

At one point Chennault was quoted as saying that he could bomb Japan into surrender with a force of 25 Mitchells. If he made the statement it was an absurdity, but it did indicate that he was thinking beyond his pursuit origins. Eventually his theater would operate the most significant bomber in the AAF inventory.

Mediterranean and Middle East

By 1942, Colonel Harry Halvorsen (of the 1929 endurance record in the Fokker *Question Mark*) commanded a detachment of B-24s that was diverted to the Middle East to bolster British defenses against the *Afrika Korps*. On June 28, Major General Lewis Brereton arrived with additional units for the emerging Middle East Air Force, later designated the 9th Army Air Force. Halvorsen made AAF history on June 11 when he led 13 Egyptian-based Liberators against Ploesti, Romania's, oil fields—the first U.S. heavy bomber mission over Europe and the first at night.

The "Halpro" (Halvorsen Project) mission inflicted little damage, and aircraft losses were disproportionate. Eight planes landed safely in Iraq and Syria, but one crash-landed and four were interned in Turkey. While the first Ploesti mission could not be counted a notable success, it showed the way into the distant future with far greater efforts 14 months later.

Halvorsen's detachment remained in the Middle East, forming the basis of the 376th Bomb Group. Through the end of the year his Liberators logged more than 80 missions, dropping some 1,300 tons of bombs.

Throughout July, the Anglo-American Middle East Air Force bombed the German bastion at Tobruk, Libya, and targeted Axis shipping in the Mediterranean.

By far the biggest event in North Africa that year was Operation Torch, the Allied landings in French Morocco. American troops went ashore on November 8, encountering sporadic resistance from the Vichy forces nominally allied with Germany. However, the diplomatic complexities were sorted out, and 33rd Fighter Group P-40s launched from the escort carrier USS *Chenango* to begin operating on the west flank of the *Afrika Korps*. The Warhawks became the first in a growing list of AAF aircraft operating in the Western Desert.

Torch included two airborne assaults, the first in AAF history. On November 8, flying 1,500 miles from Britain, 39 C-47s carried 556 troopers of the 509th Parachute Battalion to seize 2 Algerian airfields. The mission turned to hash. Several planes landed in the desert, nearly out of fuel; three or four were shot down by French fighters; some troopers jumped early and were interned in Spanish Morocco. With the remainder of his force, the battalion commander jumped prematurely, hitting the ground 35 miles from the objective. A forced march got the troopers to both fields, which had been taken by ground forces in the interim.

Undaunted, 8 days later 350 men of the 509th were dropped on Youks Les Bains Airfield, Algeria. It was a cakewalk, with the French-held field secured in 20 minutes. More airborne operations would follow.

European Theater

President Roosevelt and Prime Minister Churchill had already agreed that Nazi Germany posed the greater threat and must be defeated before Japan. However, long months would pass before even a token U.S. air presence could be established in Great Britain; many more before a combined allied air campaign could be launched against Occupied Europe, let alone the *Reich* itself. If the adage that great endeavors arise from humble origins is true, the beginning of the U.S. Army Strategic Air Forces was humble indeed.

On February 29, Brigadier General Ira C. Eaker arrived in Britain with six hand-picked officers, the pioneers of the 8th Air Force. Eaker was a 45-year-old professional who had been flying since 1918. He had made the Pan American Goodwill Flight in 1926-1927 and was a pilot on the Fokker *Question Mark*'s endurance record in 1929. A thinker as well as a practitioner, he had written three prewar books about military aviation.

Eaker chose his staff wisely: They included future standouts such as Captains Fred Castle (who would receive a posthumous Medal of Honor as a brigadier general in 1944) and Beirne Lay (a future B-24 group commander and author of *Twelve O'Clock High*). Lieutenant Colonel Frank Armstrong also became a significant leader, commanding the 97th Bomb Group from July to September 1942 and the 306th in early 1943.

Fred Castle had a huge job: assessing base requirements for the fledgling air force and coordinating materials, schedules, and construction. As much as anyone, he built the Mighty 8th from the ground up. Meanwhile, the Americans (perhaps uncharacteristically) told their RAF hosts, "We won't say much until we've done something."

Five weeks later, on March 25, Major Cecil Lessig became the first 8th Air Force pilot to log a combat mission, in a "guest appearance" with No. 64 Squadron, RAF. Flying a Spitfire on a 36-plane sweep over France, the British withdrew in the face of an estimated 50 *Luftwaffe* fighters.

At first there was little to occupy American airmen in Europe. On February 15, Lieutenant Colonel Townsend Griffiss became the first AAF flier to die in the European Theater of Operations (ETO) when he was tragically killed by "friendly forces" over the North Sea. He was lost with all the crew and passengers of a British Overseas Airways Liberator en route from Cairo to Britain. Poor air-ground coordination and the extreme aggressiveness of two Polish fighter pilots led to the tragedy.

Meanwhile, the British had identified 87 potential airfields for American use. However, some early U.S. arrivals shared quarters with the RAF. One such unit was the 31st Fighter Group, the first combat element of what became VIII Fighter Command. The group had sailed to Britain, gratefully leaving behind its Bell P-39s. The pilots were especially pleased, as they had been slated to ferry their Airacobras "across the pond." Reportedly, the fighter commander, a Great War ace named Frank O'Driscoll Hunter, had reckoned that a 25 percent attrition would be "acceptable."

Among the 31st pilots was Lieutenant Jerry Collinsworth, a future ace in North Africa. He recalls, "We were planning on the first attempt in history to fly the Atlantic Ocean in a single-engine fighter. We were going to attempt to follow B-17s across. Fortunately, the Japs did us a favor by surfacing a sub that shelled the California coast. The B-17s were sent there and we sailed across the Atlantic, which was fine with us!

"I clearly remember touching my first Spitfire. I was amazed that it had a wooden propeller! I took the wingtip and could shake the airplane. We cracked up about 20 of them the first 3 weeks we were checking out because of the unusual braking system. We were used to brakes on the rudder pedals. Not so with the Spit. You squeezed a lever on the control column and at the same time pushing one rudder or the other for the direction you wished to take. After we got used to it, no problem."

Meanwhile, other fighters were making the transatlantic flight. On July 9, seven P-38Fs flew from Dow Field, Maine, to bases in Lincolnshire and Hampshire. It was the first time that single-seaters had ferried that route as part of Operation Bolero, the buildup of U.S. air power in Britain. Late that month the 97th Group became the first U.S. heavy-bomber unit operational in the ETO.

First over Europe

The first combat mission by USAAF aircrew over northwest Europe occurred on June 29 when Captain Charles Kegelman's A-20 crew manned one of No. 226 Squadron's Douglas Boston IIIs on a 12-plane mission to Hazebrouck, Belgium. The first AAF squadron-strength mission in Europe came on July 4 when six crews of the 15th Bomb Squadron borrowed RAF Bostons for a strike against *Luftwaffe* airfields in the Low Countries. Lieutenant F. A. Loehrl's plane and crew were lost to ground fire while Captain Kegelman barely got his flakked-up Douglas back to Britain. At a nearby target, Lieutenant William G. Lynn was lost with his crew and a British plane also was shot down. Kegelman received the Distinguished Service Cross, while three other pilots were awarded Distinguished Flying Crosses.

Farther west, the 27th Fighter Squadron's P-38Fs had landed in Iceland in June. With Lieutenant Joseph Shaffer, a 33rd Squadron P-39 pilot, Lieutenant Elza Shahan shared destruction of an FW-200 patrol bomber on August 14. It was the first AAF victory against Germany. Subsequently, the 27th rejoined the group and proceeded to North Africa via the United Kingdom.

The 8th's first heavy-bomber mission was launched on August 17 as six B-17Es of the 97th Group at Polebrook, Northants, flew toward the French coast, then reversed course to draw away *Luftwaffe* fighters. The strike force of 12 Boeings was led by General Eaker flying a Fortress named *Yankee Doodle*. Leading the second element was Colonel Frank Armstrong, one of Eaker's "inner six" who had arrived in Britain in February. In the right seat of *Butcher Shop* was a young major named Paul Tibbets. Three years later, in August 1945, he would fly an even more notable mission against Japan.

In clear skies, the Fortresses bombed from 23,000 feet, hitting the Rouen rail yards. All 12 bombers landed at Grafton Underwood, reporting light fighter opposition.

Two days later came Operation Jubilee, the British–Canadian landing on the coast of France. It was the largest air battle of the war to date. The Germans won a significant victory (106 to 48 by one postwar reckoning), but the amphibious force withdrew without serious ship losses. Throughout the day the 31st Group engaged FW-190s, claiming two confirmed and two probables. Subsequently the group deployed to North Africa.

At the end of September, the AAF received a godsend in the form of three squadrons of experienced American fighter pilots. The RAF Eagles were absorbed into the 8th Air Force as the basis of the 4th Fighter Group. More would be heard from them.

PLAIN ENGLISH?

When American units arrived in Britain, there were inevitable clashes. By far the most famous was the Britons' complaint that the bloody Yanks were "over paid, over sexed, and over here." However, there were also minor disputes over terminology. Despite the similarities of language and goals, AAF and RAF fliers had to adjust to one another's vocabulary.

American	British
airplane	aeroplane or machine
antenna	aerial
copilot	second pilot
fuel gauge	fuel-level indicator
gasoline	petrol
landing gear	undercart
monkey wrench	adjustable spanner
navigation	avigation
propeller	airscrew
spark plug	sparking plug
tachometer	engine-speed indicator
wing	main plane

AIR-POWER LESSONS FOR AMERICA

In his 1942 treatise *Victory Through Airpower*, Major Alexander de Seversky examined the history of military aviation (as then known) and drew "Eleven Airpower Lessons for America." Seversky was an accomplished aviator. A World War I ace in the Czarist navy, he bootstrapped his way up the American aviation establishment as an engineer and unabashed admirer of Billy Mitchell. His wartime conclusions were occasionally based on incomplete or inaccurate data, but they make interesting reading in the context of our own time:

1. *No land or sea operations are possible without first assuming control of the air.*
   Correct.

2. *Navies have lost their function of strategic offensive.*
   False then and now: Witness the 1943 through 1945 Pacific war (with heavy reliance on aircraft carriers) and postwar emergence of nuclear submarines.

3. *Blockade has become a function of air power.*
   Correct.

4. *Only air power can defeat air power.*
   Correct. However, politics often limits air power's capability.

5. *Land-based aviation is always superior to ship-borne aviation.*
   False. This is a peculiar statement, coming after Pearl Harbor and Midway. Subsequently carrier air power further disproved the assertion in the Pacific, Korea, and Vietnam.

6. *Striking radius of air power must equal the maximum dimensions of the theater operations.*
   Neither true nor false. In World War II the only such situation occurred in the Pacific with B-29s in the Marianas. Otherwise, air power affected the outcome of many campaigns without the "reach" postulated here.

7. *In air warfare, quality is relatively more decisive than quantity.*
   Generally correct. An adequate number of superior aircraft and crews frequently defeats a much larger, less-capable force. However, there is an inevitable point of diminishing returns, as with the *Luftwaffe* jets in World War II.

8. *Aircraft types must be specialized to fit not only the general strategy but the tactical problems of a specific campaign.*
   Generally incorrect. In World War II the United States did very well without specialized ground-attack aircraft, contrary to Germany and Russia. Since then, the trend has been toward "economical" multi-mission aircraft capable of performing a variety of tasks reasonably well rather than "purebred" types that concentrate on a single mission.

9. *Destruction of enemy morale from the air can only be accomplished by precision bombing.*
Uncertain. The evidence, especially from World War II, is contradictory, especially given the limitations of 1940s "precision" bombing. What effects were made on civilian morale were achieved more by saturation bombing of cities and urban industrial areas.

10. *The principle of unity of command, long recognized on land and sea, applies no less to the air.*
Correct.

11. *Air power must have its own transport.*
Correct in principle, but some notable air campaigns relied on sea power for logistics. The buildup to D-Day and the B-29 campaign are examples.

1942 Summary

At year's end, the dismal December 1941 situation had largely been redressed. Although chronically short of aircraft, crews, and supplies (one commander wrote Hap Arnold, "I need everything"), the numbered air forces were conducting offensive operations against Germany, Italy, and Japan. But despite the Allies' grand scheme to defeat Hitler first, the realities of 1942 required major effort to focus in the Pacific, where the threat was the most immediate.

At home, training bases were kicked into third gear, and factories worked around the clock, delivering 41,000 planes to the Army. AAF personnel strength had increased fivefold to 764,000 and Arnold's staff anticipated nearly doubling that figure the next year. The first steps had been taken on the long, long road back.

1943: BUILDING FOR VICTORY

For the AAF, as for America generally, the second full year of war gave the world a preview of things to come. With growing strength in every theater and monthly increases in manpower and production, the road ahead remained long and arduous, but the outcome was beyond doubt. Air power continued contributing to the overall effort in a variety of ways, and in some theaters it remained America's only significant force until 1944.

European Theater

They called it Mission 31. All of VIII Bomber Command's previous missions had been flown over Occupied Europe, but on January 27 the "heavies" went to the *Reich* itself. The first AAF raid on Germany targeted submarine building yards at Wilhelmshaven, with parts of five groups led by the 306th. The 64 Fortresses followed Colonel Frank Armstrong, who had led the first heavy bomber mission five months before. A thin cloud layer permitted 58 planes to bomb from 20,000 feet, although the Germans belatedly started smoke generators to obscure the target. Flak was "light and inaccurate," claiming one B-17, while fighter opposition ironically lacked the customary ferocity encountered over France. B-17 gunners were credited with 22 "confirmed" shootdowns, 3 times the actual *Luftwaffe* losses but still a creditable performance. Bombing was only fair, with a wide dispersion of hits over the dock area.

Germany would prove tougher next time. On February 4, enemy fighters knocked down four bombers and flak gunners notched one over Emden. Those losses would pale in comparison to what was coming.

Schweinfurt, Twice

American air power continued building its strength through the spring and summer, with 17 bomb groups operational by August. On August 17th, the Mighty 8th launched its "anniversary mission," observing one year since General Eaker led the first heavy bombers over France. The plan was a double strike against ball-bearing production at Schweinfurt and a Messerschmitt plant at Regensburg. Even more ambitiously, the 147 Fortresses targeted against Regensburg would continue to bases in North Africa, thus avoiding the worst of the defenses on the way home. The crews sweated out weather over their bases, then took off. Messerschmitts and Focke-Wulfs attacked for 90 minutes and, with flak gunners, downed 24 Boeings. The remaining Forts crossed the Alps, headed across the Mediterranean, and landed after 11 hours airborne.

Another 230 B-17s went to Schweinfurt; the Germans knocked down 36, including most of the 2 lead formations. An incredible 60 bombers were lost, a stunning figure given the previous 1-mission high of 26.

Even for those fliers who survived, the air war brought fear and physical danger. At altitude the temperature could reach −50 degrees, with frost

2 inches thick on windows. Oxygen masks and electrically heated flight suits were essential, as failure of either could result in death. Factor in flak and fighters, plus the ordinary dangers of military flying, and the risks mounted. Hot food and clean sheets only go so far under such conditions.

Despite the buildup of ETO air power, mission strength remained limited in a variety of factors: trained aircrews, replacement aircraft, and maintenance. The latter was often overlooked by war correspondents, who focused on the "glamorous flyboys." But talented mechanics and airframe specialists were crucial, especially with the heavy damage often incurred by returning aircraft. The number of available bombers was relatively low through late 1943, only averaging 257 per mission.

On October 14, a second Schweinfurt mission was launched; more than 420 heavies were dispatched but fewer than 300 got through the weather. Three of the five target factories were heavily damaged, reducing ball-bearing production by 50 percent for a time. But the defenders put up a ferocious fight. *Luftwaffe* fighters made repeated head-on attacks: Squadrons flying company front formation for maximum concentration of gunfire. Sixty-five more Forts were lost and a dozen written off: a staggering twenty percent loss rate. Aircrews began running the numbers and concluded that at current figures, it was statistically impossible to finish a 25-mission tour. However, Captain Robert Morgan's *Memphis Belle* of the 91st Group had first proved it could be done, beating the odds in May.

P-47 THUNDERBOLT

Like the Lockheed P-38, Republic's P-47 was designed as a high-altitude interceptor. However, because Axis bombers were relatively rare from 1943 onward, the Thunderbolt earned its niche in history "down on the deck" as a fighter-bomber and ground-support aircraft. With legendary toughness and awesome armament, it was superb in that role. Its nickname "Jug" is variously attributed to its resemblance of a milk bottle and a foreshortened "Juggernaut." Certainly it was an impressive single-seater with an empty weight of 5 tons and wingspan of 40 feet, 9 inches.

The T-bolt's heart was its turbo supercharged Pratt and Whitney radial engine, capable of more than 2,000 horsepower. When P-47s entered combat against Germany and Japan in 1943, the tremendous power in a rugged airframe produced exceptional dive performance. Coupled with an

unmatched battery of eight .50-caliber machine guns, the 47 made a significant impact on Axis air power. America's top two aces of the European
theater, Lieutenant Colonel Francis S. Gabreski and Captain Robert S.
Johnson, were Jug pilots.

Some 15,500 Thunderbolts were built from 1941 to 1945, serving in the
British Commonwealth air arms and in limited use in Russia.

The answer to the problem was more friendly fighters. But even with
new drop tanks, the P-47s lacked the range to escort the bombers very far
into Germany. P-38s, with the potential range, encountered repeated
engine problems, especially at high altitude. The AAF had cast around for
a solution and found it: the P-51 Mustang mated to the Spitfire's Rolls-
Royce engine. The result was the answer to a bomber crew's prayer: a
long-legged, high-performance fighter that could tackle the *Luftwaffe*'s
experten on even terms.

(Photo courtesy of the USAF via Robert F. Dorr)

*A stacked-down echelon of four P-51 Mustangs from the 361st Fighter Group heading
home after an uneventful bomber escort mission over Europe.*

The first P-51B group, attached to the 9th Air Force, was "borrowed" by the 8th, and began flying missions in November. The 354th "Pioneer Mustangs" immediately became the most popular airmen in the ETO.

More Mustang groups joined the 8th Air Force early in the new year, and the character of the daytime air war began to shift dramatically. Meanwhile, bomber attrition remained a concern for personnel and materiel officers, to say nothing of aircrew morale.

Mediterranean Theater

The North African campaign continued its see-saw pattern in the first half of 1943. On February 8, the British 8th Army entered Tunisia, but six days later Rommel counterattacked. The blow fell on fresh American units at Kasserine Pass, producing a humiliating defeat for the U.S. Army. AAF squadrons evacuated several bases; on one field the retreating Yanks burned 18 planes and 60,000 gallons of fuel to deny them to the enemy. The Germans broke through on February 20 and Tunisia was abandoned, but the Allies quickly recovered, counterattacking four days later.

That month American air power had grown to six bomb groups, seven fighter groups, three troop-carrier outfits, and two reconnaissance groups. With additional offensive capability, Lieutenant General Carl Spaatz's fliers flexed their muscles. Some were daringly aggressive: In an ultra low-level attack, one A-20 Havoc damaged its wing by scraping the radio antenna of a *panzer.*

The North African Air Forces drew an ever-tighter noose around the Axis, which was being strangled at sea and ashore. During March, the 47th Bomb Wing's Marauders and Mitchells were credited with sinking 29 Axis ships as B-25s made masthead attacks to skip their bombs into enemy hulls. Patrolling Warhawks, Lightnings, and Spitfires began finding large formations of German transport aircraft, apparently evacuating troops to Sicily. Some mini turkey shoots ensued, but none matched the "Palm Sunday Massacre."

On April 18 four squadrons of P-40s caught a massive formation of tri-motor Junkers 52 transports. Total claims were 59 Ju-52s and 16 Messerschmitts, while the *Luftwaffe* acknowledged losing 24 Junkers and 10 fighters with 35 more transports force-landed on the coast. Six Warhawks were lost, but three P-40 pilots became instant aces: Lieutenants Arthur B. Cleaveland of the 57th Group and Richard E. Duffy and MacArthur Powers of the 324th.

Continued German air evacuation presaged the inevitable end. The next month Tunis and Bizerte were captured and, cut off from outside help, the *Afrika Korps* surrendered.

With Tunisia secured, Allied planners looked north to Sicily, but first they needed some interim bases. One was Pantelleria, 63 miles from Sicily, possessing a harbor and airfield. At the end of May, the North African Air Force accelerated its efforts and began a 12-day blitz against Pantelleria, carpeting the 42 square miles with bombs. Nearly the entire command was committed: 10 bomb groups (four with B-17s) and 9 fighter groups with P-38s, '39s, '40s, and Spitfires. From May 8 to June 11, the 12th Air Force logged 5,200 sorties, dropping 6,200 tons of bombs. Fourteen planes were lost, but the 11,000 Italians surrendered shortly before any of the British assault troops set foot on the island. It was a landmark event: the first ground victory by air power alone.

One of the units entering combat at that point was the 27th Fighter-Bomber Group with A-36 Invaders, the dedicated dive-bomber version of the P-51 Mustang. Shortly another Invader group, the 86th, went operational as well. More would be heard of the North American fighter before year end.

On July 19 came the first Allied raids on Rome. Following nocturnal leaflet drops by the RAF, during the day heavy bombers from Libya flew two missions to the Eternal City. Some 170 B-17s and '24s attacked rail targets while medium bombers struck nearby airfields. Thus, Italy became the second Axis capital attacked by the AAF. Bomber crews winked at one another: "Two down, one to go."

On July 30, events climaxed over Sardinia during a 325th Fighter Group sweep. Thirty-six Warhawks tangled with 40 or more Axis fighters, claiming 21 destroyed. It was the last aerial opposition encountered over the island, which was subjected to further attacks. One new wrinkle in the 321st Bomb Group was 75mm cannon in B-25Gs, which proved devastatingly effective from low level where accuracy was optimum.

The Airborne at Sicily

The AAF's first notable airborne operation occurred in conjunction with Operation Husky, the invasion of Sicily, which marked the debut of the Waco CG-4 glider. The initial drop on July 10 went reasonably well as 3,400 troopers of the 82nd Airborne Division seized a road junction near Gela. Colonel James M. Gavin, a mission-oriented regimental commander, "scared the hell out of us" recalled one aircrewman. In the briefing Gavin said he would personally shoot anyone who refused to jump, and would court-martial any pilot who returned a healthy trooper to base.

The next night, four groups of the 52nd Troop Carrier Wing left their Tunisian bases with 144 Skytrains carrying 2,000 more troopers. It was a communications tragedy, as the speed with which the drop was planned precluded full coordination with the Navy. Additionally, the airdrome objective already had been seized by ground troops.

The Skytrains formed up in darkness and headed for Sicily, flying at 500 feet or less. Nearing the coast, two groups were sighted by U.S. Navy ships that were not informed of the AAF operation. One undisciplined gunner opened fire, having seen numerous German aircraft in recent days. The ensuing panic led to "firing contagion" and the mission came unglued. Many troop-carrier pilots broke formation to take evasive action, then were fired upon by trigger happy GIs ashore. Twenty-three C-47s were shot down, including 12 from the 316th Group alone. Some 300 paratroopers were killed or wounded. Still, the troop carriers pressed ahead. One motivated crew pushed its shot-up Douglas to the drop zone despite 2,000 medium, small, and tiny holes in the airframe.

Allied landings on the Italian mainland occurred in September, augmented by airborne forces on September 13 and 14. In support of the Salerno operation, 3 lifts were flown totaling more than 4,000 troopers of the veteran 82nd Airborne. Later that month six fighter groups, a bomb group and a recon outfit moved to Italian mainland.

An obscure but important part of the AAF's war machine was the unlikeliest of all aerial warriors: the Piper Cub. Liaison L-4s had served in North Africa where they proved their usefulness in courier and observation duty, but artillery spotting was where the civilian in warpaint shone brightest. The Germans recognized the value of the Cub, even if some U.S. Army officers did not. *Luftwaffe* fighters made determined efforts to destroy the "grasshoppers" who usually dived into the weeds, using gullys and other terrain features to survive. Occasionally the tables were turned: Over Sicily an L-4 pilot was pestered by the same Bf-109 several days in a row, sustaining gunfire damage in the process. The spotter pilot, who knew the topography well, lured his tormenter down, then dived into a winding ravine. Turning a corner, the Cub abruptly reversed course at the end of the box canyon. The Messerschmitt, easily three times faster, could not.

The 12th Air Force logged its last notable mission by heavy bombers on October 24 when 134 Fortresses and Liberators struck Wiener Neustadt, Austria. Only one B-24 group was able to bomb through the undercast. A week later the 12th's "heavies" were transferred to the new 15th Air Force, the strategic organization of the Mediterranean theater. Four fighter groups and a recon group also went to the 15th. In the reshuffling of senior officers, Major General Jimmy Doolittle "stood up" the 15th while Lieutenant General John K. Cannon became commanding officer (CO) of the 12th.

Bloody Ploesti

On August 1, the AAF launched 177 Liberators on Operation Tidal Wave, one of the most spectacular missions in Air Force history. Departing Benghazi, Libya, and flying low across the Mediterranean, the B-24s made for petroleum targets in Romania, most notably the refineries around Ploesti. It was a daringly conceived, carefully rehearsed mission: the first low-level heavy-bomber attack on a well-defended target, and the longest yet flown (1,200 miles). The attackers were from five groups: two of the "local" 9th Air Force and three borrowed from the 8th.

Tidal Wave deserved better results. Navigation errors resulted in some targets being missed while others were attacked twice. The Libs had to climb from their approach altitudes to bomb safely, and the survivors described a Dantesque situation: blazing oil tanks with thick, black smoke; heavy anti-aircraft (AA) fire; German and Romanian interceptors; even barrage balloons with steel cables that could slice off a wing. There were collisions and near misses as pilots and copilots struggled to control their big bombers in violent turbulence from blazing fires.

Leading the 98th Bomb Group in a B-24 named *Hail Columbia* was Colonel William R. "Killer" Kane, one of the 9th Air Force's most experienced combat leaders. Realizing that the mission had turned to hash, he pressed ahead at low level, determined to put the "Pyramiders" bombs on the briefed target. "We had to shoot our way in," he wrote, his gunners trading fire with flak batteries. Flying so low that he had to horse the big Liberator over trees, Kane pulled up to 200 feet for the final approach to two smokestacks marking his target. The lead bombardier toggled his loads, then Kane forced *Hail Columbia* back toward the weeds.

Kane leveled off so low that his left arm was singed by flames erupting outside his open window. Then he was clear of the AA guns; that was the good news. The bad news: German and Romanian fighters rolled in from above. Irate that his gunners were not returning fire, Kane learned they had shot up their ammo in the treetop duels with flak guns. But the Messerschmitts pulled off and Kane set course for Cyprus. Forty-seven of his bombers had taken off; twenty-one returned intact.

Five airmen, including Kane, received Medals of Honor for Ploesti (three posthumously). Some 53 Libs were lost while 7 more were interned in Turkey. Among the 1,726 airmen on the mission, 532 were killed or captured.

Oil production was reduced at Ploesti but resumed to the point that additional missions were flown into 1944. On those, two more posthumous Medals of Honor were awarded. One of the latter recipients, bombardier Lieutenant David Kingsley of the 97th Group, gave away his parachute to a wounded B-17 gunner whose own chute was ripped by flak. Kingsley's action, perhaps more than any other, defines "above and beyond the call of duty."

B-24 LIBERATOR

Uncharitable B-17 crews insisted that the big, slab-sided B-24 was "the crate the Fortress came in." But the record shows otherwise: 18,000 Liberators were built, nearly 50 percent more than the Fortress and more than any other U.S. military aircraft in history. First flown in December 1939, Consolidated's heavy bomber seemed destined to take a role in the new European war.

With its long, tapered wing (110 feet, more than 6 feet longer than the B-17), tricycle landing gear, and twin tails, the Liberator could carry more bombs than the B-17, often with better range and speed depending on the models and mission assigned. From the basic 16-ton empty weight of the D model, the Liberator grew to more than 32 tons loaded weight in the M version.

However, the '24 was more susceptible to battle damage and could be tiring to fly in formation for prolonged periods; it was said that Liberator pilots were identifiable by their overdeveloped biceps.

The Lib made history with dramatic low-level attacks on Romanian oil fields in August 1943, but it also played a notable role at sea. That year, the end of effective U-boat threat, long-range Liberators helped narrow the Mid Atlantic Gap for Allied convoys. A limited-production cargo version was designated C-87.

More than 2,300 Liberators went to Britain, while the U.S. Navy took nearly 1,000 for maritime patrol. Meanwhile, a special naval version, the PB4Y-2, was also produced. In the fall of 1944, the Liberator equipped 46 bomb groups outside the United States.

Pacific Theater

The difference a year made: In January 1942, the United States and the Allies were on the defensive throughout the Pacific and Asia. In January 1943, the Japanese began evacuating Guadalcanal. Massive land, naval, and air losses had convinced Tokyo that "Starvation Island" could not be held, and subsequent efforts were focused on holding the line farther north in the Solomons. Major General Nathan F. Twining stood up the 13th Air Force in January, headquartered at Espiritu Santo in the New Hebrides with two bomb groups and a fighter group. Others were shortly added as the Solomons campaign progressed.

Target Yamamoto

Just as the 8th Air Force logged a notable anniversary mission in August, so did "ComAirSols" in April. That month U.S. code breakers learned that Admiral Isoroku Yamamoto, chief of the Combined Fleet, would visit the Bougainville area on the 18th, the first anniversary of the Doolittle raid. Rear Admiral Marc Mitscher, Aircraft Commander, Solomon Islands, was handed the job of assassinating the architect of the Pearl Harbor attack and, lacking long-range Navy fighters, Mitscher tossed the ball to his P-38s. Sixteen Lightnings were led by Major John Mitchell of the 339th Fighter Squadron, who performed meticulous navigation planning. It seemed a long shot: a 450-mile dogleg route at 50 feet over the water to arrive at the precise place and time as Yamamoto's itinerary indicated.

It worked. Mitchell's navigation was flawless ("I couldn't do it again in 100 years," he said) and the four-plane "trigger section" climbed to intercept while the others provided top cover. The four attackers, led by Captain Tom Lanphier, brushed aside the six Zero escorts and went after the two Mitsubishi bombers carrying Yamamoto and his staff. In a short, confused combat, both Betty bombers went down while one Lockheed was lost. Although the argument still persists, evidence strongly indicates that Lieutenant Rex Barber downed the lead bomber, then shared the second with Lieutenant Besby Holmes. Lanphier insisted for the rest of his life that he shot down Yamamoto but Barber said, "Whoever got Yamamoto is less important than the fact that we accomplished our mission." Mitchell agreed.

Back at Guadalcanal, Mitscher wired the Navy Department: "Pop goes the weasel. Looks like 18 April is our day."

P-38 LIGHTNING

Lockheed's revolutionary Lightning looked like nothing else in the air in 1939. With a twin-boom airframe for its two Allison engines, counter-rotating propellers to negate torque, and a tricycle landing gear, it was a high-altitude, high-performance interceptor. When the prototype left the ground in 1939, the P-38 became the first American production aircraft to make 400 miles per hour in level flight. In high-speed dives it also introduced the World War II generation to the phenomenon of compressibility, the onset of the sound barrier.

All P-38 models spanned 52 feet with an empty weight between 12,000 and 13,000 pounds. Max cruising speed was 290 to 305 miles per hour with a service ceiling topping 40,000 feet—extremely impressive in the early 1940s, although superchargers and engines often caused problems at such extremes.

Lightnings served in every combat theater where American forces were deployed: North Africa, the Mediterranean, northern Europe, the Aleutians, the Pacific, and the Asian mainland. A P-38 combined with a Bell P-39 Airacobra to claim the first German plane shot down by U.S. forces, but ran up its best record against Japan. Flying in the southwest Pacific and eventually the Philippines and beyond, Lightnings used high-speed "shoot-and-run" tactics against the lighter, nimbler enemy fighters. America's two top aces, Majors Dick Bong and Tommy McGuire, flew P-38s exclusively in compiling their records.

Yamamoto's death did nothing to derail what he had already planned. On June 16, the Imperial Navy launched a major air attack against Guadal-canal and Tulagi: 24 dive bombers aiming for U.S. shipping escorted by a cloud of 70 Zeroes. AirSols fighters were up and waiting, including four squadrons of AAF Airacobras, Warhawks, and Lightnings.

In a swirling battle lasting about 40 minutes, AAF fighters claimed 42 victories; it would remain a PTO record for a year and a half. Belle of the brawl was a 339th Squadron P-38 pilot, Lieutenant Murray J. Shubin, who became an instant ace with five Zeroes and a probable to his credit.

The Navy Wildcats and Marine Corsairs got 33 more, while 6 defending fighters were lost (2 collided). New Zealand P-40s and various AA gunners claimed 19 shootdowns, limiting damage to 3 ships. Whatever the actual results, the Japanese losses were serious; it was their last daylight raid on "Cactus."

Two weeks later American amphibious forces landed on New Georgia, securing an additional air base in the Solomons. B-25s struck Munda airfield on New Georgia itself, while Liberators were sent against Kahili on Bougainville but could not penetrate a thick weather front. Despite that drawback, another major stepping stone toward Rabaul had been taken.

Meanwhile, the war in the north Pacific continued at its own pace. In the miserable weather of the Aleutians, the 11th Air Force fought its perennial battle against the williwaw, only occasionally incurring aerial opposition from the Japanese. Enemy resistance on Attu ended in May but repeated attacks were launched against Kiska in June. Frequently only the radar-equipped B-24s could drop their loads, as thick clouds prevented visual bombing.

Southwest Pacific Theater

The Battle of the Bismarck Sea pitted air power against sea power, and air power won decisively. Sixteen Japanese ships with 6,000 troops left Rabaul, New Britain, on February 28, bound to reinforce New Guinea. An Australian search plane spotted the convoy and called for help. The initial strike on March 2 involved 28 B-17s of the 43rd Bomb Group, which sank one ship; but the others persisted, rounding the Huon Peninsula for Lae.

On March 3, a force of 84 5th Air Force planes and 13 Royal Australian Air Force Beaufighters piled in. The Australians strafed to suppress AA fire and launched torpedoes while Lieutenant General George Kenney's squadrons mauled the convoy. Making low-level attacks, often with 50-foot pullouts, the B-25s and A-20s pummeled the Japanese. Four destroyers and the remaining transports went down.

The masthead tactics proved extremely effective. In just one attack, the 90th Bomb Squadron's B-25s claimed 17 hits from 37 quarter-ton bombs dropped. Overall, the outfit was credited with sinking two ships and damaging nine more.

One aspect of the battle that bore upon the outcome was the loss of a B-17 to Zeroes. Seven of the Fortress crew who bailed out were shot in their parachutes; the Yanks and Aussies took notice. On the third day, scores of additional Allied planes scoured the area, mercilessly strafing survivors in the water or clinging to wreckage. Barely 800 Japanese got ashore, minus equipment, while 3,600 were killed and the survivors were returned to Rabaul. U.S. losses were a dozen airmen in the one B-17 and three P-38s.

Kenney's fighters claimed 32 planes splashed during the first 2 days. Among the successful fighter pilots was the 9th Squadron's Lieutenant Richard Bong, who notched his sixth kill over the Bismarck Sea. He would be heard from repeatedly. Meanwhile, Kenney exclaimed "I'm so proud of my boys that I'm likely to blow a fuse."

Although New Guinea was far from conquered, by August there were also resources for a more focused campaign against the Japanese naval-air complex at Rabaul. The 5th Air Force repeatedly flew missions against bases there, often fighting weather as much as Zeroes. B-25s patented several techniques, including low-level delivery of "parafrags" (parachute-retarded fragmentation bombs), skip-bombing attacks on shipping, and heavily armed "gunships" with as many as 10 forward-firing .50 calibers and even a 75mm cannon in the nose. Major Paul "Pappy" Gunn, a former Navy and commercial pilot, pioneered some of the methods that turned the Mitchells from useful medium bombers into awesome platforms for delivering destruction in a variety of means.

September brought the first U.S. airborne operation against Japan. The 54th Troop Carrier Wing delivered 1,700 parachutists of the 503rd Regiment to Nadazb and the Markham Valley of New Guinea.

Meanwhile, Colonel Neel Kearby was CO of the newly arrived 348th Fighter Group, determined to prove the big Republic P-47 in the Pacific theater. He took a long stride toward that goal on October 11, claiming six victories during a sweep over Wewak. His flight added three more, and although the claims proved optimistic, the point had been made. The Thunderbolt became a major player in Kenney's air force. Kearby received the Medal of Honor.

The aerial reduction of Rabaul, New Britain, continued well into 1944, in concert with AirSols naval aircraft from Solomons bases. Liberators and Fortresses flew almost daily missions, seldom in squadron strength and occasionally alone. The usual targets were airfields and Simpson Harbor, even at night or in bad weather just to keep the pressure on. Between them, the 5th and 13th Air Forces put the New Britain area in a tightening vise that squeezed the life out of a once mighty bastion of empire.

The Cape Gloucester landings on Bougainville drew heavy Japanese response. On the day after Christmas, 5th Air Force fighters logged their heaviest day of combat thus far, claiming 61 shootdowns. Warhawks, Lightnings, and Thunderbolts fought two large combats that afternoon, repelling determined attacks by level and dive bombers. Colonel Neel Kearby's pilots mauled a Mitsubishi Betty formation, with Lieutenant L. F. O'Neill claiming four.

China-Burma-India Theater

It was known as the Hump: the long, difficult flight from India into China across some of the most forbidding geography on earth. But there was no choice. With road and rail traffic cut or impassable, and most of Burma overrun by the advancing Japanese, only the air route over the Himalayas could keep China in the war.

THE GREATEST AIRPLANE?

At the end of World War II, General Dwight Eisenhower identified the most significant tools in the American arsenal. One was the ubiquitous jeep. Another was the bazooka antitank weapon. The only aircraft he cited was the Douglas C-47 Skytrain.

Derived from the landmark DC-3 airliner, the C-47 was built in prodigious numbers for a transport: nearly 10,000 in all. Empty weight was 18,200 pounds with a span of 95 feet, 6 inches. Top speed was rated at 230 miles per hour with a 24,000-foot service ceiling and range of 1,600 miles.

The C-47 was invaluable as a cargo aircraft, as demonstrated by its crucial role in flying the Hump across the Himalayas, keeping badly needed supplies moving across some of the planet's most rugged terrain.

However, the "Gooney Bird" became best known to history for its role in air assault. C-47s delivered paratroopers in every airborne operation the U.S. Army conducted in World War II: North Africa, Sicily, Italy, France, Holland, and in the Pacific. On D-Day alone, nearly 1,000 U.S. and RAF C-47s (Dakotas to the Brits) dropped paratroops and towed gliders to Normandy. Skytrains contributed heavily to the 1948 Berlin Airlift but were still in harness 20 years later in Southeast Asia. Heavily armed with automatic weapons, AC-47 gunships were known as "Spooky" and "Puff the Magic Dragon" for the awesome amount of firepower they could place on an area larger than a football field.

The distance from airfields in the Brahmaputra Valley to Kunming in Yunnan Province was 550 miles. The lowest mountain range along the way was 10,000 feet; the Hump for which the route was known topped 15,000 feet between the Salween and Mekong Rivers. Weather was a constant worry, not to mention the problems of climbing heavily loaded planes to altitude. Fuel was always a priority, and eventually dedicated tanker aircraft were employed: C-109 Liberators plus the usual C-46s, C-47s, and C-54s.

Transport crews crossing the mountains had enough problems without the Japanese. Fortunately, interceptions were rare, but they did occur. Troop-carrier crews began speaking of a "Zero" pilot (there were no naval units in the area) who seemed to have it in for C-47s. Somehow—nobody is sure—the Japanese flier became known as "Broken-nose Charlie." If Charlie actually existed, he almost certainly flew an Army Nakajima fighter, better known to American aviators as "Oscar."

In March 1943, the China Air Task Force gained full status as the 14th Air Force with Major General Claire Chennault retaining command of the theater's air power. Supply flights over the Hump were increasingly important with continued closure of the Burma Road, with 2,800 tons delivered in February. An approximately friendly rivalry existed between the troop carriers and Air Transport Command (ATC), largely composed of experienced airline pilots. Uncharitable AAF officers opined that ATC stood for Army of Terrified Civilians, but their extensive commercial flying experience proved invaluable, especially in the region's heavy weather.

Colonel Eugene Beebe's 308th Bomb Group arrived at Kunming in February, among Chennault's first heavy bombers. The group made an unescorted attack on Hankow on August 21, pressing through fighters and flak to strike docks and warehouses. Combat operations were enhanced in May with B-24s conducting shipping strikes along the China coast.

However, the Japanese were determined to hold on to China and launched a series of offensives. In November, the U.S. forces evacuated Liuchow, a serious setback to the 14th Air Force.

1943 Summary

This was a banner year for the Army Air Forces, now numbering 1,297,000 personnel with 68,600 additional aircraft procured. Production and training were still accelerating over 1942, but sufficient growth capacity in both areas ensured that 1944 would be even more impressive. From the "we need everything" situation of 1942, new units now were being formed, trained, and deployed to combat theaters in growing numbers.

The 8th Air Force in Britain had become a major factor in the air war. At year's end, Lieutenant General Ira Eaker had 26 bomb groups and 11 fighter groups with more on the way. The 9th (tactical) Air Force had moved to Britain from the Mediterranean, gearing up for its important role in the invasion of France. Heavy, occasionally spectacular, losses were being made good in men and materiel, and morale was improving. Arrival of P-51Bs with their seven league boots promised lower bomber losses and increasing Allied air superiority in the new year.

The Mediterranean situation was much improved. The Allies now owned the "middle sea" and focused on offensive operations on European soil. Despite the bogged-down ground war in Italy, Allied air power was clearly ascendant. Germany, increasingly hard pressed in Russia and in the skies of the *Reich*, could not afford to divert significant *Luftwaffe* strength to the southern flank. The 12th (tactical) and 15th (strategic) Air Forces now were adequately supplied and expanding their bases in Italy, Sicily, and Corsica.

Increasing offensive operations in the Pacific had met with success, notably the Bismarck Sea victory. The 5th and 13th Air Forces in the New Guinea and Solomons areas, respectively, began hammering at Japan's naval air complex on New Britain. Probably nowhere else were Allied airmen so focused as in the succession of raids against Rabaul: AAF, Navy, and Marine Corps units, along with Australian and New Zealand squadrons, all played a part.

The AAF remained on the defensive in China, but the aerial lifeline over the Hump from India was an ongoing concern. Despite forbidding terrain and often treacherous weather, the airlift command kept vitally needed supplies arriving in adequate quantities.

AGE AND THE AIRMAN

A wartime trait of the AAF was extreme youth, however defined. The service expanded so fast that its officers included teenaged lieutenants, colonels in their twenties, and generals in their thirties. Brigadier General Clinton "Casey" Vincent established the record when he pinned on his star in June 1944, a wing commander at 29. Colonel John D. Landers, an ace in the Pacific and Europe, commanded a fighter group at age 24.

Wars always accelerate careers, and never more so than during World War II. Whereas 36-year-old captains were not unknown in 1938, by 1944 there were generals that age. At least one 8th Air Force B-17 crew included eight fliers too young to vote or buy a drink, including the copilot.

Some Americans were so eager to go to war that they couldn't wait till the minimum official age of 18. Sergeant DeSales Glover logged six missions as a B-24 gunner, including the first Berlin raid, before authorities caught up with him. In 1944 he was 16, and a veteran of a year and a half!

According to legend (it's probably true), the officer's club bar at a UK B-26 base posted a warning: "Lieutenant colonels under 21 must be accompanied by a parent or guardian."

1944: AIR POWER ASCENDANT

This was the year the Allies had been waiting for. The preliminaries were accomplished, the logistics provided, and the training centers and factories running in high gear. Excepting the CBI, logistics were assured in the combat theaters, including the vast Pacific. But Germany remained the primary target, and the world watched and waited for the most anticipated event of the century: D-Day.

European Theater

United States Strategic Air Forces in Europe was created in January, with General Carl Spaatz recalled from North Africa. At the same time, Lieutenant General Jimmy Doolittle arrived from the Mediterranean to relieve Ira Eaker at the helm of the 8th Air Force. Eaker, promoted to run Allied air operations in the Mediterranean, was a sentimental favorite (he had stood up the Mighty 8th and brought it to maturity), but Doolittle's stellar reputation commended him to his fliers. At least for a while. Shortly, he reviewed the declining loss rate and increased a bomber tour from 25 to 35 missions. Aircrews were understandably displeased, but the numbers bore out their commander: More crews were completing tours and consequently their greater experience would be more helpful.

Doolittle would make other changes, not least of which was to unleash his fighters. He changed escort policy, permitting his P-38s, '47s, and '51s to hunt more aggressively for *Luftwaffe* interceptors rather than remaining tied to the "big friends" full time. Some bomber commanders didn't like the idea—they felt good seeing "little friends" nearby—but the wisdom of Doolittle's tactics showed in reduced losses. He also advocated a "down-on-the-deck" campaign, permitting homeward-bound fighters to strafe targets of opportunity.

The 8th Air Force launched "Big Week," February 20 through 27, with a series of strikes against German fighter factories. Meteorologists predicted clearing weather for the effort, and generally were proven right. Three Medals of Honor were awarded on the first day: two posthumously to navigator Walter Truemper and gunner Archie Mathies, who tried to land their crippled 351st Group Fortress rather than abandon their unconscious pilot. With his copilot dead, Lieutenant William Lawley brought back his shot-up 305th Group B-17 despite severe injuries. Like Truemper and Mathies, he refused to bail out while wounded men remained aboard.

Brunswick remained a favored target that week but Oschersleben, Aschersleben, Halberstadt, and Augsburg all felt the weight of AAF bombs. Weather deteriorated on the third day, with disastrous results in Holland, where B-24s bombed in error, causing 200 Dutch deaths. Weather then closed in, canceling day four.

Schweinfurt was on the menu again on the 24th, but canny German controllers put the *Jagdwaffe* onto the bomber boxes where U.S. fighters were thinnest. Nearly 50 bombers were hacked down. Overall, during Big Week the 8th launched 3,300 bomber sorties with 6,000 tons and, although sometimes losing 40 to 50 bombers per day, reduced German fighter production by 50 percent of the planned amount.

The results of just one Big Week mission were summarized thus: "The attack on the Gothaer Waggon Fabrik AG and its Me-110 production has resulted in 400 HE and incendiary bombs landing on the target area, 93 hitting buildings; some 424 tons of which were fragmentation type designed to destroy factory equipment. The statisticians estimate that the enemy has lost 6 to 7 weeks production equal to 140 Me-110 aircraft." The cost of such success: 33 of the 239 Liberators dispatched to Gotha, a hefty 12.5 percent. It meant at least 330 empty bunks that night.

Shortly after Big Week, yet another landmark event occurred: the first major daylight raid on Berlin, on March 4. The proud claim of "First Over Big B" went to the B-17s of the 95th Bomb Group, which dropped above the cloud layer. "I'm sure we hit the place," insisted Lieutenant Colonel Harry Mumford. Two days later the Americans were back in force: 730 "heavies" plus nearly 800 fighters. But the Germans also turned up in force. Flak and fighters inflicted heavy losses on the raiders: 69 bombers and 11 fighters missing, plus others written off. Nevertheless, by now the AAF could absorb such blows and keep up the pressure. Big B shortly lost its novelty to combat aircrews.

Not so the Germans. When Hermann Goering saw P-51s over the German capital, he realized that the war was lost.

The AAF's assault on Germany's ball-bearing industry had made some inroads since the previous fall, but other priorities intervened. Schweinfurt and related targets gained not just a reprieve but a stay of execution in April when Allied air planners switched to German transportation systems in preparation for D-Day. *Reich* Armaments Minister Albert Speer later admitted that he breathed a sigh of relief that month, not wholly appreciating what was coming.

Countdown to D-Day

As the countdown to D-Day went on, other operations were afoot. On June 2, the 15th Air Force flew the first shuttle raid to Russia, as airfields had been prepared east of Kiev. The 8th's first such operation came 19 days later, with B-17s continuing eastward from Berlin. Mustangs had the range to stay with the bombers all the way to Berlin and back.

P-51 MUSTANG

Nothing else looked so beautifully lethal. North American's P-51, like its F-86 Sabre, combined form and function in one classic package to become the standard for its era.

The Mustang was ordered and named by the British, who in 1940 desperately needed fighter aircraft. The Los Angeles firm complied with a seemingly impossible goal and rolled out the prototype in four months. Originally powered by the liquid-cooled Allison, the Mustang (originally Apache in U.S. service) combined state-of-the-art aerodynamics, including a laminar flow wing that spelled s-p-e-e-d, ultimately 435 miles per hour. Reconnaissance and dive-bomber versions were produced before the classic fighter emerged by mating the airframe to the Rolls Royce Merlin engine. The result was a world beater. P-51B, C, and D models gained air supremacy over Berlin and Tokyo, enabling heavy bombers to operate without prohibitive loss. In its different guises, the Mustang accounted for more aerial kills than any plane in American history.

In all, 15,200 Mustangs were delivered, and the type soldiered on throughout the Korean War. Today, the P-51 is still widely regarded as the finest fighter of its era.

IX Troop Carrier Command had 14 groups to deliver the 82nd and 101st Airborne Divisions with their glider regiments as well. The drop zones were behind Utah Beach, the westernmost landing area, requiring 821 Skytrains and 104 Waco gliders. Their commander, Lieutenant General Lewis Brereton, watched one group take off and described it as "a model of precision flying and air discipline." Rising from their airfields from Lincolnshire to Devon, they formed up, then turned toward a 10-mile wide corridor over the Channel. It was the first combat mission for most crews, and fortunately they did not know what awaited them.

Penetrating the dark European sky at 140 miles per hour, the Skytrains began taking flak over the Channel Islands. It got worse once they were "feet dry" over Normandy. Light, medium, and even heavy "bursting stuff" began erupting in the ordered formations. Some pilots violated orders and took evasive action, ignoring airspeed and altitude requirements. However, German gunners disrupted most formations more than they inflicted actual damage, as merely 21 troop carriers and 2 glider tugs were lost.

Colonel Charles H. Young, commanding the 439th Group, flew a radar-homing C-47 with the command element of the 506th Parachute Infantry, including historian Stephen Ambrose's famous Easy Company. Young crossed the coast at 1,500 feet, then encountered a cloud bank and shoved forward on his control yoke. The group followed, briefly flying on instruments, until he found a hole and descended to 700 feet. Within a few seconds of the "green light," the 439th drew machine gun fire and flak while approaching the drop zone. Young's second element was badly shot up, and one Skytrain near the rear of the formation was destroyed. Two more were shot down in flames, but their paratroopers got out before the C-47s crashed.

Young had a bet with Lieutenant Colonel Robert Sink, commanding the 506th, that the C-47s would drop him within 300 yards of the intended spot. Three weeks later a parachute officer showed up at the 439th, making good on the bet by turning over a 10-pound note from Sink. Even without a pathfinder illuminated "T," Young's radar beacon dropped the 506th CO within 200 yards of the aimpoint.

Additional glider tows and resupply missions fully occupied the troop carriers through "D+1," by which time things were in hand. More than 500 gliders were expended while C-47 losses climbed to 41 destroyed and 450 damaged, a steep figure but still considered acceptable because most of the latter were repairable.

While the 9th Air Force delivered the airborne troops, the 8th was also busy with 1,873 fighter sorties and 2,362 bomber flights resulting in just one B-24 lost in action. Bombers began taking off at 2 A.M. for a 5:55 target time, within minutes of H Hour. But the heavies released their loads well inland, beyond the beaches, rather than risk hitting Allied shipping beneath the clouds. Infantrymen on Omaha Beach who could have used bomb craters for cover were left exposed: Hap Arnold received much of the blame for Dwight Eisenhower's caution. Nevertheless, subsequent missions targeted coastal defenses and communications routes leading to the Normandy beachhead. Air power had its moment on "the day of days."

While 8th and 9th Air Force planes continued flying from Britain, 9th Air Force ground elements were busy in France. Engineer aviation battalions laid out runways, and tractors began grading on D+3. The first advanced field was completed at Cardonville and began operating Thunderbolts of the 368th Group on D+13. By month's end, six other fields were operational; more quickly followed. They were not merely temporary landing strips but genuine airfields with 5,000-foot runways and parking for 75 fighters.

Whether in Britain or France, the pilots and aircrews flew relentlessly. They largely succeeded in isolating the beachheads by making daylight travel exceedingly dangerous for German troops. The commander of the elite *Panzer Lehr* Division described Normandy as "a fighter-bomber race course." Twin- and multi-engine bombers concentrated on transportation targets: rail yards, roads, and bridges.

Operation Cobra kicked off July 25, beginning the breakout from the Normandy lodgement. It was preceded by massive bombing by more than 2,500 8th and 9th Air Force planes, devastating the German forward positions around St. Lo. Some 3,300 tons of bombs fell in a thick "carpet" that saturated the area, leaving many defenders dead or stunned. However, airmen later criticized General Omar Bradley's staff work, citing poor coordination between "the ground" and "the air." General Leslie McNair, the four-star commander of all U.S. ground forces, was killed by American bombs during the opening hours of Cobra. He remained by far the senior American officer killed in action during World War II. About 100 other GIs also died by "friendly fire."

On August 20, the Americans and Canadians closed the Falaise Gap, trapping 50,000 German troops but about 35,000 had escaped, minus their heavy equipment. Thousands of attack and interdiction sorties were flown by fighter-bombers and medium bombers, choking off the escape route of the German army in Normandy. Ninth Air Force B-26s were especially active, dropping bridges and stemming the eastward flow of Nazi armor and vehicles. During that period, a Marauder pilot, Captain Darrell R. Lindsey, received a posthumous Medal of Honor for remaining at the controls of his doomed B-26 so the remainder of his crew could jump to safety.

B-26 MARAUDER

Martin's maligned Marauder provided a rags-to-riches story. Capable of 300 miles per hour with twin Pratt and Whitney 2,000-hp engines, it was first flown in 1940 but soon came under scrutiny. A poor safety record ("One a day in Tampa Bay") led to near cancellation of the B-26, but Martin and the Army worked out the bugs. By war's end, the alleged "Widow Maker" had established one of the lowest combat loss rates of any AAF aircraft.

Originally the B-26 had a 65-foot wingspan, but analysis determined that more wing area was needed. (Crews said that the small wing area of the "Maligned Madam" provided "no visible means of support.") Consequently, the B-26C and subsequent models had "stretched" wings spanning 71 feet. The result: better control but a loss of about 20 mph top speed. A five- or six-man crew enjoyed the advantage of a rugged, powerful aircraft that stood up well to flak and fighters—better than the more popular B-25. Britain and other Allied air forces operated limited numbers of Marauders, with 5,100 delivered by March 1945.

Some confusion still exists because the Douglas A-26 Invader was redesignated B-26 after the Marauder left service. But to the crews who flew it, Martin's Maligned Madam was the finest medium bomber of the war.

Market Garden

The largest airborne operation in history came more than three months after D-Day. A British plan to thrust deep into Holland, flanking the Siegfried Line and encircling the Ruhr, had the potential to end the war in 1944. Skeptics—both British and American—felt it had the potential to kill large numbers of paratroopers. Nevertheless, Eisenhower acceded to Field Marshal Montgomery's ambition and Operation Market Garden went ahead. In beautiful mid-September weather, 14,000 troopers of the 82nd and 101st Divisions landed at Nijmegen and Eindhoven, respectively.

The northern flank of the operation immediately fell apart. Allied intelligence missed an SS Panzer corps in the British drop zone, and the 1st Airborne Division was isolated at Arnhem. The British ground forces tried to relieve the hard-fighting Red Devils, but German resistance was too tough: 7,000 of 9,000 "paras" were killed or captured. The 1st Allied Airborne Army withdrew to regroup and absorb the obvious lessons. Dropping paratroopers on top of two armored divisions was a poor way to begin an operation.

In the air, fighters of the 8th and 9th Air Forces met relatively little resistance, claiming 130 shootdowns over Holland in 5 days.

However, the technological battle was about to take a turn for the worse. In October, Germany's Me-262 went operational; the *Luftwaffe* beat the world by a lap and a half in deploying jet fighters, while Me-163s already were the first (and only) rocket fighters committed to combat. The latter were hardly a nuisance; they shot down fewer than 20 Allied aircraft. But the 262s, expertly flown and occasionally committed in numbers, caused serious concern. They were nearly 100 miles per hour faster than piston fighters and packed four 30mm cannon. Nevertheless, years later Chuck Yeager reflected, "Hell, I shot down the first jet I ever saw!"

Still, there were too few "Turbos" to stop the massive Anglo-American air fleets. On November 2, 1944, AAF fighters claimed a record 136 kills. By all indications the air battle for northwestern Europe was coming to an end.

The indicators were wrong.

The Bulge

On December 16, the *Wehrmacht* stunned the Allies with a wholly unexpected attack through the Ardennes. Timed to take advantage of winter weather, German armored thrusts were aimed at Antwerp to force the United States and British onto the strategic defensive. Some American units were overrun; a few broke and ran. Others were bypassed and surrounded.

Air power was largely negated for more than a week. Still, some gutsy pilots responded to the urgent calls for help. Major General Pete Quesada asked one of his recon groups to brave the 10/10 fog, leading Captain Richard Cassady and Lieutenant Abraham Jaffe to take off in their Mustangs. They survived 100-foot ceilings, misty hills, and German flak to return with information on enemy armored columns. Other P-51s and P-47s risked the weather but the bombers had to remain grounded. Some bases were "socked in," while other groups lacked adequate ceilings for bombing.

When weather broke over some targets, the defenses remained vicious. One 9th Air Force B-26 group, the 391st, attacked a vital rail target in Germany on December 23. Of 30 Marauders in the formation, 16 were shot down by aggressive enemy fighters. Meanwhile, the embattled 101st Airborne hung on by its fingernails at Bastogne, Belgium.

The next day, Christmas Eve, Brigadier General Fred Castle, who had literally built the 8th Air Force from the ground up, participated in a large effort against German airfields and transport. It was his thirtieth mission, and his last. The *Luftwaffe* unexpectedly intercepted Castle's B-17 in Allied airspace and shot him down. He received a posthumous Medal of Honor.

Poor weather helped the Germans only until the skies cleared on Christmas Day. Then fighter-bombers and troop carriers flocked over the Ardennes, attacking enemy forces relentlessly while delivering much-needed supplies, especially to the embattled paratroopers at Bastogne. The Germans were clearly defeated; they had gambled everything on one roll of the dice—and lost.

But nobody told the *Luftwaffe*.

Mediterranean Theater

The year began with the 12th (tactical) and 15th (strategic) Air Forces based in Italy, Sicily, and Corsica. In January, Lieutenant General Nathan F. Twining transferred from the Pacific to relieve Jimmy Doolittle at the helm of the 15th Air Force. The highly capable Doolittle moved to Britain to assume command of the 8th Air Force, the third such command of his career.

Among Twining's fighter groups was the 332nd, which began operations early in the new year flying P-40s. Composed of black officers and men, the cadre of pilots came from Alabama's Tuskegee Institute. The group received Thunderbolts in April but exchanged them for Mustangs two months later. The red-tailed P-51s became a familiar and welcome sight to 15th Air Force bomber crews, who knew the 332nd's superb escort reputation. The original three squadrons were augmented by the independent 99th, and Colonel Benjamin O. Davis Jr. assumed command.

February was a notable period for air power in the Mediterranean Theater of Operations (MTO). Allied aircraft helped stop the German counter-attack at Anzio, where the beachhead had been under serious pressure.

Later that month occurred one of the most controversial missions of the MTO air war. Allied forces were stalled at the Rapido River less than 100 miles southwest of Rome, and commanders noted the prominent monastery atop Monte Cassino. Established by St. Benedict in 524 C.E., the abbey sat upon a 1,600-foot massif that previously had been the site of the Temple of Apollo and had hosted such un-Christian activities as assorted orgies sponsored by the emperor Tiberius. Subsequently it was razed by the Lombards, Saracens, and Normans, and a fourteenth-century earthquake for good measure. No matter. The industrious Benedictines always rebuilt.

Monte Cassino's commanding view of the surrounding area seemed to ensure that the Germans were using it as an observation post, which presumably made it a legitimate target. (Evidently the Germans respected the site's sanctity while it remained intact.) Although the monastery was treasured for its Christian history, it was targeted for destruction on February 15. The 12th and 15th Air Forces put more than 450 bombers over the target in a devastating 3-hour attack involving Flying Fortresses, Marauders, and Mitchells. The rubble was then occupied by German paratroopers, among the finest defensive infantry on earth. They held against repeated attacks until the middle of May.

In mid-August came "D-Day South," Operation Anvil-Dragoon. Anglo-American forces landed on the Mediterranean coast, beginning a squeeze play to eject the Germans from France. Consequently, the 1st Airborne Task Force's 5,600 troopers descended on the Côte d'Azur and Riviera, arguably the most glamorous venue of any airborne operation in history.

The operation required 11 troop-carrier groups, including 8 borrowed from the 9th Air Force. Air opposition was negligible while nearly 400 C-47s dropped more than 5,000 U.S. and British paratroops in the predawn of August 15. They were followed by nine waves of gliders with additional troopers and supplies. It was a fine operation: Only 37 planes missed their drop zones, and glider casualties were light. Seaborne forces joined the airborne units on August 17.

One of the MTO's more notable bombing missions involved a rare strike against enemy warships. On the 17th nearly 100 B-26s attacked Toulon, noting a battleship, cruiser, destroyer, and submarine. The next day the 321st Group's B-25s pushed through heavy weather to reach the target. The Mitchells attacked from 13,000 feet, bucking heavy AA fire that tagged 27 planes. Nevertheless, the bombers sank the battleship *Strasbourg* and the submarine while damaging the cruiser.

Operation Strangle began in March, a widespread interdiction campaign to isolate 18 enemy divisions in central Italy. Mediterranean Allied Air Force (MAAF) planners estimated that Axis supplies were reduced from 80,000 to 4,000 tons per day. Rail lines and bridges were targeted by medium bombers and fighter-bombers, and 65,000 sorties were flown with 33,000 tons of bombs delivered by May 11. P-39s and P-47s hunted anything that moved, while Mitchells and Marauders bombed relentlessly. When the Allied ground offensive pushed off, the airmen had prepared the way. Allied troops entered Rome on June 4, the first Axis capital to be conquered.

Strategic missions on July 26 produced the biggest day of air combat in the MTO for the year. Galatz, Bucharest, and Vienna all were scenes of combat as 15th Air Force Lightnings and Mustangs claimed 39 shootdowns. The 12th Air Force fighter-bombers added 7 for a total of 46; 1 more than January's high for the year.

One Day

On August 29, the 15th Air Force sent 556 bombers after another oil target: refineries and German facilities near Pardubice, Czechoslovakia. It was no different from many other missions flown in the ETO but some specifics may be considered typical. Heavy damage was inflicted on the refinery complex, but as was often the case, collateral damage occurred. Two groups totaling 52 Liberators dropped 260 500-pounders from more than 21,000 feet; perhaps 100 bombs struck the desired target area while an unknown number landed in the western part of Pardubice and the village of Svitkov, adjoining the refinery. The Czechs suffered 188 civilians killed and 271 injured. Sixty of the dead were found in two bomb shelters that took direct hits. More than 200 buildings were destroyed or badly damaged, even though some blasted areas lay a mile or more from the target. The Norden sight's vaunted pickle-barrel accuracy could not compensate for erratic winds, thick smoke, combat confusion, or lethal stress.

A survivor of Svitkov said, "Finally all is quiet. Slowly I stand up and look around. The village is a dreadful sight. The streets are blocked with tangles of broken timbers, bricks, and electric wires. Demolished houses, bomb craters, unexploded bombs, and dead bodies are everywhere." It was the height (or depth) of irony: Victims of Nazi subjugation were killed by their liberators. The situation was not at all unusual. During the Normandy campaign a U.S. Army officer took in the rubble of a French town and remarked, "We sure liberated the hell out of this place!"

Eight B-24s were lost on the Pardubice mission in exchange for 168 German planes on the ground and 14 fighters in the air. (The AAF claimed 36.) Of more than 2,200 bombs dropped, nearly 100 were duds, leaving the Germans and some prisoners to disarm or dispose of them.

It was one day in a long war.

Pacific Theater

The AAF's central Pacific war generally consisted of routine operations until nearly year's end. The 7th Air Force B-24 and B-25 bombers bypassed Japanese garrisons in the Gilberts and Marshalls as well as Wake Island. But in the summer the emphasis shifted to the Marianas.

Tinian was secured on August 1, permitting construction to press ahead for B-29 bases. That month the forward echelon of the 73rd Bomb Wing arrived as Brigadier General Emmett O'Donnell landed on Saipan. The first four groups' ground elements followed in September.

The logistics effort was immense. Apart from runways long and strong enough to take the Boeings' weight, the bases needed taxiways, hard stands, bomb dumps, fuel storage, motor pools, accommodations, administrative offices, and the varied twentieth-century requirements for waging serious war. The Navy played a major role, delivering gasoline, ordnance, and other supplies 6,000 miles from the West Coast.

By late October, Brigadier General Haywood S. Hansell's XXI Bomber Command was ready for operations. The crews opened their mission log with 18 Superforts against submarine facilities at Truk Atoll in the Carolines, "Possum" Hansell flying in the lead plane.

The long-awaited first mission to Japan was scheduled for November, but the weather dictated otherwise. Crews sat through a maddening week of briefings before they finally got the green light on November 21. Of 111 Superforts dispatched, 17 aborted but the others mostly bombed their assigned targets in the Tokyo area: factories and port facilities. F-13 recon versions of the B-29 already had been to the "Empire" and continued on each mission, occasionally spoofing the defenses by functioning as decoys. Resistance was generally light with two Boeings lost, but one was rammed by a Japanese fighter.

Haywood Hansell had helped draft AWPD-1 for Hap Arnold in 1941, and remained an advocate of high-altitude precision bombing. However, the conditions over Japan were not conducive to conventional techniques. After two months, XXI Bomber Command still had not destroyed its nine priority targets. A change was in the wind—a whirlwind.

B-29 SUPERFORTRESS

The importance of the B-29 can be judged by the fact that it was the most expensive aircraft program of the war. The unit cost of more than $600,000 was staggering; three times that of a B-17. It has been said that only the Manhattan Project that produced the atomic bomb (closely related to the B-29) was greater. The Superfortress first flew in September 1942, and in 1943 was selected to deliver the A-bomb, expected to be available in 1945.

The Superfort was huge for its day, with a 141-foot span and a maximum loaded weight of 137,000 pounds. An empty '29 weighed nearly 2 tons more than a maximum-loaded B-17, carrying more than twice the fuel yielding nearly twice the combat range. With a top speed approaching 400 miles per hour and combat ceiling of 32,000 feet, the Superfortress boasted a combat range of 3,200 miles.

Despite initially troublesome Wright engines, Boeing turned the B-29 into an awesome weapon wholly beyond anything available to any other nation. Originally based in eastern China, B-29 groups began bombing Japan in 1944. However, the logistics of supporting high-consumption aircraft in China mandated a shift to the Mariana Islands, where missions commenced in November. The 3,900 Superforts produced not only helped end World War II, but served well in Korea, where communist jet fighters forced the Superforts to fly at night. B-29s still equipped half of the Air Force's bomb wings as late as 1952.

Southwest Pacific Theater

Lieutenant General George Kenney was determined that a 5th Air Force pilot would finish the war as America's top ace. His ambition got the better of his judgment: He consistently removed excellent officers from leadership positions so they could go freelancing and run up the score. Two of his paladins perished in March: Colonel Neel Kearby, previously CO of the first P-47 group in the theater; and Lieutenant Colonel Thomas Lynch, a former P-38 squadron commander. However, Kenney had two more aces up his sleeve: Lightning pilots Richard Bong and Tommy McGuire. They would accomplish their leader's goal, but not without further loss.

In the larger scheme of things, the AAF made visible progress that spring and summer. In March and April, Kenney's bombers pounded Japanese air power to nothingness in Hollandia, Dutch New Guinea; U.S. Army troops landed unopposed and began establishing major air and support bases. In June the Americans captured Biak Island, whose airfield became another step on the path to the Philippines.

During early July the 503rd Parachute Infantry put 1,400 troopers on Noemfoor Island off New Guinea's west coast, assisting the amphibious troops. While the parachutists captured one airfield, they incurred heavy casualties in the rough, tree-studded terrain. The balance of the regiment waded ashore. It was just one of a series of obscure places with unpronounceable names that made headlines: Ambesia, Balikpapan, Boeloedowang, Halmahera, and so many more.

In October, the 5th and 13th Air Forces began striking southern Philippines targets, mainly Negros and Mindanao. The Japanese were conspicuously absent; fewer than 500 Army and Navy aircraft combined to defend the huge archipelago. All that changed in October.

The Leyte landings began on October 20 beneath an umbrella of blue carrier aircraft. Almost immediately combat engineers began developing airstrips at Tacloban and Dulag. As a result of the major fleet engagement in Leyte Gulf, the Army fields were soon crowded with Navy planes orphaned from their ships. But the crisis had passed by October 25.

Protecting Kenney's southern air flank was the 13th Air Force, harassing Japanese bases in the Celebes. Meanwhile, on October 26, two P-38 squadrons of the 49th Group arrived at the Tacloban strip, screeching their tires onto pierced steel planking. As quickly as the Lockheeds were refueled the ambitious hunters were airborne, and that afternoon Major Dick Bong added number 31 to his hit parade. But the Japanese also flew at night, and a squadron of Northrop Black Widows arrived to deal with that problem. Eventually, however, a Marine Night Hellcat squadron was needed to sort things out.

On November 22, the 13th Air Force's top shooter was lost over Makassar Strait. Lieutenant Colonel Robert Westbrook died seeking his twenty-first victim, an additional reminder (if any were needed) that aces were as mortal as fledglings. At war's end 7 of the AAF's top 19 Pacific aces had been killed in action or in flying accidents.

The 13th Air Force remained very much in the background, overshadowed by the 5th and its affiliation with MacArthur's splashy headlines. Nevertheless, the 13th made do even with its perennially small contingent: two P-38 fighter groups and three bomb groups, two with Liberators, one with Mitchells. There was also a photo group and a troop-carrier outfit. Yet Major General Clair Street's bobtailed air force got results: On October 30, Lightnings sank two Japanese tankers off Borneo, and barely a week later fighters and bombers sank two ships in Ormoc Bay, leaving another grounded.

December 7 was observed by 5th Air Force fighters claiming their greatest killing of the war with 66 shootdowns. Protecting U.S. shipping from *kamikazes* in Ormoc Bay, the fighters flew almost dawn to dusk; some pilots had two flights. Most of the shooting was done by Lightnings of the 49th and 475th Groups and Thunderbolts of the 348th. Four leading aces added to their scores over Ormoc that day: Colonel Charles MacDonald and Majors Dick Bong, Tommy McGuire, and Gerald R. Johnson. At war's end they were the top AAF Pacific aces.

Despite setbacks, the Japanese kept coming. They anticipated the occupation of Mindoro, the last step to the main island of Luzon, and acted accordingly. The area became the scene of intense naval and air activity, with the Americans hard pressed to maintain their new holdings. In the second half of the month, at least 19 U.S. ships were damaged and 3 sunk or abandoned, not counting small vessels.

The situation peaked on the evening of December 26. Air power was still building in the area, and the Japanese moved to chop it off. Two cruisers and six destroyers steamed offshore to begin a bombardment of the two airstrips. More than 100 planes responded: B-25s, P-38s, P-40s, P-47s, and even P-61 night fighters. Although ill trained for nocturnal shipping attacks, the aircrews pressed through the darkness and flak, making repeated runs. Pilots kept their running lights on to avoid collisions in the congested airspace over the enemy task force, so AA gunners easily tracked them. The cost was heavy: 26 of the available planes were lost. However, the Japanese inflicted relatively little damage and withdrew, being distracted by repeated low-level attacks. The Army fliers claimed three ships sunk but in truth the only Japanese loss was a destroyer struck by U.S. Navy torpedo boats.

Meanwhile, 13th Air Force bombers were taking a toll on Japanese shipping in the East Indies and Borneo. On December 22, Liberators sank five of six transports in a convoy, further choking off enemy supply lines.

China-Burma-India

General Chennault had always been short of heavy bombers. In early 1944 he got them. The XX Bomber Command's 58th Wing began assembling B-29 groups and logistics in India, anticipating operations against Japan from Chinese bases. Concurrently, the 20th Air Force was established at General Arnold's headquarters in Washington, as the Superfortress program was by far the largest in the AAF.

Preparations for XX Bomber Command were substantial, involving support bases in India and operating bases in China. Tens of thousands of "coolies" were employed building, lengthening, and strengthening runways to accept the big Boeings with their 70-ton gross weights. Photographers loved the contrast: gleaming multi-engine aircraft parked alongside runways being constructed by gangs of tireless peasants bearing crushed rock in wicker baskets; the occasional water buffalo hitched to a roller.

The East-meets-West contrast was not limited to technological differences. Some Chinese held the ancient belief of a personal devil that clung grimly to an individual's back. A theory evolved that if the afflicted person ran close enough to a whirling propeller, the devil would be slain. Consequently, several incidents were reported of Chinese dashing across the nose of aircraft while taxiing or—worse—taking off. Some wrecks resulted as pilots clamped on the brakes, risking a nose over, or swerved into a ground loop. Therefore, at Kunming (and probably elsewhere) the word went out: Pilots committed to a takeoff run were to proceed without regard to human life. "It's a pretty spectacular object lesson when a P-40 chops up a coolie," said one flier.

GENERAL CURTIS E. LEMAY (1906–1990)

Curt LeMay was described by an American KGB operative as "a caveman in a bomber." But LeMay played a significant role in ending World War II and an even greater role in preventing World War III. Upon receiving his wings in 1929, he became a fighter pilot but converted to bombers and made headlines by leading a B-17 formation to South America in 1938.

He logged a notable combat tour commanding the 305th Bomb Group in Britain during 1942 and 1943, developing tactics and procedures that reduced potentially crippling losses while improving bombing accuracy. Soon promoted to the rank of general, in 1944 he went to China to lead XX Bomber Command's B-29 operations. When the logistics proved excessive, the CBI Superfortresses transferred to the Mariana Islands. In January 1945, LeMay preceded the groups to Guam, and XXI Bomber Command proceeded to torch most of Japan's industrial areas.

In 1947, LeMay assumed command of U.S. Air Forces in Europe and presided over the Berlin Airlift. He returned to America in 1948 to lead the Strategic Air Command, arguably turning SAC into the most professional military organization in history. SAC's motto, "Peace is our profession," referred to nuclear deterrence with B-36s, '47s, and '52s. LeMay, the youngest four-star general since Grant, remained at the helm until 1957 when he was made vice chief of staff; he became chief of staff in 1961, remaining until mandatory retirement in 1965. It has been said that he was the only member of the Joint Chiefs who would have stood up to President Lyndon Johnson, and LeMay's retirement at the start of the Vietnam War probably was a factor in the prolonged agony of that fruitless conflict.

In late April, the big Boeings began flying to Kwangshan, China, in preparation for their first mission. It came on June 5 when XX Bomber Command took the offensive, launching 98 B-29s against Bangkok. Poor weather required radar bombing by the 77 planes that got through: an inauspicious start, perhaps, but still a beginning.

The first raid on Japan was flown in mid-June, but the theater's serious logistics problems prevented adequate support. Many B-29s flew Hump missions to provide the enormous amount of fuel necessary for a single combat mission.

That spring the Japanese army took the offensive again in China. In April it launched an operation to control the Peking-Hankow railway, and in late May it began a massive attack in Eastern China. Intended to overrun U.S. bomber bases, the latter offensive largely succeeded. Air-power pundits noted (wryly, no doubt) that the situation proved that strategic bombers really could have an effect upon the ground war!

A significant factor arrived in September in the cigar-chomping form of Major General Curtis LeMay. A no-nonsense professional in every respect, he analyzed the situation and set about improving things. "Bean counters" in the United States began noting a steady improvement in XX Bomber Command's serviceability rates. One of them was Lieutenant Colonel Robert Strange McNamara.

Still, there were limits to what was possible. Seven B-29s had to ferry fuel across the Hump for each sortie to Japan, which was bad enough. Beyond that, some major bases were threatened by the Japanese Army. Another means had to be found to optimize the Superfort's awesome potential.

Meanwhile, an innovative aerial operation began in Burma: supply of British Brigadier Orde Wingate's "Chindits," dropped far behind Japanese lines in February. Wingate had proven that isolated columns could sustain themselves the year before, although only with heavy losses. Now, with air support virtually guaranteed, he crossed the Chindwin River as part of the overall effort to recapture Burma. From March to May, Colonel Philip G. Cochran's 1st Air Commandos delivered 9,000 men, 1,300 animals (mostly mules), and 250 tons of vital supplies in northern Burma. It was truly a commando operation, with Allied aircraft operating well behind enemy lines at thinly defended landing strips. Wingate died in March but his concept was proven.

The 10th Air Force committed P-38s, '40s, and '51s to cover the transports, resulting in some spirited dogfights over Japanese airfields. On March 27, the Warhawks of the 80th Fighter Group and Allison-powered Mustangs of the 311th claimed 27 kills, the highest daily tally of the CBI war.

Little noted at the time, the Army's first combat helicopter operation was conducted in Burma that April. A Sikorski R-4B, one of four assigned the 1st Air Commandos, thrashed its way through the humid air to rescue four men behind enemy lines. Lieutenant Carter Harman needed two days to lift the pilot and three casualties of a Vultee L-1 out of Japanese territory, requiring four risky trips in the two-seat flying machine. Reported Colonel "Flip" Cochran, "Today the 'egg beater' went into action and it acted like it had good sense." The chopper met the challenge, with nearly 20 rescues or evacuations accomplished that year.

Allied airmen in India had their hands full even without the Japanese. In March, the British outpost at Imphal in Manipur Province was surrounded, and air power often made the difference to the defenders. Imphal turned into a bloody, muddy slogging match, especially when the monsoon season arrived in May, severely limiting flying weather. The siege was not lifted until late June.

Meanwhile, 14th Air Force fighters and bombers contributed to the defense of Hengyang in June, defending the rail center against six-to-one odds. But the Japanese were too strong and their western advance continued. In early November, the Americans evacuated the field at Kweilin in Kwangsi Province; Eastern China was untenable for heavy-bomber operations. Consequently, the CBI B-29s began planning a move to the newly won Mariana Islands although the Superforts remained in-theater until early 1945.

Despite the setbacks in China and the slugfest in Burma, Japanese resistance in India largely ended during August.

In December, the Air Transport Command and Troop Carrier Command began flying two Chinese infantry divisions from Burma back to China. The buildup led to a Nationalist offensive in five months, beginning to retake much of the land lost to the advancing Japanese. Meanwhile, the Hump operation increased in volume and efficiency, with 12,000 tons lifted per month early in the year.

The success had its cost. Transport aircrews called their route "the Aluminum Trail" for the hundreds of aircraft littering the route. But they kept China in the war.

WAFS + WFTD = WASPS

America faced a manpower shortage in 1942. Consequently, women were mobilized as never before, taking an increasingly active part in supporting the war effort. "Rosie the Riveter" became an icon of female dedication to cause and country, producing prodigious quantities of materiel: literally everything from bedpans to battleships.

An early effort to employ women in military aviation was the Warning Auxiliary Corps, established in May 1942 as a nationwide observer service. Although America was subjected to very few air raids (Japanese submarine-launched aircraft off the Pacific coast), vigilance was important in watching wartime skies.

That summer a noted woman pilot, Nancy Harkness Love, established the Women's Auxiliary Ferrying Squadron. Qualified applicants already had a commercial pilot's license, providing the AAF with a ready-made pool of pilots who could relieve male aviators for overseas duty.

Another AAF program was the Women's Flying Training Detachment formed by air racer Jacqueline Cochran. With the backing of General Hap Arnold, she advocated a training program for young women interested in becoming wartime pilots—a larger potential than the small number of pre-war female fliers. The two organizations were merged in August 1943, forming the Women Air Service Pilots, or WASPs. Of 25,000 applicants, 1,830 were accepted for training and nearly 60 percent (1,074) graduated from Avenger Field at Sweetwater, Texas. Nearly 40 WASPS were killed in the line of duty.

During the war some WASPs made greater contributions than many people realized. Perhaps the best example occurred in the summer of 1944 when Lieutenant Colonel Paul Tibbets sought to alleviate crews' increasing concern about the B-29. With unreliable Wright engines, the Superfortress program faced serious setbacks as bomber pilots naturally worried about in-flight fires.

Figuring that sometimes the best man for the job is a woman, Tibbets selected two WASPs as B-29 demonstration pilots. Without much fanfare he landed at various bomber bases, casually allowing male crews to see "two little girls" flying the notorious bomber. It was perfect psychology. Combat aircrews drew the obvious conclusion: If "mere" women could fly the Superfort, so could they!

By late 1944, the shortage of male pilots was over, as training had already kicked into high gear. Consequently, the WASPs were released to civilian life. As Civil Service employees they were ineligible for veterans' benefits, and 28 years passed before the U.S. government finally recognized their contribution to World War II with veterans' benefits.

Another feminine aspect of the AAF was 6,000 nurses assigned to various airfields in the United States and overseas. Some 500 became flight nurses, serving aboard transport aircraft that evacuated casualties from combat zones.

1944 Summary

In the third full year of war, the AAF boasted 2,372,000 men and women, almost double the 1943 figure. Arnold and Company had become a growth industry, and the Air Forces were recognized as such by the upper management on Pennsylvania Avenue. Before year end, Arnold was elevated to five-star rank, putting the AAF on equal footing with the ground forces. In typical Hap fashion, he accepted the accolade on behalf of his airmen.

Although D-Day was unquestionably *the* event of 1944, it overshadowed important developments everywhere else. With air superiority ensured over Europe, the 8th and 15th Air Forces increased their tempo, pounding the *Reich* with larger and larger formations. On some days more than 1,000 4-engine bombers were airborne with half as many fighters. German industry, exceptionally resilient, continued producing massive amounts of war stocks but less and less was delivered to the battle fronts. The *Luftwaffe*, although always dangerous, was being hammered into defeat. Meanwhile, the 9th and 12th Air Forces were relentless as their fighters and medium bombers hounded the *Wehrmacht*'s troops, supplies, and communications. At year end, the final plans were in place for an invasion into Germany, and GIs began jiving, "Home alive in '45."

In the Pacific and Asia, B-29s were operational in growing numbers. While the China situation proved a reversal, it was soon made good, and long-range bombers in the Marianas spelled serious trouble for Japan. The situation was recognized in Tokyo as early as July when Guam, Tinian, and Saipan were secured. The emperor's warlords felt they knew what was coming; they hadn't a clue.

The far reaches of the Western Pacific also demonstrated the inexorable progress of American air power. Long steps up from the New Guinea theater provided the springboards to the Philippines, where the 5th Air Force came to roost. Again, although the enemy recognized the futility of further resistance, his philosophy and disposition permitted no thought of surrender.

The balance of the Philippines and all of Okinawa lay ahead.

1945: MISSION ACCOMPLISHED

In the final eight months of the war, the AAF and aviation generally would play even greater roles than before. The full potential of America's air arm was realized: technically, strategically, and institutionally. Massive bomber fleets dominated the skies of Europe and the Western Pacific, affording an even greater aerial umbrella for land and sea operations. Combined with the stunning power of the atom, military aviation had proven its war-winning potential beyond all doubt. Somewhere far above the contrail level, even the shade of Billy Mitchell must have watched in awestruck wonder.

European Theater

The new year opened with a bang—literally. On January 1, more than 800 German fighters swarmed over airfields in Belgium and northern France, hoping to cripple Allied air power in one massive blow. Many raiders achieved surprise, and about 150 British or American planes were destroyed. However, the *Luftwaffe* lost as many as 300, nearly 70 in a series of low-level dogfights with U.S. fighters. Allied AA gunners accounted for most of the tally—with their German counterparts who assumed anything airborne was hostile!

(Photo courtesy of the USAF via Robert F. Dorr)

Two pilots from the 94th Fighter Squadron stationed in Italy in 1943 watch as their squadronmate explains a dogfight.

While the Allied losses were heavy, they were replaced. A 9th Air Force P-47 pilot turned up after being declared missing. Hopping off his "borrowed" bicycle, the young lieutenant exclaimed, "They got me, but I got two of them first!"

Germany was still pulling out of the Ardennes on January 14, which brought the biggest 1-day haul of aerial kills in the ETO: 174. Fifty-six were credited to the 357th Fighter Group in "The Great Mousetrap Play."

Escorting B-17s near Brandenburg, the Mustangs overcame numeric and altitude disadvantages to turn the tables on the defenders, losing three P-51s. Lieutenant Colonel Andy Evans and Lieutenant John Kirla got four kills each; five others scored triples.

Two 357th aces ended their tours that day, landing at dusk to find Leiston Airdrome in an uproarious celebration. Captains Bud Anderson and Chuck Yeager had flown an impromptu tour of Western Europe, realizing too late that they had missed the biggest dogfight in recent history.

During February, the 8th Air Force repeatedly hammered Berlin; on February 22 came the largest daylight raid on the capital yet. Of 1,411 bombers dispatched, only 4 were lost despite bombing from as low as 10,000 feet to minimize civilian casualties. Nearly 1,200 "heavies" were up the next day, again encountering almost no opposition. When weather prevented visual bombing, radar usually enabled dropping through the clouds.

RADAR

Electronic identification of airborne objects is called *radar*, an acronym for radio detection and ranging. Radar revolutionized aerial warfare, beginning in World War II. It was absolutely crucial to the Royal Air Force victory in the 1940 Battle of Britain and quickly became a matter of intense scientific and military research. Airborne radar was especially important in darkness or poor weather, as it allowed night fighters to locate enemy bombers and enabled bombers to drop with reasonable accuracy against targets that were otherwise invisible.

Radar works by emitting a pulse of electromagnetic energy that strikes an object and returns to the emitter. The time of "flight" for the electronic pulse tells the radar operator the distance of the target; the azimuth provides the bearing. Thus, it is possible to track even a supersonic target as long as there is a return "paint" off the object.

During 1944, the 8th and 15th Air Forces increasingly relied on radar bombing in European weather. As many as 80 percent of heavy bomber missions relied on some sort of blind bombing, which kept the pressure on Germany. However, results were usually disappointing, as half the bombs dropped "in the blind" struck more than two miles from the intended target.

Stealth technology was developed to reduce the effectiveness of radar, enabling friendly aircraft to get closer to their targets before being "painted" by enemy radar. The press often erroneously defines stealth as "radar evading," but the only way to evade radar is to fly at tremendous height or extremely low, beneath the coverage. Relying on composite materials and carefully sculpted surfaces that deflect rather than reflect electronic beams, stealth aircraft reduce the effective range of radar.

Airborne and satellite radar can provide tremendous information on friendly and enemy forces over a wide area. Aerial command posts such as the E-3 AWACS (Airborne Warning and Control System) scan hundreds of square miles at a time, enabling commanders to make fast decisions based on real-time data.

The ground war continued its eastward drive. On February 9, the Allies cracked the Siegfried Line, and that month Anglo-American air forces began Operation Clarion against German transport systems.

Tactical reconnaissance squadrons were exceedingly active; some pilots logged nearly 100 hours per month. In fact, the top air-to-air score of 1945 was recorded by Captain Clyde East of the 15th Recon Squadron: 11 shoot-downs for a career total of 13.

March brought more gloom to Germany. On March 7, the U.S. Army captured an intact bridge across the Rhine at Remagen and the British crossed on March 23. The next day Operation Varsity involved 1,800 C-46s and '47s plus 1,300 gliders of IX Troop Carrier Command. Witnesses on the ground said it took more than three hours for the procession to pass one point. The U.S. transports delivered 17,000 troops of the 17th Airborne Division, also providing 1,200 vehicles and 130 artillery pieces in an area of 25 square miles.

Watching from the west bank of the river, General Brereton said, "The first air columns over the river were approximately five minutes early. The formation was excellent, all units in good order ... Intense flak was encountered and I saw during the first 25 minutes at least 9 flamers and 6 crashes. Not a single plane was attacked by the *Luftwaffe*. Of the 46 aircraft lost by 9th Troop Carrier Command, 39 were lost to flak and 1 by accident; the cause of the other 6 losses is unknown. The impact of the vertical envelopment was a stunning blow to the enemy. The way was opened to Berlin."

By now, 8th Air Force thousand-bomber missions were common. On March 11 over Essen, 1,079 bombers dropped 4,738 tons on rail and communication targets. A week later, 1,250 heavies with 670 fighters delivered 3,000 tons of bombs on Berlin. German jets took a mounting toll (24 B-17s in March) but it was much too little, far too late.

CEP

In bombing, the standard of comparison is called circular error probable (CEP), a quantifiable figure based on direct observation of bomb impacts within a prescribed distance of the target. The CEP is therefore the distance from the aimpoint within which 50 percent of the bombs are expected to strike. During World War II the standard was 1,000 feet, meaning that half the bombs dropped on a particular target were expected to hit in a radius of 333 yards.

That was the standard. It was not always met.

Visual bombing was one thing, blind bombing quite another. Even with radar guidance, bombs dropped "on top" could be spread across miles of countryside below the cloud deck. It was even worse before radar. Early in the war the Royal Air Force found that only about 20 percent of its nocturnal sorties over Occupied Europe placed bombs within 5 miles of the intended spot. The biggest factor was navigation: Flying in hostile skies, at night, seeking targets that devoutly wished not to be found was immensely challenging. That was the main reason that the RAF resorted to "area attacks" (carpet bombing) rather than "precision" attacks advocated by the AAF.

Nevertheless, under proper conditions the CEP could be surprisingly small. On April 15, 1945, within three weeks of VE-Day, the 467th Bomb Group's Liberators placed all of their bombs inside 1,000 feet on an artillery battery; half within 500 feet, thereby halving the traditional CEP.

Today, with precision-guided munitions (PGMs), the CEP has shrunk to less than the size of a typical structure. The resulting anomaly is such that a "miss" still might destroy the target.

Meanwhile, 9th Air Force fighter-bombers continued hammering German forces. In two weeks of March, Thunderbolts and other fighters claimed nearly 900 armored vehicles, almost 900 locomotives, 19,000 railroad cars, and more than 10,000 motor vehicles. Even allowing for inevitable error, it was an awesome toll. The command's 14 fighter and 3 recce groups kept advancing with the ground forces, moving from France, Belgium, and

Holland into Germany itself in April. The 11 bomb groups, with greater range, continued operating from the liberated countries.

Independent night-fighter squadrons also made their mark. One unit, the 422nd, logged 13 kills with its big Northrop Black Widows in less than a week.

On April 1, ground forces completed encirclement of the Ruhr Gap, forcing more *Wehrmacht* units to retreat. As German territory dwindled, aircraft were concentrated on fewer available fields, and the Mighty 8th's fighter groups licked their chops at the juicy targets. Daily bags of 100 and more were turned in by one group after another. Losses were often heavy— the *Luftwaffe* could still put up a lot of flak—but the end drew closer with each takeoff. On April 19, the 447th Group lost the last 8th Air Force bomber destroyed by enemy aircraft.

On May 8, the final ETO aerial kills were scored by 9th Air Force fighters. The last was credited to Second Lieutenant Kenneth L. Swift, a P-38 pilot of the 474th Group.

That same day, Nazi Germany ceased to exist. But even before the surrender, some bomb groups were conducting low-level sightseeing tours of Europe and the devastated *Reich*. Dedicated mechanics who had sent bombers on hundreds of sorties finally got to see the result of their contribution to ending the war. Gazing down at shattered cities, one man summarized it for all: "I never knew that Germany was so beat to hell."

Mediterranean Theater

The 12th and 15th Air Forces were beating the Germans day by day. The weather, however, was an implacable opponent. Through most of the first four months of 1945, low ceilings and high winds kept heavy bombers grounded as much as a week at a time. Mediums and fighters could operate more freely but there were times when the sky of the MTO was vacant except for occasional reconnaissance sorties.

On one occasion in January, 70 Liberators took off to bomb Zagreb, Yugoslavia's railroad yards and other targets. Sixty-nine B-24s aborted; the seventieth pushed through to drop its load unescorted.

Although not quite the strength of the Mighty 8th, the 15th Air Force grew to sizeable proportions by VE-Day. Lieutenant General Nathan

Twining commanded 5 bomber wings (4 with B-24s) totaling 21 groups and a fighter wing with 7 groups. Missions with 800 bombers were not unknown, far eclipsing Germany's ability to protect its southern aerial flank.

Much of the period preceding Germany's capitulation in Italy focused on the Bologna region and the Po River Valley. The 12th Air Force kept busy attacking tactical targets day and night when the weather cooperated: P-47s, B-25s, and B-26s by day; A-20s and new Douglas A-26s by night. Enemy transport was the most frequent target system, especially bridges allowing reinforcements to reach the front.

The 12th Air Force's mediums operated an often tedious "bomb shuttle service" between Corsica and the Brenner Pass. B-25 crews grew impatient with unimaginative operations orders repeating routes and schedules day after day. Although losses were considered acceptable, fliers naturally resented anything that made life easier for Germany's highly practiced flak gunners. Most Mitchell groups forsook Corsica's barren environment for the mainland that spring, putting them closer to their targets.

On days of decent weather the 15th Air Force put up increasing numbers of heavies: 790 Fortresses and Liberators to Vienna and environs on March 12. On March 24, escorted by Lightnings and Mustangs, the MTO bombers got a rare look at Berlin as 660 "big friends" bombed a tank factory and other targets in the capital of the shrinking *Reich*.

In mid-April, the 5th Army broke out of the Bologna region and the 15th Air Force launched 830 bombers against highways and supply routes. The German army was in retreat, although occasionally still fighting with the skill for which it was famous.

On April 14, the 5th Army attacked in the Po Valley, crossing the river to maintain pressure on the *Wehrmacht*. Fighters, especially P-38s, flew repeated dive-bombing missions against bridges in the area, delaying the enemy's withdrawal. Meanwhile, Mitchells and Marauders went after ferries and pontoons pressed into German service.

Late April brought a return of adverse weather as the war was winding down. On May 2, the German armies in Italy surrendered. Over the next few days bombers dropped German-language leaflets to isolated units that may have lost contact with higher headquarters. The war in Europe was over.

Der Krieg ist vorbei.

Southwest Pacific Theater

Logically and factually, the Southwest Pacific theater ceased to exist when MacArthur's forces advanced north of the equator. Naturally, that included the entire Philippine archipelago where attention had been focused since fall 1944.

The new year got off to a poor start as the last of Kenney's paladins was killed on January 7. Major Tommy McGuire, arguably the hottest P-38 pilot in the Pacific, had notched his 38th victory and was gunning for Dick Bong's spot as ace of aces. In a low-level dogfight over Negros Island, McGuire stalled his P-38 and crashed into the trees. He received a posthumous Medal of Honor; Bong survived him seven months before a P-80 accident claimed his life.

By January 25, the U.S. Army had captured an airfield on Luzon, a necessary preliminary step toward Manila.

Although Pacific airborne operations received precious little ink in comparison to the ETO, Kenney's troop carriers remained active. On February 3 and 4, the 317th Troop Carrier Group dropped 1,830 troopers of the 11th Airborne Division on Tagaytay Ridge, northwest of Lake Taal, preceding the advance on Manila. The second and third drops were five miles off, requiring additional lifts over two days.

Meanwhile, 5th Air Force fighters and bombers relentlessly pounded Corregidor Island in Manila Bay. On the 16th, Colonel Jack Lackey's 317th Group again lifted elements of the 11th Airborne, delivering 2,050 paratroopers on "the Rock." Most landed where intended: on the parade ground and golf course, although some were blown over the cliffs. Following two weeks of rock climbing and fighting, Corregidor was back in American hands after three years. Subsequently the drive on Manila succeeded; resistance ended on March 4.

On February 10, one of the most bizarre episodes of the Pacific air war occurred. Lieutenant Louis E. Curdes of the 3rd Air Commando Group was scouting near Batan Island when he spotted a C-47 descending for a landing. Curdes knew that Bataan was held by the Japanese but he was unable to raise the Skytrain by radio. Running out of time, he took desperate measures.

Three days before, Curdes had scored against his third Axis power. Now he jockeyed his Mustang behind the C-47, took careful aim and shot out both engines, forcing the transport into a premature landing. Eventually the

13 passengers and crew were rescued, and Curdes received a rare honor. Already a Mediterranean ace, he added to the enemy totems painted on his P-51D. His final score: seven German planes, one Italian, one Japanese, and one American!

The last U.S. airborne operation of the war occurred in June as the veteran 317th Group used 67 aircraft and 8 gliders to deliver 1,030 troopers to Lipa Airstrip at Aparri on Luzon's north coast. The object, to prevent Japanese forces escaping the Cagayan Valley, succeeded. It was the only combined parachute-glider operation of the Pacific war.

China-Burma-India

On January 6, China-based B-29s flew their last mission to Japan. That month LeMay departed for Guam, taking over XXI Bomber Command, while Brigadier General Roger M. Ramey "shook the stick" to run XX Bomber Command. At higher echelons, control of CBI Superfortresses fell to the theater commander, British Admiral Louis Mountbatten.

Almost immediately, Ramey began mine-laying operations in earnest with expanded operations throughout Southeast Asia. Preferring to fly on moonlit nights, the Superforts dropped parachute mines from 2,000 to 6,000 feet. Coastal and inland waters of Indochina, Singapore, and Ceylon were sown with thousands of mines that further impeded Japan's already crippled merchant marine. However, when Japanese ground forces overran or threatened many 14th Air Force bases, mining operations were limited to the Upper Yangtze.

A major event occurred on January 22 when the Burma Road reopened. Japanese troops pulled back to the coast in some areas but kept up the pressure elsewhere.

The 14th Air Force continued taking the war to the Japanese—a nice change of pace for Chennault's often hard-pressed airmen. They did so on the deck as well as in the air, leading to the top American fighter score for enemy planes destroyed on the ground. Major Thomas A. Reynolds flew P-40s and P-51s with the 5th Fighter Group during 1944 and 1945, logging 92 missions with the Chinese-American Composite Wing (CACW). By far his best day occurred in February when, attacking three airfields in the Shangtung area, Reynolds shot up 25 Japanese planes with 10 assessed as destroyed. His final tally was reckoned at 38½ ground and four air.

Despite such successes, the Japanese remained on the offensive in China nearly to the end. CACW squadrons had to vacate several airfields in southern China as the enemy had long since learned the advantage of moving at night. Laohokow, almost 600 miles west of Shanghai, was abandoned on March 25, but it was the last base the 14th Air Force ceded to the enemy.

The China B-29 operation closed down in March and April, as the groups were more profitably used elsewhere. That meant the Marianas. Departing from Luliang, crews endured the tedium of 18-hour flights to the central Pacific. The transition was made in complete safety, demonstrating just how far the trouble-plagued B-29 program had come.

In July, the Hump operation lifted 71,000 tons to China—more than the Burma Road provided during the 7 months it was open that year. With both air and ground logistics in place, the allies enjoyed a far stronger position than at any time in the theater's turbulent history.

The war on the Asian mainland continued taking a huge toll even as military operations abated. Later estimates reckoned more than 100,000 deaths per month—mostly civilian—owing to war-related disease and starvation. The estimate of lives saved by the atomic bombs seldom includes Chinese, Burmese, Indians, and others who would have perished if the war had progressed into 1946.

Pacific Theater

In the Pacific, 1945 was the year of the Superfortress. It was also the year of Curtis LeMay.

Transferred from XX Bomber Command in China, LeMay arrived at Guam in January to take over from "Possum" Hansell. General Arnold felt that XXI Bomber Command was not getting results commensurate with the effort and expense invested. He believed that LeMay's hard-boiled attitude and extensive knowledge would make a difference. He was right.

Among other things, LeMay gave increasing emphasis to mining operations. Mining had been done by XX Bomber Command from India, mainly from January to March. Although some AAF leaders balked at supporting naval or ground forces, LeMay recognized the benefits. He advocated mining operations in Japan's home waters, raising the ante from one group conducting mining to a full wing.

Meanwhile, LeMay inherited a growth industry. In addition to the original B-29s from China, four other B-29 wings arrived in the Marianas. The 73rd, 313th, 314th, and 315th added 17 Superfortress groups to the original 58th Wing's 4 outfits. There were plenty of Superforts in the Pacific: Now they had a firm hand on the controls.

MISSION SUMMARY

The massive human and material investment in just one B-29 mission is provided in this official document for XXI Bomber Command's Mission 188 of June 5, 1945.

Mission # 188.

Date: 5 June 1945

Target: Kobe Urban Area (90.25—11)

Participating Units: 58th BW, 73rd BW, 313th BW, 314th BW

Number of A/C Airborne: 530 (including 7 Super Dumbos)

% A/C Bombing Primary: 89.37% (473 Primary and 8 Opportunity)

Type of Bombs and Fuzes: E-46, nondelay nose and varied delay tails; T4E4, varied delay nose and nondelay tail; AN-M47A2, instantaneous nose and nondelay tails and M17-A1, 24 sec. nose and nondelay tail.

Tons of Bombs Dropped: 3,079.1 Primary (target) and 54.7 on Opportunity (targets)

Time Over Primary: 050822K—050947K

Altitude of Attack: 13,650—18,800

Weather Over Target: 0/10—8/10

Total A/C Lost: 11

Resume of Mission: About 3.8 square miles of the city were destroyed and about ½ square mile east of Kobe. Nine numbered industrial targets were damaged. Total damage to city is 8 square miles, about 51% of the built up portion of the city. Of the B-29s lost, 3 were due to E/AC, 3 to enemy AA, 3 to E/A and AA, 1 crashed at Iwo Jima and 1 to unknown causes. Forty-nine A/C were noneffective. The 125 E/AC sighted made 672 attacks. Claims were 86-31-78. E/AA was heavy, meager to intense, generally accurate and damaged 139 B-29s. Forty-three A/C landed at Iwo Jima.

Average Bomb Load: 13,178 lbs.

Average Fuel Reserve: 677 gallons.

Explanation: A/C, aircraft; E/AC, enemy aircraft; E/AA, enemy anti-aircraft fire. Claims by B-29 gunners: 86 destroyed, 31 probably destroyed, 78 damaged.

Meanwhile, XXI Bomber Command continued shaking out the bugs. On February 10, of 84 effective sorties, a dozen were lost. That was bad enough, but only one was attributable to enemy action. The B-29 was proving its own worst enemy, especially owing to the troublesome Wright engines.

LeMay started working a small miracle in the crucial area of maintenance. Whereas B-29 availability had been running under 60 percent, he eventually got the in-commission figure up to 80 percent and more. Analysts in Washington were goggle-eyed at XXI Bomber Command's statistics: The Marianas B-29s had a higher operational rate than most stateside units.

Other changes were in the wind. After much discussion with his staff, LeMay decided to roll the dice with a dramatic change of tactics. On a successful mission in late February, dropping incendiaries rather than high explosives, 230 B-29s burned a square mile of Tokyo with only 3 losses. However, weather and the relatively small force prevented any conclusive lessons. Clearly incendiaries were the weapon of choice in Japan, but other factors were considered. LeMay's analysts noted that weather often precluded accurate high-altitude bombing, as per AAF doctrine, so he opted to go in low, at night. It was a risky venture: The bombers would be well inside the range of flak guns, which were more dangerous than enemy fighters.

On the night of March 9 and 10, the "fire blitz" began as 325 Boeings were dispatched to destroy Tokyo and largely succeeded. The 279 that reached the target released 1,665 tons of ordnance, burning out 15 square miles of urban area. Nearly 84,000 Japanese died while 22 industrial targets were destroyed. The bombers attacked from unusually low altitude: 4,900 to 9,200 feet, taking the defenses by surprise.

Although LeMay usually gets credit for the change in tactics, it was suggested by his staff analysts, who noted that weather often required radar bombing through clouds. Furthermore, the jet stream (little understood before the war) could cause dispersion of bombs dropped from 20,000 feet. Without having to climb so high, less fuel and more bombs could be carried. LeMay grasped the advantages and went even further: He took some guns and gunners out of the Boeings, reducing weight even more.

The low-level attack was proven. One of LeMay's wing commanders, Brigadier General Thomas S. Power, dropped his own bombs then orbited the capital to assess the results. He was impressed with the flak—it barely existed—and enemy aircraft were hardly seen. Even more impressive was the way Tokyo ignited. Wind-whipped fires swept across the city, fed by wooden buildings and violent winds whipped by the flames. Some pilots and copilots had to fight for control of their big bombers even at 6,000 feet. En route southward, airmen could still see the glow of Tokyo's flames 150 miles at sea.

The price was stiff: 14 planes missing with their well-trained crews. Twelve more went down on March 14 and 15 during a daylight fire raid on Nagoya. Nevertheless, urban Japan was systematically being burned to the ground.

Meanwhile, on March 4 the blood-soaked volcanic ash of Iwo Jima began paying for itself. A 9th Group B-29 named *Dinah Might* landed on the newly won island, unable to transfer fuel. Some 2,400 other Superforts followed over the next 5 months.

On March 6, Brigadier General Ernest M. Moore led VII Fighter Command to Iwo, landing the island's first P-51. He brought two Mustang groups with him; a third would follow. Moore, a 37-year-old West Pointer, had been in Hawaii in December 1941 and knew his way around the Pacific.

The Iwo Mustangs got their first taste of combat on April 7, notching 27 kills. Two future aces scored that day: Major Jim Tapp of the 15th Fighter Group nailed four while Captain Harry Crim of the 21st got two. It was especially gratifying for Crim, who had flown a North African P-38 tour without a kill. Later he said, "I fought the Germans for patriotism and the Japs for fun. Next time I'm fighting for money."

April 1 was Easter and April Fool's Day. It was also L-Day at Okinawa. Amphibious troops got ashore with almost no resistance but as they moved inland, the Japanese turned up with customary ferocity. Okinawa became a slugfest—the bloodiest battle of the Pacific, both ashore and at sea.

May was the worst month yet for XXI Bomber Command. Eleven Superforts were lost on the 14th and 17 on the 23rd. It was a stunning toll despite the 3.2 percent loss among 520 reaching the target area. But in 1945 a B-29 cost more than half a million dollars; one AAF survey suggested treating very heavy bombers more like ships than aircraft.

Worse was just around the corner. On May 25, 464 bombers released. 3,262 tons on Tokyo, creating another firestorm, but an appalling 23 Superfortresses were written off: nearly 5 percent of the attacking force. Furthermore, 60 B-29 crewmen in enemy hands were left to die in the flames or were beheaded by fleeing guards. Throughout the year, "B-San" fliers were murdered by their captors as a matter of course.

Mickey Moore's Sunsetters also were taking losses. On June 1 they sustained their worst loss of the war, and not from enemy action. Of 148 Mustangs sent to escort bombers to Osaka, only 27 got through a severe weather front to make rendezvous. An equal number of fighters succumbed to turbulence and zero-visibility conditions; only three pilots were rescued.

On June 22, Japanese resistance ended on Okinawa, and existing airfields were expanded while others were laid out. The island was to become the aerial springboard for the invasion of the home islands, beginning in late fall. That same month Pacific fighters squeezed Japanese air power in a two-pronged attack from the Ryukyus and Iwo Jima. On June 10, Okinawa P-47Ns of the 318th Group claimed 17 kills while Sunsetter Mustangs nailed 27 for a total of 44. It topped the year's record established two weeks before.

Meanwhile, B-29 operations increased. In June it was not unusual for 500 or more Superforts to launch from the Marianas. Late that month, 510 bombers and 148 fighters were sent against 8 targets with just 5 B-29s lost. Not even Japanese ramming tactics dented the huge formations; *bushido* enthusiasm was a poor match for technological know-how.

Administrative changes also occurred that summer. In July, XX Bomber Command was inactivated while Headquarters 20th Air Force moved from Washington to Guam with Lieutenant General Nate Twining in command. At the same time U.S. Army Strategic Air Forces, Pacific, was established there under General "Tooey" Spaatz.

The war news remained grim. On July 30, Japan refused the Allies' Potsdam Declaration calling for unconditional surrender. Two days later, 836 B-29s launched one mining and five incendiary raids with only one loss. Toyama, a steel-producing city, was erased; three others were 65 to 80 percent destroyed. However, Tokyo's war cabinet decided to continue fighting.

Bad idea.

Splitting Atoms

The 509th Composite Group had received some pointed joshing by the other B-29 outfits at North Field, Tinian. The group had been formed at desolate Wendover Field, Utah, in December, under 29-year-old Colonel Paul Tibbets. The 509th was like no other organization in the AAF. It was incredibly small for so grand a title as "group": just one bomb squadron, the 393rd, plus a troop carrier and headquarters squadron and support units. At its height, the 509th comprised merely 1,829 men with 15 bombers. They were B-29s with names such as *Full House*, *Strange Cargo*, *Straight Flush*, and (appropriately) *Top Secret*. One aircraft, call sign Dimples 82, would remain unnamed until its most famous mission. Tibbets would name it for his mother.

Arriving in June, the Boeings with the black arrow on their tails (later a "circle R") flew few combat missions and the crews generally kept to themselves. Some 509th men felt like outcasts. Until August 6.

Accompanied by two other planes, Tibbets took the newly named *Enola Gay* to Honshu that morning. He carried one bomb: a 10,000-pound city slayer called Little Boy. It was a uranium weapon, which yielded the equivalent of 12,000 tons of TNT. Although only Tibbets and the Navy weapons officer knew the physics of the weapon, one crew member was uncommonly astute: "Colonel, are we splitting atoms today?"

When bombardier Major Tom Ferebee released the bomb from 32,000 feet, Tibbets hauled the '29 into his practiced escape. He had been told that optimum tangency was 159 degrees from release heading, and he got every foot of turn possible from the airplane.

Forty-three seconds later, a man-made sun burst over Hiroshima. Among other things, it was a military district headquarters and home of the Japanese Army submarine school. The tail gunner's fervent "My God" spoke volumes. According to Japanese sources, 71,000 people died; nearly as many were seared or blasted. A broiling mushroom cloud churned its way up to 50,000 feet, leaving rubble across an area of 5 square miles.

The American political and military leaders hoped that an atomic bomb would convince Japan to surrender. Three days later, with apparently no word forthcoming from Tokyo, the 509th sent Major Charles Sweeney in *Bock's Car* to Kokura. His weapon was Fat Man, a plutonium bomb, but the primary was obscured. Therefore, Sweeney opted for his alternate and obliterated 43 percent of Nagasaki. As many as 35,000 Japanese died.

That same day Russia declared war on Japan. The emperor, if not all his advisors, recognized the appalling reality of the situation. On August 14, he announced acceptance of the Potsdam Declaration while 750 Superforts were still airborne. That day, the AAF scored its final aerial victories of the war. Operating from the Ryukyus, P-38s and P-47s claimed 18 kills before the Japanese message was received. The last four victors were 8th Group Lightning pilots: Captains R. F. Meyer and B. G. Moore with Lieutenants D. E. Hollister and G. I. Stevens, who downed four Nakajima Franks. (P-61 night fighters claimed two kills after midnight, but no credit was awarded.)

On September 2, some 500 B-29s and more than 1,000 Navy aircraft overflew Tokyo Bay while the surrender ceremony ended aboard the battleship *Missouri*. Standing with the victors were Carl Spaatz, chief of the Strategic Air Forces; George Kenney, who was MacArthur's senior airman most of the war; and Jimmy Doolittle, who had arrived on Okinawa to oversee conversion of the 8th Air Force to a B-29 organization. Their presence was tacit tribute to the AAF's contribution to winning the war.

The question has been asked, what would have happened if the war continued? One thing is known: General Leslie Groves, manager of the Manhattan Project, expected seven atom bombs available by year end. However, LeMay probably would have run out of target cities worth an A-bomb by then.

VJ-DAY CELEBRATION

On the day that Japan agreed to surrender, hundreds of AAF airmen were tugged in opposite directions. Emotionally torn, they rejoiced at the end of the war while regretting limited opportunity to fly a combat mission. Some B-29 crews recently assigned to the transplanted 8th Air Force attended successive briefings that last week only to have each flight canceled.

On Okinawa, the 348th Fighter Group accepted some new P-51 pilots. One of them was Lieutenant Robert Stevens, later a professional cartoonist. As an eager young stud, Stevens relished the status of fighter pilot and sported a .45-caliber pistol in a shoulder holster. "They'll never take me alive," he declared, insisting that he would shoot it out with any Japanese intent on capturing him. However, other priorities always prevented him from test firing his big Colt.

On VJ night, amid suitable celebrations, Stevens determined that there would be no better time to break in his .45. He loaded a magazine into the pistol, chambered a round, and pointed at the sky. "All I got was a very loud *click,*" he recalled ruefully. Repeated tries brought the same result. Eventually Stevens took his M1911 to the armorers, who found it had a broken firing pin. "The Japs would've got me after all," he laughed.

On August 27, B-29s began hundreds of sorties dropping something besides bombs and incendiaries. POW relief flights spread over Japan, Korea, and eastern China, locating prison camps and providing urgently needed food and medical supplies. Throughout the duration of the "campaign," 77 airmen lost their lives in 8 aircraft.

1945 Summary

Few would dispute that the B-29 mated with the atom bomb was the most impressive aviation development of the war. Even without two nuclear attacks, the Superfortress demonstrated its awesome ability to destroy entire cities in one night. Unlike other nations, Japan's economy depended to a large extent on cottage industries located in homes or private shops. The combustible nature of Japanese cities ensured that firestorms devastated huge segments of the nation's urban areas, while B-29 mining operations reduced the efficiency of an already crippled merchant marine. Air power emerged clearly triumphant in the Pacific; less so in China, where bases remained potentially vulnerable.

The end of the European war four months earlier also gave the AAF a major boost in prestige. Although the merits of strategic bombing were argued during the war and for decades thereafter, Hap Arnold's airmen made a significant contribution to victory. Air superiority was a prime requirement for the Normandy landings, and the AAF public relations machine made certain that American citizens—and Congress—absorbed that fact.

Air Force strength in 1945 peaked at 2,282,000, down slightly from 1944. Mainly it was because many long-service men were discharged as the United States wrapped up the European war and prepared to end the fight in the Pacific. As noted, Hiroshima and Nagasaki meant that a horrific invasion of Japan was unnecessary.

As it was, the butcher's bill was bad enough. Just over 40,000 AAF personnel were known dead in combat theaters, while 63,500 were prisoners or missing in action. Some 12,000 missing men were dead. Another 18,000 were wounded. More than 41,000 airmen were captured; half of the 5,400 in Japanese hands died in captivity compared to about one tenth in Nazi hands. AAF combat casualties of 121,867 did not include another 13,000 "stateside" deaths.

THE PRICE OF VICTORY

The AAF obtained 230,200 airplanes from 1940 to 1945, including 138,320 combat types. The numbers included 34,763 multi-engine bombers, 25,904 twin-engine bombers, 68,259 fighters, 1,117 recon planes, 22,698 transports, 55,712 trainers, and 13,558 "Cub"-type liaison planes.

The taxpayers footed a huge bill in those 45 months, and for AAF aircraft the typical 1944 prices (including GFE, or government-furnished equipment, such as guns and bomb sights) were as follows:

B-17 Flying Fortress	$204,370
B-24 Liberator	$215,516
B-29 Superfortress	$605,360
B-25 Mitchell	$142,194
B-26 Marauder	$192,427
P-38 Lightning	$97,147
P-40 Warhawk	$44,892
P-47 Thunderbolt	$85,578
P-51 Mustang	$51,572
P-59 Airacomet	$236,299
C-47 Skytrain	$88,574
PT-17 Kaydet	$15,052
AT-6 Texan	$22,952

On average, 6,600 American servicemen died per month from December 1941 through August 1945—220 a day. But apart from the toll in lives, the American war effort accounted for billions of dollars per month.

During the spring and summer of 1944, the AAF was losing 1,000 to 1,500 planes per month in the European and Mediterranean theaters. The highest monthly toll against Japan was 256 in May 1945.

Combat losses totaled 22,948 aircraft: 18,418 against Germany and Italy plus 4,530 against Japan.

WINNERS AND LOSERS

Six decades or more after World War II, it is almost impossible to envision a time when the world teetered on the brink of totalitarianism. But the national socialists in Germany, fascists in Italy, and imperialists in Japan formed a global triad dedicated to the extinction of democracy, and the rest of the world needed six years to defeat them. On the opposite side of the same coin was Soviet Russia, held in communism's steel grip, with the same purpose in a different guise.

In geopolitical terms, the big winners were America and Russia. In 1945, the United States was the only superpower on earth, possessing the strongest economy, the greatest navy and air force, and the atom bomb. Almost wholly untouched by war, America led the way into a resurgent postwar world with enormous economic, political, and moral authority. Those factors placed it squarely on a collision course with Stalinist Russia.

Although wartime allies, the United States and Soviet Union shared almost nothing in common. With no tradition of democratic rule, Russia proceeded to annex vast territories of Eastern Europe for itself as a buffer against the West. Still struggling to regain its full industrial potential, Moscow had one item for export: revolution.

The colonial powers such as Britain and France quickly lost or abandoned their previous holdings. In their place, Communist China emerged as the dominant power in Asia with occasionally tenuous ties to Moscow. Wars of "national liberation" emerged around the post-colonial periphery in Asia and Africa. When Russia obtained atomic weapons in 1949, a balance of terror ensued for half a century.

Within the U.S. armed forces, the AAF emerged fully fledged. Of necessity it had been granted de facto independent status under Army administration, and General Hap Arnold sat as one among equals on the Joint Chiefs. Arnold was an excellent example of the youngest branch: on VJ-Day he was only 59; General of the Army George Marshall was 65, while Fleet Admiral Ernest King was 67. Aviation's enormous contribution to winning the war virtually ensured full autonomy, a promise realized in the new Department of Defense in 1947.

As in World War I, aviation was a big winner with enormous strides during World War II. Although air power was vastly more influential in "War Two," technical progress was not as dramatic, with one exception. The war began and ended with all-metal monoplanes that climbed higher and flew faster than those six years previously, but the only true innovation occurred in propulsion. Development of jet engines and the attendant aerodynamic studies pointed to the future—and beyond.

Although airplanes themselves underwent a propulsion revolution, the way they performed their missions represented a significant improvement. Primary was the emergence of electronics, especially radio and radar. Once mated, they enabled unparalleled communication and navigation in darkness or bad weather. The tactical advantages of radio and radar were first proved in the Battle of Britain in 1940, and only increased thereafter.

CHAPTER 5

THE JET AGE

The inevitable postwar demobilization was dramatic. From a manpower total of 2,282,000 in 1945, the Army Air Force (AAF) dropped to 455,000 in one year, remaining at approximately that level through 1950. Over the next three years, the demands of the Korean War pushed manning levels to nearly one million, with more than 800,000 through 1969 (a high of 904,000 was achieved in 1968).

Among the major innovations in the postwar AAF was the establishment of the Strategic Air Command (SAC) in March 1946. The first commander was General George C. Kenney, who defined SAC's mission as "long-range offensive operations in any part of the world." Toward that end he had 1,300 aircraft (including 300 B-29s) and 100,000 personnel. Over the next few years, SAC would continue growing in importance to the Air Force and the nation.

As of 1945, piston combat aircraft were fast becoming obsolescent. Ten years later they were obsolete (and ten years thereafter they were invaluable again). Jet propulsion brought a renaissance and a revolution to military aviation.

America's first jet aircraft was the Bell P-59 Airacomet, powered by two anemic General Electric engines. Also known as the "Lead Sled," it was no faster than most piston fighters but provided much-needed experience with new engine technology. Security surrounding the P-59 program was such that a fake four-bladed propeller was affixed to the jet's nose when it was towed from the hangar.

Based on original research and European data, the United States began fielding a stable of more capable jet fighters. The first useful design was Lockheed's P-80 Shooting Star, followed by Republic's P/F-84 Thunderjet. Although generally underpowered, they offered a significant combat capability that shortly would be tested in Asian skies.

P-80 SHOOTING STAR

America's first serious jet fighter was Lockheed's follow-up to the excellent P-38 Lightning. Although Bell's P-59 had flown in 1943, the P-80 became the first U.S. jet built in useful numbers (a total of 1,700). A relatively advanced airframe mated to the General Electric J33 engine with 4,000 pounds of thrust resulted in a genuinely useful aircraft.

First flown in 1944, the P-80 showed considerable promise. Five thousand were ordered, but by VJ-Day only a handful had been delivered. Armament was the World War II–standard six .50-caliber guns, plus 2,000 pounds of bombs or rockets, with a top speed of about 575 miles per hour in the C model. Meanwhile, the B model became the first U.S.-production aircraft equipped with an ejection seat. Reconnaissance models were equipped with cameras in place of machine guns.

Shooting Stars established postwar speed records (nearly 600 miles per hour) and, owing to the 1947 designation change, the P-80 became the F-80 in time for the Korean War. The type saw heavy use in Korea, where Shooting Stars logged nearly 100,000 sorties. An F-80C featured in history's first jet-versus-jet combat, over Korea in November 1950.

The F-80 was the basis of the T-33, the Air Force's first jet trainer, which remained in production until 1959.

PUSHING THE ENVELOPE

Between 1949 and 1951, the Air Force test pilot school was moved from Dayton, Ohio, to Edwards Air Force Base, partly because California offered excellent weather year-round. Although the name of the organization changed frequently (it was the Air Materiel Command Test Pilot School in 1949), its mission remained consistent: to provide skilled pilots capable of evaluating new designs and techniques in the military aviation and aerospace fields.

(Photo courtesy of the USAF via Robert F. Dorr)

Korean War ace Iven C. Kincheloe, who later became a famous test pilot for the Air Force.

Those were heady days in the high desert, with exciting experimental concepts to be tested as well as a succession of new fighters and other types. The challenge and satisfaction of mastering complex, often dangerous, equipment attracted many of the finest pilots in the Air Force.

The dean of test pilots was Colonel (later Major General) Albert Boyd, an extremely capable flier and leader who oversaw most Air Force test functions during the 1940s and beyond. It was said that from 1945 to 1957, the AAF and U.S. Air Force (USAF) never bought an airplane without his endorsement. Boyd was known as a stern taskmaster but he was also acknowledged as the complete master of his field. The Tennessean had been at Pearl Harbor in 1941 and already enjoyed a reputation as a "can-do" maintenance and engineering officer. Rated in an incredible 25 aircraft types simultaneously, in June 1947 he returned the world speed record to America for the first time in 24 years. Piloting a modified P-80, he recorded a respectable 623 miles per hour in June 1947. When Major General Boyd retired, he had logged an awesome 23,000 military flight hours in hundreds of aircraft types.

In 1947, the Navy and AAF both had progressive flight test programs, "pushing the envelope" of jet- and rocket-powered aircraft. The high desert of Southern California provided a natural airfield, the miles-long Muroc Dry Lake, which seemed designed for high-speed airplanes. A variety of experimental designs was tested at Muroc, which later became part of the complex for Edwards Air Force Base, named for Captain Glenn Edwards, who died testing Northrop's innovative YB-49 "Flying Wing" in 1948. By tradition, AAF and USAF bases were named for dead airmen, leading Brigadier General Chuck Yeager to explain his longevity: "I never let a pathologist examine me and I never let them name an air base after me." They did, however, make an exception and name a street for him.

The Navy's lead program was built around two sexy red Douglas D-558 Skystreaks. They were turbine-powered machines able to take off under their own power, and in August 1947 they established back-to-back speed records of 640 and 650 miles per hour. The program was ready to attempt a Mach One record, but the Navy declined, balking at the $50,000 price per flight.

That left the field wide open to the Air Force. Like the D-558, the Bell X-1 was a straight-wing design, but any similarity ended there. The orange rocket's fuselage was based on the shape of a .50-caliber bullet, and the machine had to be air-launched from a B-29. Nevertheless, it demonstrated excellent potential with a four-chamber, liquid-fuel engine.

Bell began unpowered flights in 1946 with the first use of rocket power before year's end. The AAF took over the project in July 1947 with progressively faster speeds being recorded. The X-1's mission was to explore compressibility effects beyond a conventional jet's Mach .85, pushing ever closer to the "sound barrier." Despite initial doubts that the straight-wing design could punch through the Mach, some pilots and engineers believed it possible. Among them was 24-year-old Captain Charles E. Yeager, previously a Mustang ace, who achieved lasting fame when he flew *Glamorous Glennis* to 700 miles per hour on October 14, 1947.

BRIGADIER GENERAL CHARLES E. YEAGER (1922–)

Among the most significant airmen of all time, Chuck Yeager seemed to define the indefinable mystique of "the right stuff." He gained notice as an 8th Air Force P-51 pilot in 1943 through 1944, not only as a double ace but as one of the few who bagged a German jet. Although lacking formal education, by persistence and innate ability he established himself in the postwar Air Force as a knowledgeable, analytical test pilot. In 1947, he flew the Bell X-1 to Mach 1, proving the viability of supersonic flight and ensuring his place in history. Six years later he reached Mach 2 as well.

During the Vietnam War, Yeager commanded the 405th Fighter Wing, a composite unit flying a variety of aircraft from bases in South Vietnam, Thailand, and Taiwan. Subsequently he served as U.S. Defense Representative to Pakistan, where he used a helicopter to count wrecks of downed aircraft during the 1971 war with India.

Yeager continued flying until retirement in 1975, but kept current in tactical jets as a consultant at Edwards Air Force Base. On October 14, 1997, he went supersonic in an F-15 Eagle, half a century after his historic flight in *Glamorous Glennis*.

Like most military pilots, Chuck Yeager knew how to have a good time. The night before his flight into history, he had taken a nasty spill while horse racing with his wife, wrenching a shoulder and cracking two ribs. However, he was not about to let such inconvenient developments keep him out of the X-1. A doctor taped his ribs, so "the pain was at least manageable."

Before takeoff Yeager confided in his fellow test pilot, Jack Ridley, concerned that his injuries would prevent him from closing the high-tension lock on the X-1's canopy. Ridley's solution was inspired. He sawed off a broom handle and suggested that Yeager use it as a lever for more mechanical advantage on the canopy. It worked like a charm.

After release from the B-29, Yeager rode the rocket to 42,000 feet, indicating .96 Mach with three chambers firing. He found that the faster he flew, the smoother the ride. "Suddenly the Mach needle began to fluctuate," he related. "It went up to .965 Mach—then tipped right off the scale.

I thought I was seeing things! We were flying supersonic! It was as smooth as a baby's bottom: Grandma could be sitting up there sipping lemonade." He maintained supersonic speed for about 20 seconds, and then raised the nose to decelerate.

Yeager radioed Jack Ridley, saying that the meter had been pegged. Ridley replied that Yeager must be seeing things. Characteristically unconcerned, Yeager allowed that he was still wearing his ears, and nothing fell off the airplane. On the ground, the National Advisory Council on Aeronautics (NACA) monitoring crew reported distant thunder. It was the sound of the future: a man-made sonic boom. Data showed that Yeager had pushed *Glamorous Glennis* to 1.07 times the speed of sound.

Yeager's feat was kept secret for a time, but word leaked out and the Air Force publicly acknowledged the record. Eventually, the X-1 achieved 967 miles per hour and reached 73,000 feet.

In late 1953, Yeager flew the upgraded X-1A to 1,650 miles per hour, becoming the first pilot to achieve Mach 2 as well. Neither X-1 variant had an ejection seat, and at typical speeds a conventional bailout was almost impossible—proof of the courage and dedication of the test pilots involved.

EJECTION SEATS

With the very high speeds possible in jet aircraft, the old-fashioned method of manual bailout was no longer a reliable means of escape. Therefore, rocket-powered ejection seats were developed which catapulted airmen up and out of an imperiled airplane; some seats dropped out the bottom. In any case, mechanical assistance greatly increased the odds of survival, even at airspeeds as high as 700 miles per hour.

The earliest ejection seats were compressed-air devices in advanced German aircraft of World War II, notably the Dornier 335 with front- and rear-mounted propellers. However, even the more sophisticated U.S. and British seats of early jets had limitations with minimum safe altitudes, airspeeds, and angle of bank. Later, "zero zero" seats were developed, which could be activated with the airplane on the runway with zero altitude and zero airspeed. More recently, sophisticated self-stabilizing seats permit safe ejection from an inverted aircraft with the seat righting itself before deploying the parachute.

Two entrants in the "ejection seat hall of fame" are little known elsewhere. In 1954, an Air Force flight surgeon, Lieutenant Colonel John P. Stapp, strapped himself onto a rocket sled that braked from 632 miles per hour to 0 in 1.4 seconds. He was subjected to an incredible 40 Gs, but survived to prove the concept of supersonic ejections. Previous ejection tests involved weighted dummies, apes, and even bears.

The first genuine supersonic ejection occurred in February 1955 when North American test pilot George Smith pulled the handle, leaving a doomed F-100 at Mach 1.05. He was injured but returned to flying.

A newer philosophy in ejection seats is an enclosed capsule containing the entire cockpit. The most famous Air Force aircraft to employ the option is the General Dynamics F-111, designed as a low-altitude supersonic bomber. Flying at very high speed and treetop level, conventional ejection seats provide marginal survivability. The F-111's system afforded additional protection to the pilot and navigator-bombardier.

More than 12,000 lives have been saved by ejection seats worldwide.

Other X planes followed through the 1950s into the 1960s. The X-2 further "pushed the envelope" of supersonic flight, gaining additional knowledge of structures, materials and heat, flight control, and propulsion. Among the record setters was Captain Frank "Pete" Everest, an erstwhile P-40 pilot, who logged Mach 2.87 (1,900 miles per hour) in July 1956.

After a breakfast of eggnog and toast, Everest climbed into the B-50 mother ship and rode it to 33,000 feet. There he eased himself into the X-2's cramped cockpit, completed his checklist, and waited while the Boeing gained speed in a 3,000-foot descent. Then the rocket plane was dropped.

Everest fired both chambers of the rocket engine, which ignited with such force that he was slammed back against his seat, his helmet striking the cockpit wall. He shook his head to clear the shock of sudden acceleration, and then slowly pulled the stick back to begin his climb for more altitude.

Trying to maintain his planned climb schedule, Everest found the X-2 seemingly running away from him. Fighting the controls, struggling to hold a steady flight path, he was already supersonic.

Pete Everest watched the Mach meter climb to a speed that he knew had never been seen before. Still in level flight, the rocket continued the astonishing momentum of its climb. Telemetry proved that his top speed was more than 1,900 miles per hour. Subsequently, Everest wrote that he felt like an explorer, like Columbus and Magellan. He felt "both awed and proud."

Eventually the X-2 became the first plane to achieve Mach 3 (2,094 miles per hour).

The Air Force and the National Air and Space Administration (NASA) combined on the ultimate X plane, the X-15, which (in *Star Trek* terms) literally went where no man had gone before. With a design specification of 4,000 miles per hour and more than 50 miles altitude, it was unlike anything else. The builder, North American, teamed with the Air Force, Navy, and NASA to produce a succession of spectacular flights during 1961, increasing speed from Mach 4 to Mach 6 that year alone. Air Force Captain Pete Knight capped the program with his October 1967 record of 6.7 times the speed of sound.

INTERSERVICE RIVALRY AND INDEPENDENCE

For airmen, the most significant postwar event was the restructuring of America's military with a Department of Defense (DoD) and an independent Air Force. However, for a sense of perspective, the science fiction writer Robert Heinlein had an astute perception. "No department of defense ever won a war," he wrote. "Check your histories."

The change had been a long time coming. A unified defense department had been suggested as early as 1925, and some serious planning ensued. The pressures of World War II forced a delay, but some wartime glitches were cited as necessary by DoD advocates to avoid repetitions. Perhaps the major example was Army-Navy confusion in the critical hours leading up to Pearl Harbor.

There was little doubt that the military-unification act would pass, especially with President Truman and General Eisenhower as backers. The admirals, however, feared (rightly, it turned out) that some senior Air Force leaders would try poaching in Navy waters. General Carl Spaatz, for instance, advocated taking over long-range reconnaissance and antisubmarine work to avoid Navy duplication of those roles. The Navy was justifiably concerned: Exactly the same thing had occurred in Britain in 1918 when the Royal Naval Air Service was incorporated into the Royal Air Force. Other generals looked at carrier aviation and saw room for acquisition. Again, Britain was an example as the Royal Air Force provided aircrews for Royal Navy carriers until the brink of World War II.

Thus, when the War Department became the Department of the Army, the stage was set for an extraordinarily bitter dispute: Army against Navy, Navy against Air Force, and Marines against everybody. (Harry Truman, a World War I Army officer, compared the Leathernecks' propaganda machine to Stalin's.) It was an ugly turf war. Generals and admirals sought to make their respective service the first among equals, especially with the advent of nuclear weapons. The Air Force, of course, got a head start in 1945 when it dropped the only two A-bombs ever used in earnest. The Navy scurried to play catch-up, developing both land- and carrier-based aircraft capable of delivering the big, heavy nukes of the era.

During 1946, the Joint Chiefs directed the AAF's Major General Lauris Norstad and Vice Admiral Forrest Sherman to draft a unification plan, which went to the president and Congress. The National Security Act of 1947 was signed into law that September, allowing the Navy to keep its own aviation while the Marine Corps was preserved.

The first Secretary of Defense was a Great War naval aviator, James Forrestal (who shortly died in office), while the Department of the Air Force proceeded under Stuart Symington. Spaatz remained chief of staff. At the squadron level, much of the change was superficial: New uniforms appeared and a red stripe was added to the horizontal bar in the national insignia.

B-36 PEACEMAKER

In 1943, the AAF began thinking of an intercontinental bomber, a replacement for the already revolutionary Boeing B-29. The answer was Consolidated's mammoth B-36, an innovative design with six powerful Pratt and Whitney "pusher" engines mounted on the trailing edge of the 230-foot wings. It first flew in 1946 with a gross weight of 100 tons, then an American record. Deliveries of production aircraft began in 1948, and gross weight of the definitive J model was 410,000 pounds—more than 200 tons.

With a 9- or 10-man crew and an internal fuel capacity of at least 21,000 gallons, the Peacemaker had an 8,000-mile range with a 10,000-pound bomb load. In the D model, jet engines were mounted outboard on each wing to boost takeoff power. When deliveries ended in 1954, 385 Peacemakers had armed 10 wings of Strategic Air Command (SAC), including 114 long-range reconnaissance versions with as many as 14 cameras. The investment in research, construction, and manning was enormous for the time, with each bomber costing between $4 and $7 million.

When the Peacemaker was retired in 1959, SAC became an all-jet force. Nevertheless, the B-36 provided the credibility of nuclear deterrence during a crucial period of the Cold War.

The grace and beauty of the B-36 is best captured in the 1955 Jimmy Stewart film *Strategic Air Command*. The gorgeous color photography is still seen on cable TV.

No sooner had the new scheme been adopted than more feuding broke out. The "blue suiters" had the inside track, as Truman's new Secretary of Defense was a political hack more than willing to do as told. In 1948 and 1949, the dispute became an argument as to whether large aircraft carriers or the B-36 bomber should represent America's first line of defense. General Hoyt Vandenberg, speaking for the Air Force, supported carriers for anti-submarine warfare, but added (perhaps disingenuously) that the nation could not justify a large peacetime carrier fleet. The flaw in his argument was obvious: Presumably no future war could last long enough to produce the numbers of ships necessary.

When the Truman administration canceled the supercarrier USS *United States* ("the only time the Air Force sank a carrier"), the chief of naval operations resigned in protest. Other admirals retaliated by urging a congressional investigation of the B-36. Fortunately, cooler heads prevailed. By the time of the next war (in Korea), there was plenty of work for everyone.

C-54 SKYMASTER

Following up the Douglas DC-3/C-47 was extremely tough, but the C-54 lived up to its billing. Developed from the DC-4A of 1938, the Skymaster became America's first four-engine military cargo plane early in World War II. Following its first flight in March 1942, it was valued by Army and Navy transport services. Some 1,160 were delivered through 1947.

The C-54 had a 117-foot, 6-inch wingspan, weighing 37,000 pounds empty with a gross weight of 62,000 pounds. Four Pratt and Whitney 1,290-horsepower engines drove the transport at a maximum 265 miles per hour. It could fly 3,900 miles with 14 tons of cargo or 49 passengers, but a "flying ambulance" version was specially equipped for evacuating combat casualties as well.

Skymasters were found everywhere on the globe during World War II. Eventually they logged a million miles per month across the North Atlantic with as many as 20 round trips per day, yet only 3 C-54s were lost in nearly

80,000 ocean crossings through 1945. While C-46s and C-47s flew most of the trips over the Hump from India to China, C-54s with their greater cargo capacity also made important contributions to the China-Burma-India (CBI) theater.

Ironically, perhaps, the Skymaster's most notable role occurred three years after the war. In 1948, when the Soviets shut down land access to Berlin, C-54s carried most of the load during the highly successful airlift. "Operation Vittles" probably could not have succeeded without a round-the-clock flights into the isolated German city.

C-54s and their R5D Navy counterparts remained in operational service through the 1960s.

BERLIN AIRLIFT

The claim has often been made that air power never won a war. Wrong. Aviation not only won a major campaign single-handedly, but prevented a wider war in the process.

On June 24, 1948, the Soviet Union blocked Allied access to Berlin by ground transportation. With the former Nazi capital deep inside East Germany, the American, British, and French sectors of the city faced eventual starvation—which is precisely what Moscow desired. The Russians well knew that the Allied sectors of Berlin required 4,500 tons of supplies a day, including coal. The *Luftwaffe* had been unable to deliver 300 tons per day to Stalingrad six years before.

The Russians expected the Western allies to abandon Berlin, leaving the key city wholly in Soviet hands. General Lucius D. Clay, U.S. military governor in Germany, drafted plans for a breakthrough that had the potential for World War III, but he consulted with his allies. The British suggested an air bridge into the city, and the word went down.

Clay tossed the ball to U.S. Air Forces, Europe (USAFE). Lieutenant General Curtis LeMay, the tough-as-nails USAFE commander who had bombed Germany and nuked Japan, probably saw no little irony in the situation. Having reduced the Axis to smoking rubble, he now prepared to save 2,500,000 Germans from starvation.

With other pressing concerns (including a possible Russian invasion), LeMay designated Brigadier General Joseph Smith as the initial airlift commander. At the same time Clay used his influence (and probably exceeded his authority) by starting to draft most of the 400 C-54s in the Air Force inventory. Then he asked permission of President Truman. The results were almost immediate as Operation Vittles (Smith's famous phrase) began just two days later.

On June 26, Royal Air Force Dakotas (C-47s) landed with 6.5 tons of supplies for Berlin's British garrison. Immediately thereafter, the U.S. Military Airlift Command began gathering Douglas C-54s from as far afield as Alaska, Hawaii, and the Caribbean. Operation Vittles was literally pulled out of midair to meet the challenge of feeding a city that would soon be in desperate need of food, fuel, and most other supplies.

In July, Major General William H. Tunner took over direction of the airlift. Tunner had an extensive transport background: He had helped establish Ferrying Command during the war and later ran the Hump operation. He streamlined the airlift even more, reducing landing intervals from three minutes to two in some instances.

LIEUTENANT GENERAL WILLIAM H. TUNNER
(1906–1983)

If Bill Tunner hated anything, it was a cargo plane sitting on the ramp. He believed in keeping aircraft airborne, delivering their loads where needed, and getting the planes off for another run.

A West Pointer drawn to flying, Tunner won his wings in 1929 in an Air Corps that had no transport aircraft worthy of the name. Nevertheless, in 1941 he helped establish Ferry Command, delivering aircraft to U.S. allies (notably Britain) before direct American involvement in World War II. Subsequently the organization became Air Transport Command, with Colonel Tunner in charge of the ferrying division, which delivered 10,000 aircraft overseas per month.

In September 1944, Tunner was sent to India to run the CBI's famous Hump flights. By the end of the war a year later, his command was delivering an astonishing 70,000 tons per month. The record was based on disciplined flying, excellent maintenance, and more efficient loading and unloading procedures.

Tunner was named Aviation Man of the Year for 1949 but his work was far from done. He led Combat Cargo Command during the Korean War and on the last day of that conflict (July 27, 1953), as a lieutenant general, he became commander of U.S. Air Forces in Europe. He retired in 1960, having run the two largest airlift operations ever conducted at that time.

Although winter was months away, inventories had to be maintained, and the first coal flights began on July 2. It took time, but by October the American and British efforts were unified under one command for greatest possible efficiency, using all suitable airfields in the Allied zones. Limited to flight paths defined by the Soviets, the U.S., U.K., and French planes operated in crowded airways and worsening weather. However, the burden was eased the following month when Naval Air Transport Command added its R5Cs to the effort.

Whether Air Force or Navy, the Douglas Globemaster hauled the majority of the freight to Berlin. Air Force strength peaked in January 1949 with 225 C-54s committed to the airlift, leading up to a maximum-effort "Easter Parade" on April 16 when nearly 1,400 sorties delivered almost 13,000 tons to Berlin. It was a prodigious affair, with Allied planes logging not quite one landing per minute throughout the day.

After nearly a year of ineffectual obstruction, the Soviets finally ended their illegal blockade on May 12, 1949. However, Operation Vittles continued until September as a precaution against Communist backsliding, as Moscow had repeatedly demonstrated that its word was not to be trusted.

From June 1948 through August 1949, some 278,000 flights delivered 2,300,000 tons of food, fuel, and supplies (an average of 160,000 tons per month) to the western sectors of Berlin. It was a signal success for air power—not only for the aircrews but for maintenance men who worked around the clock to keep "up" airplanes available. The enormous logistical effort also required a high order of planning and coordination among three main services: the U.S. Air Force and Navy and the Royal Air Force.

The victory was not without cost: 31 Americans (28 Air Force) and 39 Britons lost their lives supplying Berlin.

The magnitude of the Berlin Airlift almost defies description in today's context. For example, the multinational NATO supply effort to Sarajevo lasted three and a half years, from 1992 to 1996. In those 42 months, the allied air forces delivered 180,000 tons to the Yugoslav capital—a figure exceeded in one month's airlift to Berlin.

The Berlin Wall became a stern, mute testament to the true nature of communism. It was not built to keep West Germans out; it only kept East Germans in.

RENOVATION OF THE AIR GUARD

In 1950, the Air National Guard was a poor relation to the Regular Air Force. Typically operating obsolescent fighter aircraft, in some states the Air Guard was little more than a glorified flying club. However, by necessity that situation changed during the Korean War, when reservists and guardsmen filled cockpits with pilots and aircrew that the regulars could not provide. Subsequently, the Guard steadily grew in importance during the Cold War.

The man most responsible for the Guard's transition was Major General Winston P. Wilson, a former mechanic who possessed the vision for the organization to reach its potential. Between 1950 and 1971, when he retired, Wilson guided the Guard Bureau away from its largely parochial status into a modern, capable force fully integrated into Regular Air Force operations. Among his greatest achievements was expanding the Guard's structure to include airlift and tanker units.

C-124 GLOBEMASTER II

The C-5 of its era, the Globemaster II (named for Douglas Aircraft's abortive C-74) was the heavy lifter of the 1950s Air Force. The C-124 first flew in 1949 and was a huge airplane for its day: The 174-foot wingspan and towering, 48-foot tail led to the nickname "Aluminum Overcast." Powered by four Pratt and Whitney 3,800-horsepower radial engines, the 124 was capable of 270 miles per hour but cruised at 230. Its 101,000-pound empty weight was nearly doubled with fuel and 35 tons of cargo, being rated at nearly 195,000 pounds. Total production was 445 aircraft, which enjoyed extensive use not only with Military Air Transport Service but Strategic Air Command (SAC), Tactical Air Command (TAC), and Air Materiel Command as well. All benefited from the Globemaster's long-range capability: 4,000 miles with 13 tons of cargo. At its height, the 124 equipped 20 transport squadrons with a total of 377 aircraft.

In the early 1960s, C-124s were assigned to troop carrier squadrons of the Air Force Reserve. In that configuration, the Globemaster II carried 200 passengers or 127 litters for casualty evacuation. The last Guard and Reserve C-124s were retired in 1974.

KOREA: BACKGROUND TO CONFLICT

In 1945, following the defeat of Japan, the Korean Peninsula was divided along the 38th parallel. The Soviet-backed Democratic Republic of Korea held blatantly aggressive intentions of "reuniting" the nation by force, while to the south the Republic of Korea (ROK) was recognized by the United States and most Western nations. Following a diplomatic blunder by the Truman administration, Pyongyang wrongly decided that the ROK was available for the taking and attacked in June 1950.

American response was rapid, if initially ineffective. Post–World War II policies had reduced the U.S. armed forces in the Far East to little more than garrison status, with inadequate equipment and training. The main event was expected in Europe, but with the Cold War suddenly turned hot in Asia, priorities had to be rearranged. A Soviet error in the United Nations enabled the United Nations to commit allied troops to the defense of South Korea, and a seesaw battle was waged the length of the peninsula. In late 1950, the Americans and ROKs were nearly pushed into the sea, but General Douglas MacArthur's masterful amphibious landing at Inchon reversed the situation. Allied forces quickly advanced toward the Chinese border.

Then it was MacArthur's turn to err. Ignoring tacit and overt evidence to the contrary, he determined that Mao tse Tung's huge army would not come south. In December 1950, the UN troops were pushed backward again, and the battle lines stabilized generally along the prewar border. Prolonged, frustrating negotiations with the North Koreans finally reached a tenuous armistice in July 1953.

Korea has been called "the forgotten war," and it is an apt title, although nearly six million Americans served there, including 1,285,000 Air Force personnel. For about 40 years, the Pentagon bean counters pegged American dead at 58,000; only in the 1990s was it discovered that the actual toll was 34,000 dead, although thousands of missing men were written off as nonreturned prisoners.

Despite occasional violent outbreaks, the defense of South Korea has proven a democratic success for more than half a century.

A WHOLE NEW WAR

One Army historian noted that after World War II, institutional knowledge seemed to disappear "at the speed of light." Less than five years after VJ-Day, the U.S. armed forces were not only ill prepared to fight a major war, but in many cases they had forgotten how to do so. Basic mistakes were committed; essential lessons had to be relearned. One example was communications: Frequently, the Army and Air Force could not talk to one another owing to different radio equipment.

Air power was politically restrained in Korea, prohibited from striking lucrative targets across the Yalu River in Manchuria. However, tactical air power demonstrated its effectiveness in interdicting Communist communications and supplies in North Korea.

When war erupted in Korea, the 5th Air Force in Japan had three wings of F-80 Shooting Stars, two all-weather fighter squadrons with F-82 Twin Mustangs, an RF-80 recce squadron, two light bomber squadrons with Douglas B-26s, and a troop carrier wing. The 20th Air Force in the Marianas and Okinawa had a bobtailed B-29 wing with two squadrons plus a long-range recce squadron, an F-80 wing, and an all-weather F-82 outfit. In the Philippines, the 13th Air Force owned an F-80 wing and a troop carrier squadron. The Far East Air Forces commander, General George E. Stratemeyer, was returning from a conference when things popped. Confusion reigned for some hours. There was no help from the ROK Air Force, which possessed about 60 trainers.

The North Korean Air Force had 130-odd combat aircraft, all Soviet built and nearly half devoted to ground attack. On the first day, Yak fighters strafed Seoul and Kimpo. That night, Communist tanks were less than 20 miles from Seoul and the U.S. ambassador ordered an evacuation from the port of Inchon. The theater commander, General Douglas MacArthur of World War II fame, directed long-range fighters to cover the embarkation but remain offshore unless the ships were directly threatened. It was an absurd order, depriving the F-82 Twin Mustangs of the initiative necessary in fighter combat.

Meanwhile, other measures were enacted that included deployment of jet and piston fighters. F-80s and F-82s "capped" a formation of C-47s that helped evacuate American civilians from Korean airfields. Lieutenant

William G. Hudson won the first aerial victory of the war when he bagged an intruding Yak-7 on June 27; two of his Twin Mustang companions added to the score. Later that day, F-80s downed four more Communist planes, but the enemy offensive continued largely unabated.

However, in the summer of 1950, clear-cut success lay in the future. The Pyongyang steamroller bulldozed its way south, very nearly pushing Allied forces into the sea. The Pusan pocket was barely held, with relief only coming in September when General MacArthur pulled off his masterpiece— the almost-impossible amphibious landing at Inchon. Meanwhile, suitable airfields in South Korea were overrun one by one, forcing fighter-bomber squadrons in Japan to stretch their endurance almost to the limit. On-call TacAir became increasingly difficult to coordinate, but slowly order was built from near-chaos. Communications and procedures were established, leading to much greater teamwork between the Army and the Air Force.

That summer was one of confusion, adaptation, and improvisation. F-80s could not operate from most South Korean airfields owing to vulnerability of jet engines to dirt and foreign objects. Additionally, with useful loadouts the Shooting Stars were limited to about a 100-mile radius of action, which further restricted their utility. Consequently, six jet squadrons hastily reverted to F-51D Mustangs, which, although lacking the Lockheeds' speed, could reach almost anywhere they were needed and could operate from unim-proved fields. Amid the catch-as-catch-can operating environment, some officers thrived on being left to their own devices. Said one jet jockey, "I learned in Korea you want to get in on the early part of a war, before things get too organized."

By far the most publicized aspect of the Korean air war was fighter com-bat. The world's first jet-versus-jet dogfight occurred on November 8, 1950, when Lieutenant Russell Brown of the 16th Fighter Interceptor Squadron was credited with destruction of a "Korean" MiG-15. In truth, Brown's opponent was a Russian, Senior Lieutenant Kharitonov, who motored home with his MiG's tough hide ventilated by .50-caliber rounds. (One Soviet ace said it was not unusual to find 40 or 50 hits on returning MiGs.) The first authenticated jet-to-jet kill occurred the next day when Lieu-tenant Commander W. T. Amen, in a Grumman F9F-2 Panther off the carrier USS *Philipine Sea*, bagged a MiG harassing Navy attack aircraft.

For decades, the true identity of MiG pilots was an open "secret," but the end of the Cold War opened many Russian files. Chinese MiGs began operation in late 1951 and North Korean's in early 1952; neither was ever as significant as their Soviet counterparts.

Whatever the nationality of the Communist pilots, transonic F-86s and MiG-15s represented the same public perception as SPADs and Fokkers 40 years before. There were other similarities as well: a strategic stalemate on the ground that led to a meatgrinder war of attrition and an almost wholly one-sided naval war.

F-86 SABRE

MiG Alley. *The Hunters.* "The fighter pilot's fighter." Probably no aircraft in history has proved such a seamless blend of form and function as North American's classic Sabrejet. Ironically, for an Air Force icon, the design began as a straight-wing Navy project but benefited from German aerodynamic research after World War II. Revised with a 35-degree swept wing, the prototype XP-86 first flew in October 1947, and quickly demonstrated supersonic speed in a dive. The next year the Sabre set a world speed record of 670 miles per hour.

After war erupted in Korea in 1950, Sabres were rushed to the combat zone to meet the Communist MiG threat. Although nearly always outnumbered, aggressive F-86 pilots took a heavy toll of the Soviet-built fighters and earned a lasting place in air combat history with America's first 39 jet aces. Eventually, some 25 countries flew F-86s in various models, with 6,200 built in the United States and 2,200 more in Canada, Australia, and Japan.

The F-86 was succeeded by North American's bigger, faster F-100 Super Sabre, which became operational in 1954 and served well into the 1970s.

The main air combat arena was called MiG Alley in the northwestern corner of North Korea. Owing to political considerations, Communist air bases in Manchuria were off limits to Sabre jocks, who were officially forbidden to cross the Yalu River into Chinese airspace. The fact was, however, that aggressive young (and not so young) fighter pilots who got their teeth into a MiG could develop tunnel vision, disregarding the meandering Yalu beneath their wings. It became a bragging point for some pilots that they checked their wristwatches by the clock on the Antung control tower.

Nevertheless, most F-86 pilots played by the rules. They had a big job to do, and on occasion they were hard pressed. The two Sabre wings dedicated to the air-to-air mission were faced by hundreds of Chinese, Soviet, and North Korean MiGs only about 200 miles from South Korean airfields. Because tactical air power was the Allied trump card in Korea, it was essential to give the fighter-bombers, mediums, and heavies as much latitude as possible. Otherwise, Communist ground forces might have gained enough logistical support to mount a major offensive that would drive the UN forces off the peninsula.

Professionalism was the keystone in the Korean air war. For example, of the top 10 Sabre aces, seven were World War II combat veterans, including Captains Joe McConnell (16 MiGs) and Lonnie Moore (10), who had been in bombers. Colonels Royal Baker (13) and Jimmy Johnson (10), Majors Jim Jabara (15) and George Davis (12), and Captain Ralph Parr (10) were career fighter pilots who had flown against the Axis. Captains Manuel Fernandez (14.5), Frederick Blesse (10), and Harold Fischer (10) were new to aerial combat.

America's first jet ace was a 27-year-old former P-51 pilot, cigar-chomping Captain "Jabby" Jabara of the 4th Fighter Wing. He bagged his first four MiGs in April 1951, but by late May he was getting frustrated. "I'd begun to think that I never was going to get a chance at that fifth MiG," he related. The MiGs had been playing coy, unwilling to fight without a significant advantage.

On May 20, Jabara led his F-86 flight over the Yalu, hearing another formation engaged in a fight. He ordered his three pilots to drop their external tanks, but one of his hung up. Disregarding standing orders, the aggressive Jabara pressed ahead, insisting, "I wasn't about to lose what may be my last shot at becoming an ace." (Technically, he was already an ace by virtue of 1.5 kills in Europe seven years before. But among F-86 jocks, only jet scores were accorded full honors in Korea.)

Jabara's Sabre was hampered by the hung-up drop tank, but he found 12 or more MiGs approaching. When another pair of Sabres split the MiG formation, his flight tackled three bandits. He was lining up a shot when three more MiGs jumped his flight.

Jabara turned hard into the threat, forcing the MiGs to overshoot. Although two broke away, he latched onto the tail of the third one, which maneuvered violently. Absolutely determined, Jabara hung on, closing to within 1,500 feet distance. He pressed his trigger three times, seeing his armor-piercing incendiary rounds light up the MiG's fuselage and left wing. The batwinged jet did two violent snap rolls, then started to spin. Circling at 10,000 feet, Jabara and his wingman watched the MiG pilot "pull the handle." The canopy came off, followed by the seat and the pilot's parachute opening. The MiG exploded a few seconds later.

That was not the end of the fight. For the next several minutes, 28 Sabres sparred with an estimated 50 MiGs venting their anger. Jabara climbed back to 20,000 feet and spotted 6 more MiGs. Again disregarding the odds, he picked a target, closed in and opened fire. As before, hits registered across the target's fuselage and tail. The Klimov engine flamed out almost immediately, emitting thick smoke. Jabara still had the gunsight "pipper" on the MiG, so he fired again. Number six gushed flames and went down burning.

Jabara was the first Korean War jet ace, with one to spare. He returned to combat in 1953 and rang up nine more MiGs, finishing as the second-ranking U.S. ace of the war. He also flew briefly in Vietnam, but after surviving three wars Colonel Jabara died in a 1966 traffic accident.

Even with frequent air superiority, the Korean campaign did not always favor the Americans. B-29s were first employed in large numbers on November 19, 1950, bombing a barracks complex at Musan near the Tumen River. However, during the next year the Superfortresses were driven from daylight skies owing to losses that would not have evoked a "golly" in 1945. The MiG-15 had practically been invented to destroy B-29s over postwar Europe, and the fact that the venue was relocated to Asia mattered not at all. There simply were not enough F-86s and F-84s in-theater to provide all the protection necessary, and each B-29 lost was irreplaceable; Boeing was no longer building them.

On October 23, 1951, 8 Superforts were escorted by 55 F-84s with 34 Sabres as an advance screen. More than 100 MiGs tied up the F-86s while another 50 Red fighters attacked the main formation. Making good use of superior speed, the MiGs penetrated the Thunderjet perimeter and hacked down three B-29s. The five survivors all landed with serious to severe damage. Even after switching to nocturnal missions, the big Boeings were not immune to interception: Two were lost in one night during June 1952.

More and more of the air war was fought at night, often at low level in mountainous terrain. Communist logisticians knew that trucks and trains could move more safely in darkness, leading to a hide-and-seek campaign that favored moonless nights, preferably in bad weather. Air Force B-26s with Navy or Marine Skyraiders and night fighters searched beneath the eerie, harsh glow of parachute flares, seeking worthwhile targets.

Fighter-bomber pilots took enormous risks to support friendly ground forces. No better examples exist than the first two Medals of Honor awarded to Air Force recipients: Major Louis Sebille and Captain Charles Loring both dived their damaged planes into their targets rather than return to base or bail out. Whether either pilot was able to pull out of his attack will never be known, but their example of self-sacrifice remains an inspiration. In fact, all four Air Force Medals of Honor were posthumous awards.

It was that kind of war.

Airborne operations were a notable feature of AAF contributions to World War II, but they were not unknown in Korea. Two significant "drops" were made: at Sunchon in October 1950 (2,860 troopers) and near Munsan-ni in March 1951 (3,486 troopers). Although small by 1944 standards, they demonstrated the Air Force's continuing role in supporting the U.S. Army and kept airborne options before senior American commanders.

Air Force manpower tripled in Korea: from 33,600 Far East Air Force (FEAF) personnel at the start of the war to more than 112,000 at the end. In three years, Air Force squadrons logged 721,000 sorties while losing 1,180 men killed and 1,466 aircraft. Other airmen remained missing or unaccounted for—a sore point with friends and relatives half a century later.

In the aftermath of the three-year Korean experience, the Air Force examined the lessons—and drew the wrong conclusion. Institutionally, the service decided, "We won't have to do that again!" Despite the purely tactical nature of the conflict, and continuing U.S. treaty obligations in the region, the Air Force remained convinced that its future lay in long-range, strategic missions of deterrence and, perhaps, full-scale war in Europe.

Conversely, the Navy and Marine Corps did better. Partly because of the fully integrated sea-air-ground nature of amphibious operations, the naval services not only retained their tactical emphasis, but improved upon doctrine, technique, and equipment. Carrier squadrons still trained for Armageddon, but they were prepared for lesser scenarios as well.

A decade later, the Air Force had to relearn the same hard lessons.

WINNERS AND LOSERS

The Korean War ended in a truce after three years of bitter struggle. The fact that the demarcation line remained where it had at the start of the war proved the futility of the Communist goal of "reuniting" Korea under Pyongyang's authoritarian rule. In that respect, the loser was not only Kim Il Sung but communism in general, as the blatant aggression of 1950 demonstrated the true nature of the threat. The fact that UN forces contributed significantly to preserving Seoul's independence was further reason for regret in the Moscow-Peking axis. Moscow's subsequent suppression of democratic movements in Hungary and Czechoslovakia reinforced the lesson, although international socialists retained their enthusiasm for decades to come.

The true winners of the Korean War were the people of South Korea. They had suffered enormous losses and hardship but retained their independence thanks to substantial military and economic aid from the United States.

Air power emerged a winner from Korea, but it was a tenuous victory. Tactical air support proved crucial to holding the line against the enemy's terrific manpower advantage, but strategic air power played no significant role. In fact, B-29s were largely driven from daytime skies by swift, well-armed MiG-15s. However, North Korea possessed no industry to speak of, and the potentially lucrative targets across the Yalu in Manchuria were artificially denied the Superfortresses. Washington's concern of "provoking" China, which already had nearly a million men in Korea, resulted in operating regulations that presaged even more onerous restrictions in Vietnam.

Still, air power paid its way in Korea. The Chinese and North Koreans were unable to move sufficient supplies into the forward areas and stockpile them for a major offensive. Flying night and day, Air Force fighter-bombers and attack aircraft destroyed or deterred sufficient truck and rail traffic to permit the hard-pressed infantry to hold the MLR, the main line of resistance. Transport aircraft also were important in keeping an adequate flow of urgently needed supplies "in theater," while the helicopter emerged as a viable military tool rather than a novelty. It would be heard from again.

THE WAR OF THE FERRETS

A separate conflict lasted nearly 20 years, a hot war within the Cold War. It centered upon surveillance flights around the world, usually on the periphery of the Communist bloc but occasionally inside hostile airspace. Surveillance or "ferret" aircraft mostly monitored enemy electronics (communications and radar frequencies) seeking not only information but technical capabilities.

The Air Force planes involved in electronic intelligence or ElInt missions were enormously varied: from converted B-29 and B-50 bombers to recon B-36s, '47s and '57s, modified C-130s, C-121s, and KC-135s to dedicated U-2 "spy planes." It became a bragging point in reconnaissance wings that "I have more sack time over Siberia than I do at home."

The Cold War casualty count was "light" by most standards, but heavy within the ElInt community. From 1950 to 1969, 16 American surveillance aircraft were shot down by Soviet, Chinese, or North Korean fighters—nearly one a year. Nine were USAF planes carrying 79 airmen to their deaths. Additionally, at least 84 naval aircrew were killed on ElInt flights, although the U.S. government frequently lied to relatives, citing weather or "accident" as cause of the loss. Several other ferret aircraft landed with battle damage, bearing dead or wounded crewmen.

There was, of course, no reciprocity. Other than stiffly worded diplomatic communiqués, nothing came of the shootdowns that occurred in international airspace. Ferret operators became familiar with the choreographed disingenuousness of the governments involved: a ritual of indignant accusation, self-righteous denial, and obfuscation. The politicians and diplomats breathed forth hot air; ElInt operators bled and died.

NEW PLANES, NEW MISSIONS

The Air Force had been busy at home during the Korean War. New designs were tested and entered service while others were improved or modified for additional roles.

Successor to the F-86 was North American's bigger, faster F-100 Super Sabre. The "Hun" (for hundred) became a mainstay of the post–Korean

War service, and Colonel Horace A. Hanes set a landmark pace in August 1955 when he flew an F-100C at 822 miles per hour, the first supersonic speed record by a production aircraft. The speed was computed as the average of multiple runs at 40,000 feet. As lead ship of the Century series, the F-100 established the precedent for Mach-plus performance in every successive fighter.

(Photo courtesy of the U.S.A.F. via Robert F. Dorr)

A top view of an RF-86F Sabrejet, based in Komaki, Japan, in 1955.

One of the most important developments was the emergence of America's first large-scale production jet bomber, the Boeing B-47. With greater range and performance than other types, it continued Boeing's dominance of the bomber field.

B-47 STRATOJET

A jet bomber was conceived by the Air Force late in World War II, but U.S. engineers wanted the benefit of German test data. Consequently, Boeing's beautiful B-47 received 116-foot, 35-degree swept wings and 6 GE J47 engines in 4 underwing pods. The three-man crew included pilot and copilot beneath a fighterlike canopy with bombardier in the nose. In the E model, the empty weight jumped from 80,750 pounds to 206,700 pounds gross—mostly in fuel.

The Stratojet first flew in 1947 and soon demonstrated a 600 miles per hour top speed. Its internal fuel permitted a 2,300-mile combat radius but was capable of in-flight refueling from Boeing KC-97 tankers, thus achieving true "global reach." Gradually introduced to service from 1951 to 1953, the streamlined bomber possessed a capability unique at the time. More than 2,000 Strato-jets had been delivered when production ended in 1957, equipping 28 bomb wings and 5 reconnaissance wings. Although replaced by the B-52, the Stratojet remained in service, primarily as a recon platform, until about 1965. Brigadier General Paul Tibbets, who flew the Hiroshima atomic bomb mission, regarded the B-47 as his favorite aircraft.

STRATEGIC AIR COMMAND

The Strategic Air Command had been established in 1946, still part of the AAF. When General Curtis LeMay assumed command in 1948 he began rebuilding SAC in his image: thorough, tough, and supremely professional. He ran SAC pretty much as a fiefdom, largely because of his enviable reputation as a no-nonsense commander who got things done. He was, after all, the general who had burned the industrial heart out of Japan.

LeMay knew the value of looking out for his people, especially because his bomber wings lived in a twilight world of around-the-clock readiness. He expected his combat crews and "wrench benders" to spare no effort in meeting his exacting standards, but he rewarded success. Spot promotions, better pay, and improved housing all figured in his philosophy.

By 1960, one third of SAC bombers were on 15-minute alert with others airborne, circling near their "go" points in case of Soviet attack. SAC's command and control was reinforced in 1961 with advent of the "Looking Glass" EC-135, an airborne command post largely immune to nuclear blast.

B-52 STRATOFORTRESS

When you think air power, think B-52. The ultimate Cold War weapon, the Boeing Stratofortress appears ageless, and it has become a convention among B-52 crews that they "don't trust an airplane under 30." At the end of the twentieth century, a third generation of Stratofortress crews was entering service.

The '52 was enormous for its day, with nearly 70 feet more wingspan than the B-47 and well over twice the gross weight. Eight Pratt and Whitney jet engines propel the Stratofort at speeds upward of 650 miles per hour, and its upgraded armament now includes "standoff" (long range) and precision-guided munitions as well as "gravity bombs."

Nearly 750 "BUFFs" (Big Ugly Fat Fellows) were delivered from 1955 to 1962, representing seven production models. As of 2002, the Air Force retained about 85 H models. However, Stratofortresses always will be associated with nuclear deterrence. In the doomsday scenario, a six-man B-52 crew would penetrate the layered air defenses of the Soviet Union, not unlike the seriocomic Colonel Kong in *Dr. Strangelove*. Both high- and low-level attacks in the USSR were envisioned, but the B-52's major combat occurred in an unlikely spot in an unlikely role. Tens of thousands of sorties were logged during the Vietnam War, with B-52s modified to haul as many as 108 "dumb" bombs internally and externally. Serious losses occurred during attacks against North Vietnam in December 1972, but the bombing was a factor in convincing Hanoi to negotiate a settlement.

The heavy bomb tonnage that B-52s delivered against Iraqi forces during Desert Storm reminded any doubters of the BUFF's longevity, which now may extend to 2025 or even 2040. In the latter instance, the immortal Boeing will have served more than 80 years.

While the B-52 was the star of SAC's arsenal, it needed a cast of supporting players. Not the least of those was another Seattle product, the KC-135 Stratotanker. Aerial refueling had fully come of age in the mid-1950s, and acquisition of the '135 added tremendously to SAC's global reach. Stratotankers were incorporated into strategic bomb wings to enhance tactical efficiency, and they appear as ageless as their bomber stablemates.

KC-135 STRATOTANKER

With transition to an all-jet bomber force, the need for a jet tanker was obvious. Boeing met the demand with the KC-135, based on the successful 707 airliner with an airframe 136 feet long and a wingspan of 131 feet. First flown in 1956, some 730 Stratotankers were built through the 1960s. Boeing modified 88 other '135 airframes for a wide variety of roles including transports, aerial command posts, and reconnaissance or mapping.

The '135 is rated for 322,000 pounds maximum takeoff weight with 120,000 pounds of transferable fuel. Four Pratt and Whitney J57s permit cruise speeds of 600 miles per hour or more. The crew of four to six (depending on the mission) includes the boom operator, or "boomer," who flies the refueling probe into the receptacle of the receiving aircraft.

Other tankers such as the Lockheed KC-10 have entered service, but they have a long way to go. Already active nearly 50 years, the '135 stands an excellent chance of establishing a longevity record comparable to the C-130.

The late 1950s proved an era of immense technological progress, which is little appreciated today. Two Air Force projects in particular have been overlooked: the air-launched Hound Dog cruise missile and the XB-70 Valkyrie bomber, both from North American Aviation.

The first was the GMM-77 Hound Dog, allegedly named for the Elvis Presley hit. By the late 1950s, the Air Force realized that traditional high-altitude bombing profiles played to the strength of the Soviet defenses. Developed between 1956 and 1959, Hound Dog (later AGM-28) was a delta-winged "standoff" weapon capable of Mach 2 speed at 55,000 feet. Its J52 engine propelled a 4-megaton warhead and, with a range of up to 500 miles (depending on speed and altitude), it permitted a B-52 to launch 2 missiles beyond the range of the most likely defenses, especially enemy interceptors.

Hound Dog proved a successful program. Many of the 600 missiles delivered through 1963 remained in the Air Force inventory well into the 1970s.

North American's other program was even more spectacular. In 1957, the combination of airframe, materials, and propulsion merged for a useful Mach 3 aircraft. The result was the XB-70, a graceful white behemoth almost 200 feet long with a 105-foot wingspan. Powered by 6 advanced jet engines, the Valkyrie's 260 tons could sustain cruise at three times the speed of sound. However, its high-altitude flight profile made it vulnerable to the Soviet SAMs entering service, and evasive maneuvering at 2,000 miles per hour was impossible. The program was canceled in 1961 with two prototypes built, one of which was lost in 1966. Nevertheless, the threat of a high-flying, super-fast bomber caused Moscow to invest billions in a counter, as in the MiG-25 Foxbat.

Another "penetrator" was Convair's sleek B-58 Hustler, intended as an interim design pending the B-70's arrival. Bearing a family resemblance to the F-102/106 series of fighters, the Hustler was a four-man, delta design powered by four GE engines, capable of nearly 1,400 miles per hour at 40,000 feet. It first flew in 1956 and entered service four years later when the 43rd Bomb Wing demonstrated sustained Mach 2 speed in a well-publicized cross-country dash. The "wing king," Colonel James K. Johnson, was a Korean War double ace whose first operational aircraft had been the Boeing P-26!

Despite its sensational performance (19 speed and altitude records), the Hustler was expensive and troublesome. Production was limited to 116 aircraft, with service ending in 1970 when the FB-111 went operational.

Subsequent bombers, notably the B-1, were designed for either high- or low-level penetration of enemy airspace. Meanwhile, in a doctrinal reversal, the supremely reliable B-52 was made into a potentially effective under-the-radar attacker as well.

BALLISTIC MISSILES

The Army, Navy, and Air Force all had missile programs underway in the late 1950s and early 1960s. As an interim, a variety of surface-launched cruise missiles entered service, such as Matador, Snark, and Regulus, but they lacked performance and range. Each service wanted a slice of the glamorous new pie, for both strategic weapons and space exploration. It took several years for things to shake out: The Air Force got land-based nuclear missiles, the Navy got submarine-launched missiles, and the Army got out of the long-range missile business. The National Aeronautics and Space Administration was established to take over the space program.

The major weapon in the new arsenal was the intercontinental ballistic missile (ICBM). With range to reach the interior of the Soviet Union from the United States, and powerful warheads to destroy hardened targets, the family of intermediate- and long-range missiles recast the nature of the Cold War.

If one man drove the ICBM program, it was Bernard Schriever. An Air Corps pilot of 1933 vintage, he survived the airmail debacle the next year and later flew for Northwest Airlines. Recalled in 1938, he served as a test pilot and earned a Master's degree in engineering. During the war he flew B-17s in the Southwest Pacific theater but his talents led elsewhere. After the war, he became a scientific liaison officer, placing him in the right place at the right time.

When the Soviets exploded their first thermonuclear weapon in 1953, the United States began considering missiles as an adjunct to manned bombers. Bernie Schriever established the Air Force ICBM program headquarters at Inglewood, California, theorizing that long-range missiles were a relatively cheap means of maintaining nuclear deterrence. Fewer men, equipment, and bases all argued convincingly for operational and budgetary reasons. The results of Schriever's work led to the Thor, Atlas, Titan, and Minuteman programs. Subsequently he became director of the Manned Orbiting Laboratory and retired in 1966. The Atlas constituted his legacy: It launched America into serious space exploration.

Ballistic missiles entered SAC's arsenal in 1958 as the intermediate-range Thor and intercontinental Atlas went operational in 1959. Over the next four decades, they were replaced by even more capable Titan and Minuteman ICBMs. Possessing bombers and ICBMs, SAC represented two thirds of America's nuclear triad, while ballistic missile submarines provided the third leg.

As depicted in novels and films, the eerie world of ICBM launch silos was a combination of mind-numbing boredom and apocalyptic decision-making. In their underground cubicles, two-man launch crews practiced for doomsday while seated at consoles too far apart for one officer to initiate the launch sequence. However, each was armed with a revolver, obliged to shoot his partner if the other refused to turn the key when The Word came down.

Psychological screening was deemed essential for missile crews, which required stable, mature personalities. The missileers handled the stress of their work in different ways; some were professionally curious about the targets for their "birds," while others did not want to know. At any rate, they stood watch in their hardened silos for more than 30 years and accomplished their goal of deterrence.

IRBMS AND ICBMS

The Air Force's first ballistic missile was the intermediate-range Thor, a 65-foot, single-stage weapon weighing 105,000 pounds at launch. Because of its 2,000-mile range, Thor had to be deployed in Britain to provide any deterrence against Russia. British forces also adopted the type, which was retired from U.S. service in 1963.

The more powerful Atlas had been tested in 1957 and was deployed from 1959 to 1965. At 82 feet long and 267,000 pounds launch weight, Atlas ultimately was rated at 9,000 miles range with an accuracy of 2 miles. However, it was most noted as the vehicle for NASA's Mercury orbital program.

A fully developed ICBM was Titan, first launched in 1959 and going operational three years later. It was a two-stage rocket and the first used in hardened underground silos. Titan II appeared in 1965 with more range and payload, contributing to the Gemini manned space program. Nearly 100 feet long, with an all-up weight of 221,500 pounds, its 2 liquid-fueled engines propelled it some 6,300 miles with a mean miss distance of less than 1 mile.

The Minuteman series was a solid-fuel design, smaller and easier to maintain than Atlas or Titan. At 56 feet long and 65,000 pounds weight it was tested in 1961 and deployed in 1962. The Minuteman II entered service 4 years later with more range, load, and 200-yard accuracy. Minuteman III, deployed in 1970, reportedly is capable of hitting within 150 yards of a target 8,000 miles from launch. It is a multi-warhead missile, able to deliver 10 or more multiple independently targeted re-entry vehicles (MIRV) weapons, although international treaties are reducing the number carried.

Eventually, SAC achieved full integration of bombers and missiles by consolidating both weapons in strategic aerospace wings. SAC's peak ICBM inventory probably occurred around 1975 with 1,054 missiles.

However, manned bombers remained an important part of the Strategic Integrated Operational Plan (SIOP).

MAD, MIRV, SALT, AND START

The strategic-weapons lexicon involved a jumble of acronyms that still confuse American citizens decades later. "Peaceniks" were fond of citing the policy of mutually assured destruction as MAD, but it kept the balance of terror for the duration of the Cold War. Neither East nor West could mount enough megatons for a successful first strike without incurring unacceptable losses in retaliation. If it was mad, at least it averted nuclear war.

In the 1970s, missile technology had advanced to the point that multiple warheads could be mounted on one rocket. With MIRVs, one ICBM could lift as many as 10 warheads, providing more bang for the nuclear buck. Circa 1999, the United States had 982 ICBMs (432 in submarines) with 8,300 warheads.

The proliferation of thermonuclear weapons finally resulted in a series of discussions between America and Russia. The Strategic Arms Limitation Talks (SALT) sought to freeze the opponents' respective arsenals before undertaking actual reductions. President Richard Nixon and Premier Leonid Brezhnev signed SALT I in 1972. SALT II remained unratified with both sides presumably abiding by the terms of the draft.

After additional SALT negotiations, the United States and the USSR entered discussions for a Strategic Arms Reduction Treaty (START) in 1979. However, after Russia's invasion of Afghanistan that year, President Jimmy Carter curtailed negotiations. The Reagan administration subsequently determined that the Soviets were not abiding by the draft of SALT II, and those talks ended.

However, under new leaders the United States and the Soviet Union signed START I in 1991. Months later the USSR collapsed, leaving a void on the Russian side that was only redressed over the next decade. In 2001, the United States and Russian Federation reached parity at 6,000 deployable warheads. START II, completed in 2000, calls for elimination of heavy ICBMs with no more than 3,500 warheads per side in 2004, including elimination of MIRVs.

NORAD

In the 1950s, during the chilliest portion of the Cold War, the United States and Canada formed the North American Air Defence Command (NORAD), headquartered in Colorado. Long-range Soviet bombers were capable of striking both countries via the polar route, and precautions were taken. In 1954, President Eisenhower authorized establishment of the Distant Early Warning (DEW) Line of 58 radar sites astride the 70th parallel across Alaska, Canada, and Greenland. A huge construction program was completed in Arctic temperatures between 1955 and 1957, with the DEW Line going operational in July 1957. At typical speeds of the era, a three-hour warning was anticipated for any major metropolitan area in Canada or the United States. Additional radar systems were the Pine Tree and McGill Lines in southern Canada, with better coverage at low altitude.

The USAF's contribution to the Continental Air Command was Air Defence Command (ADC), serving on an equal footing with the Royal Canadian Air Force and U.S. Navy interceptor squadrons. (At one point the hottest outfit in ADC was a Navy F3D Skyray squadron.)

ADC typically flew single-seat fighters such as the General Dynamics F-102 and F-106 Delta series. Sitting in their ready rooms, crewcut interceptor pilots lounged with paperback novels or newspapers, or just dozed, awaiting the word to scramble into Armageddon.

F-102 AND 106 SERIES

One of the standbys of the "Steve Canyon Air Force" of the 1950s and 1960s, the Convair Delta series of fighters made its reputation with NORAD's Air Defense Command.

The YF-102 Delta Dagger first flew in 1953, with delivery in 1955. Convair built 986 including two-seaters, all with missile or rocket armament. The single Pratt and Whitney J57 engine gave the Dagger supersonic speed of 820 miles per hour. Although the "dash speed" was notable, its greater operational advantage was an excellent rate of climb, important for an interceptor.

Almost seven tons heavier when loaded and nearly twice as fast with a J75 engine, the Delta Dart differed visibly from the Dagger with flat-top tail. It first flew in late 1956, going operational in 1959. The Dart's innovative Genie missile carried a small nuclear warhead that would destroy a formation of bombers within 1,000 feet of detonation. Delivery ended in 1961 with total production of 340 Darts. Combined production for the Delta fighters was 1,326, a figure exceeded in the Century series aircraft only by the F-100 Super Sabre.

As always, the fliers got the ink but they were supported by thousands of anonymous NORAD staffers and radar operators. By the early 1960s, a quarter-million personnel worked under NORAD, keeping a watchful eye on northern skies for the threat that never emerged. However, over-flights by Tupelov "Bear" reconnaissance aircraft were not unknown.

Around this time, the Air Force became seriously interested in space. Following the Soviet Union's successful *Sputnik* satellite launch in 1957, the air staff envisioned the need to command the heavens as well as the skies. NORAD's mission expanded to include space concerns in 1959, leading to origin of the term "aerospace" as a unified concept of aviation and space exploration. Admiral Arleigh Burke, chief of naval operations, suggested a unified space command for greater efficiency, and was supported by the U.S. Army. However, the Air Force balked at losing some of its hard-won autonomy and continued with its own program. Failure of the Vanguard missile in 1957 led to establishment of the National Air and Space Admin-istration, which took over America's manned space program.

AIRMEN IN SPACE

In 1960, President John F. Kennedy launched America on the path to the moon, calling for a lunar landing within 10 years. The obvious source of astronauts was military aviation, and hundreds of Air Force, Navy, and Marine fliers applied for the program.

Originally, selection for astronaut training required a degree in physical science or engineering; test pilot school with at least 1,500 hours flight time, preferably in high-performance aircraft; under age 40 and less than 6 feet tall; superb physical condition; and suitable psychological characteristics.

While combat experience was not required, it was definitely preferred. Deke Slayton was an experienced bomber pilot, having flown B-25s against Germany and A-26s against Japan. F-86 pilot Gus Grissom had chased MiGs in Korea. (Somewhat ironically, his middle name was Ivan.) Among the four naval aviators, John Glenn and Wally Schirra also had MiGs to their credit.

Air Force pilots were heavily represented in the first three manned space programs. *Mercury* was the original single-seat capsule permitting orbital flights. *Gemini*, as the name implies, was a two-man vehicle leading to rendezvous and docking. *Apollo* was the ultimate leap, taking humans to the moon and back.

Of the dozen men who have walked on the moon, four were Air Force officers: Buzz Aldrin (1969), David Scott (1971), Jim Irwin (1971), and Charles Duke (1972).

THE FIRST 25 AIR FORCE ASTRONAUTS

Group I, 1959 (7 total)
Captain L. Gordon Cooper Jr., *Mercury, Gemini*
Captain Virgil I. "Gus" Grissom, *Mercury,* died in *Apollo 1* fire, 1967
Captain Donald K. "Deke" Slayton, *Apollo*

Group II, 1962 (9 total)
Major Frank F. Borman II, *Gemini, Apollo*
Captain James A. McDivitt, *Gemini, Apollo*
Captain Thomas P. Stafford, *Gemini, Apollo*
Captain Edward P. White, *Gemini,* died in *Apollo 1* fire

Group III, 1963 (13 total)
Major Edwin E. "Buzz" Aldrin Jr., *Gemini, Apollo*
Captain William A. Anders, *Apollo*
Captain Charles A. Bassett II, killed in aircraft, 1966
Captain Michael Collins, *Gemini, Apollo*
Captain Donn F. Eisele, *Apollo*
Captain Theodore C. Freeman, killed in aircraft, 1964
Captain David R. Scott, *Gemini, Apollo*

Group IV, 1965 (6 civilians and Navy)

Group V, 1966 (19 total)
Captain Charles M. Duke Jr., *Apollo*
Captain Joseph H. Engle, shuttle
Major Edward G. Givens Jr., killed in auto, 1967
Major James B. Irwin, *Apollo*
Major William R. Pogue, *Skylab*
Captain Stuart A. Roosa, *Apollo*
Captain Alfred M. Worden, *Apollo*

Group VI, 1967 (11 civilians)

Group VII, 1969 (7 total)
Major Karol J. Bobko, shuttle
Major Charles G. Fullerton, shuttle
Major Henry W. Hartsfield Jr., shuttle
Major Donald H. Peterson, shuttle

25 of 72

THE AIR FORCE ACADEMY: A DREAM REALIZED

Forward-looking airmen began considering likely curriculum subjects for an Air Force Academy (AFA) in 1948. Of necessity, West Point provided most of the senior airmen while aviation was a branch of the Army, but the postwar restructuring of the armed forces opened the door to a dedicated academy for the newest service. President Eisenhower approved funds for an AFA in August 1954, and the first class convened at Lowry Air Force Base near Denver in 1955.

Lieutenant General Hubert R. Harmon, a 1915 West Pointer and wartime commander of the 13th Air Force, was recalled from retirement to serve as the academy's first superintendent. He insisted, "The mission of the academy will be to train generals, not second lieutenants." Another AFA philosophy is found in the academy's motto, "Man is sustained in his flight through life by the power of his knowledge."

The cadets moved to the beautiful new Colorado Springs campus in August 1958, with the first class graduating in June 1959. At that time, the first U.S. AFA graduates were six years from combat in Southeast Asia.

VIETNAM ON THE HORIZON

On the eve of the Vietnam War, two very different aircraft entered service. The most sensational by any standard was Lockheed's SR-71 "spy plane." Capable of extreme speeds and altitudes, equipped with state-of-the-art sensors, the long, lanky Blackbird was unmatched by any other aircraft then flying.

Far more utilitarian, but enormously valuable, was another Lockheed product, the C-141 Starlifter. An innovation in its time, the first military jet transport proved a long-lived, reliable aircraft that spanned the era from the 1960s beyond the 1990s.

SR-71 BLACKBIRD

Lockheed's chief designer, Kelly Johnson, produced an astonishing variety of important, innovative aircraft, from the P-38 Lightning to the U-2. But none were as technologically impressive as the SR-71 (SR standing for strategic reconnaissance).

A late-1950s concept with early 1960s construction, the Blackbird's combination of design, materials, and propulsion remained a world standard into the twenty-first century. The original models were designated A-12s, but production versions were SR-71s. Measuring 107 feet long with a 55-foot span, the wickedly beautiful Lockheed first flew in 1964 and entered service 2 years later. With twin Pratt and Whitney J58s, its speed (certainly more than the admitted Mach 3) and ceiling made it invulnerable to conventional defenses, which permitted Blackbird crews (pilot and systems operator) to photograph any spot on earth with extreme clarity. Onboard sensors also were capable of analyzing targets by infrared and other systems. From 80,000 feet, the SR-71 can scan 100,000 square miles per hour.

SR-71s were withdrawn from service in 1990, due to high maintenance cost and the conventional wisdom that satellites finally had overtaken the aircraft's capabilities. However, the Blackbird returned five years later and reportedly resumed missions in 1997. Despite subsequent retirement, persistent reports indicated that some '71s were kept available for special contingencies.

Fifty Blackbirds of all models were produced, with twenty lost in accidents. None were ever downed by hostile action.

The SR-71 held the absolute speed record of 2,193 miles per hour and an altitude record of 85,000 feet. As one pilot said of the impressive speed, "You've never been lost until you've been lost at Mach 3!"

The U.S. commitment in Southeast Asia increased gradually during 1962 and 1963. In February 1962, a Fairchild C-123 Provider was shot down while engaged in Operation Ranch Hand, spraying chemicals to defoliate a Viet Cong ambush site. Captains Fergus C. Groves and Robert P. Larson and Staff Sergeant M. B. Coghill were all killed, the first Air Force men killed in action (KIA) in South Vietnam.

Ranch Hand became a controversial program once the public learned more about it. Concern over environmental impact on friendlies, neutrals, and even enemies, was raised. In a few years, the defoliant "Agent Orange" would join napalm as a favorite target of antiwar or pro-Communist elements in the United States and Europe.

C-141 STARLIFTER

Lockheed's C-141A Starlifter, the first jet transport aircraft, was delivered in 1964 and created an immediate world standard in military airlift. The follow-on B model, with in-flight refueling ability, appeared in 1979 with a larger airframe permitting one third more cargo load. Powered by four Pratt and Whitney turbofans, the '141 has a long-range cruise speed of 465 knots (535 miles per hour) and a 5,500-mile ferry range.

During Operations Desert Shield and Desert Storm, the immense burden of transporting troops and equipment to the Middle East fell heavily upon the Starlifter fleet. The workload was such that much of the type's remaining service life was used up as thousands of hours of flight time were required, flying round trips halfway around the world. Despite extremely heavy use, the 141 has established one of the best safety records in aviation history. The Starlifter is expected to be fully retired in 2006.

CRISIS IN CUBA

In the fall of 1962, the Soviet Union did an incredibly stupid thing: It installed medium-range ballistic missiles (MRBMs) and nuclear-capable bombers in Cuba. The presence of such a threat less than 100 miles from the American mainland simply could not be ignored.

President John F. Kennedy was made aware of the situation by a combination of intelligence sources, but the most convincing came from the Air Force. Lockheed U-2s of the 4080th Strategic Reconnaissance Wing overflew Cuba several times in August. The first of 24 SAM sites was found by U-2s in October.

The Soviets were familiar with the U-2. It had begun penetrating Russian airspace in 1956 and four years later a CIA pilot, Francis Gary Powers, was shot down by surface-to-air (SAM) missiles. (Fourteen were needed to do the job; two MiGs also were downed.) Powers was captured and put on trial. Officially he was a "civilian," but his Air Force service had been formally terminated for purposes of tenuous "deniability." He was exchanged for a Soviet agent in 1962.

Additionally, at least 18 U-2s were provided to Nationalist China beginning in 1961. Eventually 14 were lost through 1970, including 5 shot down over Communist China.

Meanwhile, surveillance flights continued over Cuba. On October 14, Major Richard S. Heyser took off from Edwards Air Force Base, California, overflew western Cuba, and landed at McCoy Air Force Base, Florida. The long flight was worth the effort: He returned with the first photos of MRBM sites. Major Rudolf Anderson Jr. obtained more images the next day.

Keenly aware of the threat posed by SA-2 SAMs that had bagged Powers, the Air Force, Navy, and Marine Corps began more than 150 low-level "Blue Moon" flights on October 23. They averaged eight a day, scorching along at 500 feet, making 700 miles per hour or more. The Air Force contribution came from the 363rd Tactical Reconnaissance Wing at Shaw Air Force Base, South Carolina. Its RF-101 Voodoos were the first supersonic "recce birds" ever built.

Voodoos flew scores of sorties over Cuba, but with marginal success. Pilots were livid when they learned that at least half of the images they had risked their lives to obtain were lost in processing. Most of the useful photography was obtained by Navy and Marine Corps RF-8 Crusaders.

Aircraft immunity to Russian and Cuban defenses ended on October 27 when Major Anderson was killed by an SA-2 missile, although Soviet Premier Nikita Krushchev had ordered no launches against U-2s lest the crisis escalate. Most accounts say that the decision to fire was made by a local Russian commander; at least one version states that Cuban dictator Fidel Castro was involved. Anderson received a posthumous Air Force Cross, the first ever awarded.

Faced with an unwinnable situation, Krushchev agreed to remove his missiles and bombers. In a back-channel arrangement kept secret for years, the United States reciprocated by removing Jupiter missiles from Turkey.

CHAPTER 6

THE LONGEST WAR

Following France's defeat by Vietnamese Communists in 1954, Vietnam was (like Korea) divided north and south. As in Korea, the north was aligned with China and the Soviet Union while the south was nominally democratic with U.S. backing. During the early 1960s, increasing Communist activity in Laos focused attention on Southeast Asia, leading to commitment of U.S. military advisors in the region. In August 1964—three months before the presidential election—the Tonkin Gulf Incident spurred Democratic President Lyndon Johnson to order air strikes against North Vietnam in retaliation for two alleged torpedo attacks on U.S. warships. In the second incident, nervous American sailors reported more hostile torpedo boats, and Washington used the dubious account as a means of demonstrating resolve to resist Communist aggression.

Johnson had no plan to win the Vietnam War. In fact, the admiral commanding the U.S. Pacific Forces described Washington's policy as "a strategy for defeat." America's primary goal was the mere avoidance of defeat, hoping that by bolstering Saigon indefinitely, Hanoi would eventually abandon its aggressive aims. It was an extraordinarily short-sighted policy, especially since the Vietnamese had already outlasted the Chinese, Japanese, and French.

From 1965 to 1968 the Air Force was engaged in Operation Rolling Thunder, an on-again, off-again campaign against North Vietnam. However, Defense Secretary Robert Strange McNamara's rules of engagement (ROE) limited targets available to aircrews and prevented attacks on MiG bases and surface-to-air missile sites until the Communist defense network was nearly complete. Possible Chinese and Russian reaction to U.S. air strikes was an overriding concern driving the restrictive ROE, while American airmen sustained unnecessary casualties. In 1966, McNamara told pilots that they must continue absorbing "unlimited losses in pursuit of limited goals."

Growing discontent within the United States about the war led to Johnson's decision not to run for election in 1968. His successor, Republican Richard Nixon, was elected on the basis of a "secret plan" to end the war, the so-called Vietnamization program with a phased withdrawal of U.S. forces. Thus emboldened, Hanoi launched a massive attack in the spring of 1972, resulting in a return to bombing "up north." Massive air operations throughout Indochina blunted the Communist offensive, and a final campaign in December resulted in the previously intransigent Hanoi delegation signing a "peace accord" that it had no intention of honoring. Nevertheless, the agreement provided the Nixon administration with a face-saving document necessary to complete the withdrawal. Hanoi finished its conquest of the south in 1975, after the United States had mostly ended its support of Saigon.

During the prolonged, undeclared war in Southeast Asia, 8,744,000 Americans were engaged, including 1,740,000 Air Force personnel. More than 58,000 Americans died in the process, including 10,700 noncombat deaths. The Air Force toll was ultimately pegged at 2,580 from all causes.

THE IN-COUNTRY WAR

American servicemen in South Vietnam distinguished between the "in-country war" and those campaigns elsewhere in Southeast Asia. America got into Vietnam via the back door in Laos and eventually operated in Cambodia as well, but North Vietnam drove the entire effort. Hanoi's patience and willingness to sustain serious losses for a decade eventually eroded American commitment, especially because the North was never in danger of invasion. That situation permitted the hard-eyed pragmatists in Hanoi to export North Vietnamese Army (NVA) troops and supplies throughout the region.

The Communists' main logistic effort was focused upon the so-called Ho Chi Minh Trail, actually a cordon of hundreds of paths leading southward into eastern Cambodia, Laos, and western South Vietnam. The effort was stunning in its commitment and variety: everything from bicycles to trucks; there were even reports of NVA-controlled elephants.

However, in 1961 most of that was in the future. U.S. Air Force advisors arrived in Saigon to train and develop an indigenous South Vietnamese Air Force with suitable aircraft. They included small Cessna spotter planes, armed North American T-28 trainers, and Douglas A-1 Skyraiders, powerful piston engine attack aircraft developed by the U.S. Navy. The country's sometime premier, Nguyen Cao Ky, led a flamboyant Skyraider squadron under U.S. Air Force (USAF) direction, complete with his beautiful wife in form-fitting lavender flight suit.

For reasons of policy and deniability, regulations usually required a South Vietnamese or Laotian in the appropriate aircraft during strike missions. More often than not, the USAF officer did nearly all the flying, but gradually the "locals" developed their skills. A decade or more of combat flying produced some extremely competent "indigenous personnel."

However, Hanoi's escalation of intrusions throughout the region led to greater American commitment. Combined with the Viet Cong (VC) in South Vietnam, the Communist threat against the fragile Saigon government steadily increased. The martyred American president, John F. Kennedy, had stated his country's resolve to "bear any burden" in defense of antiCommunist allies, and his successor, Lyndon B. Johnson, followed suit. With the second "Tonkin Gulf Incident" off North Vietnam in August 1964, Johnson ordered a series of air attacks on North Vietnam.

In response to the incident in the gulf, the Air Force committed growing numbers and types of aircraft to South Vietnam. That same month, Martin B-57s were deployed to Bien Hoa Air Base from Clark Field in the Philippines while a squadron of F-100s landed at Danang. Additionally, a squadron of F-105 Thunderchiefs flew from Japan to Korat Royal Thai Air Force Base.

(Photo courtesy of the USAF via Robert F. Dorr)

Four F-105 Thunderchiefs release their ordnance over Vietnam.

By year's end, Air Force planes were flying armed reconnaissance missions over Laos. Operation Barrell Roll in northern and central Laos lasted for years, attempting to interdict Communist bases and supply lines leading to South Vietnam, while supporting government forces as well. Similar operations were conducted in the southern panhandle under the code name Steel Tiger. Because the United States was not at war with neutral Laos, the missions were considered semi-secret, but they soon became well known. It was just another absurdity in an already absurd war: The United States never declared war on North Vietnam, either.

Early in the new year, Air Force crews were engaged over North and South Vietnam. On February 8, Super Sabres provided top cover for South Vietnamese aircraft attacking targets in the north. Ten days later, F-100s and B-57s bombed and strafed hostile forces around An Khe, South Vietnam.

Viet Cong rocket attacks and commando raids on U.S. facilities resulted in a tit-for-tat escalation. By 1965, the Air Force was fully committed to

Southeast Asia with an enormous variety of aircraft and capabilities. Special operations helicopters, "bird dog" spotter planes flown by forward air controllers, "fast movers" such as F-100 Super Sabres and F-4 Phantoms, and even B-52s from Thailand and Guam all featured during the in-country war.

(Photo courtesy of the USAF via Robert F. Dorr)

USAF Colonel Daniel James Jr. in front of his F-4C Phantom during the Vietnam War. "Chappie" James retired as a four-star general.

Thailand was increasingly important to Air Force operations in Southeast Asia. Major bases at Ubon, Udorn, Korat, and U-Tapao supported the air war against Hanoi, with increasing numbers of men and aircraft. From barely 9,000 Air Force personnel in the kingdom of Siam in 1965, numbers leapt to 26,000 the next year and grew to more than 35,000 by 1968. Throughout the war, Air Force personnel accounted for about three quarters of American military forces in Thailand. Aircraft at the major Thai bases grew from 340 in 1967 to 450 in 1972.

Thailand also featured in the morale of American fighting men. Rest and recuperation leave in the Thai capital was reckoned the best in Asia, and it became a saying, "I'll bet you an R&R in Bangkok."

FACS

Forward air controllers (FACs) are among the least appreciated of all airmen. Their primary weapons include radios and smoke rockets to mark targets for the "fast movers" with guns and bombs. Frequently flying well within the range of enemy weapons, FACs often "trolled" for hostile forces to shoot at them. The most familiar depiction of an FAC is Danny Glover's role in *Bat 21*, with Gene Hackman as the downed flier he guides to safety. Glover's character is pure fiction, but the dedication he displayed rings true.

Despite the dangers of flying low and slow in vulnerable airplanes, the mission was often valued by junior officers. It carried a good deal of independence and responsibility, which appealed to some lieutenants and captains who otherwise chafed under the more structured atmosphere of most fighter units.

If anybody loved FACs, it was infantrymen. Time and again airborne controllers called in fighters to save a rifle platoon from "deep serious." Frequently an FAC could not buy a drink if a rifleman was present in the bar.

It was a long, frustrating effort. The enemy, whether NVA or VC, devoutly did not wish to be found, and rare was the occasion that FACs could report significant numbers of enemy in the open. More often, infantry units radioed the contact while FACs trolled overhead at barely 100 miles per hour, developing more specific information and marking the spot with smoke. They then summoned fighters or "Spooky" gunships, which could bomb or strafe through double- or triple-canopy jungle. More than 200 FACs lost their lives in Southeast Asia, and both FAC Medals of Honor were posthumous.

At the other end of the aircraft spectrum from O-1s, O-2s, and OV-10s were B-52 Stratofortresses. Designed to carry thermonuclear weapons into the Soviet Union, the "BUFFs" (Big Ugly Fat Fellows) conducted awesome "arc light" operations throughout Indochina. Flying 4,000 miles round trip from Andersen AFB on Guam (and frequently from Thailand), the Stratofortresses could drop as many as 108 bombs of 500- to 750-pound size. Beginning in late 1965, their bombs erupted with abrupt violence in jungled areas, leaving a cratered landscape similar to the moon. Surviving VC and NVA troops reported that they feared B-52s more than anything else, partly because the Boeings flew too high to be heard. However, arc light operations were expensive and often ineffective owing to the chain of command. Frequently, 72 hours elapsed between a target request and execution, and as one noncommissioned officer (NCO) at Strategic Air Command (SAC) headquarters noted, "The VC could move to America in three days."

Meanwhile, the "out-country" war continued largely unabated. The Laotian interdiction campaign against the Ho Chi Minh Trail involved hundreds of aircraft in startling variety, from FACs on up. Assorted methods were employed, ranging from electronic sensors and "people sniffers" to defoliants such as the infamous "Agent Orange." Special forces "trail watch" teams surveyed parts of the supply route almost constantly, reporting on Communist activity and calling in fighters or gunships. Despite impressive claims for vehicles destroyed, the campaign never succeeded in choking off enough supplies to prevent enemy activity in South Vietnam.

The tremendous logistics required to sustain half a million men in South Vietnam ensured a major role for transport aircraft. Aged types such as Fairchild C-123 Providers from the 1950s delivered troops and supplies in-country, as did the bigger, faster Lockheed C-130 Hercules, which doubled as a gunship. Jet-propelled Lockheed C-141 Starlifters carried much of the transpacific load in both directions, delivering supplies and personnel westbound while returning with wounded men and caskets eastbound.

UP NORTH AND DOWNTOWN

Two Air Force planes carried most of the load "Up North." The McDonnell Douglas F-4 Phantom was a highly versatile fighter-bomber that got most of the glory because of its MiG-killing record. However, the Republic F-105 Thunderchief was the main strike aircraft over North Vietnam, capable of exceptional speed and awesome bomb loads. The "Thuds" were based in Thailand, immune from the frequent enemy attacks on South Vietnamese airfields, and earned a lasting reputation as bombers, fighters, and SAM-hunting "Wild Weasels."

F-105 THUNDERCHIEF

The largest American single-seat aircraft ever built, Republic's mighty "Thud" flew more sorties and sustained more losses than any aircraft over North Vietnam. Sixty-three feet long with a wingspan of only 34 feet, the F-105 weighed 12 tons empty and 17 tons combat loaded. Yet the Pratt and Whitney J57 with 24,500 pounds of thrust propelled the big, sleek jet to Mach 2 at altitude and more than 700 miles per hour at sea level.

The original F-105 flew in 1955 but improved aerodynamics resulted in the superior B model of 1957. Designed as the first fighter with an internal bomb bay, its expected role was low-level strike, including nuclear delivery. History dictated otherwise. The Thud was one of the major players in Southeast Asia from 1965 to 1973, logging thousands of sorties in nearly eight years. At the height of their combat career in 1966 and 1967, about 130 Thunderchiefs were based at Korat and Takhli, Thailand. Two-seat F models were flown by the "Wild Weasels" who trolled for SAM sites, waiting for the Soviet-made missiles to fire at the Thuds, which then destroyed the radars and launchers. Thunderchiefs sustained 321 losses in combat and 61 operationally, or nearly half of 833 built.

The Thud remained in Air National Guard service until 1984.

The Johnson administration oversaw Operation Rolling Thunder against North Vietnam from 1965 to 1968. Reportedly taking its name from a hymn, the ill-managed affair drew the condemnation of the most devout airmen committed to the enterprise. Tactical air crews sustained growing losses for little visible result, largely owing to Defense Secretary McNamara's rules of engagement. The ROE prohibited attacks on MiG fields until 1967, ensuring that Vietnamese interceptors could operate freely, with sanctuary available in China. Meanwhile, Soviet-built surface-to-air missile (SAM) sites were immune to attack until after they were completed and manned by trained Vietnamese operators, lest Moscow become riled. Postwar Soviet data showed that only 16 Russians died in Vietnam from 1965 to 1972.

During the interim, reconnaissance flights monitored the construction of sites and installation of radar vans and launchers. The 7th Air Force realized it was only a matter of time until the SA-2 missiles began flying. It was not a long wait.

On July 24, 1965, an F-4C from Ubon, Thailand, was destroyed by an SA-2 northeast of Hanoi. It was the first known loss to Vietnamese SAMs; Captain Roscoe H. Fobair and his back seater, Captain Richard P. Keirn, both ejected although Fobair subsequently was reported killed. "Pop" Keirn was on his second war, flying a fifth "guest appearance" mission with the 15th Fighter Wing. He spent the next seven and a half years in captivity, a state not entirely unknown to him. As a 20-year-old B-17 copilot, he had flown "fourteen and a half" missions in 1944, spending nearly a year in the bag in Germany. Thus, his two-war total comprised 20 combat missions in 21 years.

Apart from Keirn's string of bad luck (he was one of only two American POWs in both World War II and Vietnam), the shootdown held other notoriety. McNamara had forbidden preemptive strikes on SAM sites lest the Soviets protest the risk to their advisors. Now that the sites were "up," they could be attacked if they tracked or fired upon U.S. aircraft.

Although only three more Air Force planes were known lost to SAMs for the balance of the year, the missiles still exerted an effect. Three days after Fobair and Keirn went down, the Thailand-based F-105s went after SAM sites and other targets in the Hanoi area. Seven Thunderchiefs were lost, all to antiaircraft guns.

SAMs got the press but gunfire would remain the primary threat for the rest of the war. However, aircrews still could be unnerved by SA-2s. After the war, Brigadier General Robin Olds said, "The truth is you never do get used to the SAMs. I had about 250 shot at me and the last one was as inspiring as the first. Sure, I got cagey, and I was able to wait longer and longer, but I never got overconfident. I mean, if you're one or two seconds slow, you've had the schnitzel."

F-4 PHANTOM

The Phantom was a U.S. Navy design that became an Air Force standard. It was a big two-seat interceptor with twin Pratt and Whitney engines that left a smoky trail across the sky. The Navy's first flight occurred in 1958 but the Air Force got F-4Cs in 1964, including reconnaissance versions. It was designated F-110 before the 1963 Department of Defense (DoD) aircraft system change (allegedly because Secretary of Defense

McNamara could not manage the Air Force and Navy designations). Mach 2 performance included a 60-second climb to 40,000 feet. By comparison, the much lighter F-104 with the same engine took more than 90 seconds to 35,000 feet. Originally, USAF Phantoms had two pilots but the back seater (GIB, or guy in back) handled radar.

The Phantom became the premier MiG killer in Vietnam, both with the Air Force and Navy. However, it also carried a substantial bomb load and introduced laser-guided "smart" weapons to combat as well. Additionally, RF-4s largely replaced the older McDonnell RF-101 Voodoo in the photo reconnaissance role.

From a single squadron in Vietnam in 1965, the F-4 grew in importance to three wings seven years later. During most of the war, the Air Force deployed more than 200 Phantoms to Southeast Asia, and by 1972 the 355 Phantoms "in theater" represented more than one third of Air Force strength in South Vietnam and Thailand. Including "recce birds," 458 USAF Phantoms were destroyed in combat (half of them over North Vietnam) and 70 more were lost in operational accidents.

When Phantom production ended in 1979, more than 5,100 had been delivered, including 2,900 to the Air Force. The F-4 was also flown by 11 nations before being retired from Air Force service in 1996.

The galling rules of engagement only continued. In 1967, Johnson asserted that he was applying "a maximum amount of pressure with minimum danger to our own people." It was a lie. By then Operation Rolling Thunder was two years old, and results were discouraging to say the least. With the administration concerned about Chinese and Soviet reaction, a carrot-and-stick approach was employed, trying to induce Hanoi to negotiate in good faith. The Paris "peace" talks were a farce; it took two years to decide who could sit at the conference table.

Of even more importance were prohibited zones in the two most important areas: "downtown" in Hanoi and the main port, Haiphong. U.S. pilots inbound to targets on the periphery of those safe areas angrily reported dozens of ships waiting to offload supplies in Haiphong, including more antiaircraft guns, ammunition, and SAMs.

Despite the high-tech threat posed by SAMs and supersonic MiGs, the huge majority of Air Force combat losses fell to various types of gunfire: 1,443 of 1,804 total. Surface-to-air missiles accounted for 110 known losses followed by 96 destroyed in ground attacks against South Vietnamese air bases. At least 67 Air Force planes were shot down by MiGs while the cause of loss remains unknown in the remaining instances. Thus, the generic term "ground fire" accounted for 80 percent of USAF aircraft losses to enemy action.

Operational or combat-related losses included everything from premature detonation of ordnance to collisions, stall-spin accidents, and "controlled flight into terrain"—always a risk in mountainous areas at night. Weather was also a factor in operational losses. The region's monsoon season limited decent flying weather to only about six months per year, so the useful window for offensive operations was even more constrained. The 7th Air Force planners had to allow for such considerations in addition to the rules of engagement.

Occasionally the Americans were able to combine initiative with opportunity to overcome the enemy—and the ROE. On January 2, 1967, Colonel Robin Olds, the charismatic leader of the 8th Tactical Fighter Wing in Thailand, led a mission that quickly became legendary. Operation Bolo was conceived as a means of luring Vietnamese MiGs into combat, as they seldom engaged in pure fighter affairs. They preferred (rightly, from their perspective) to concentrate on the "strikers," usually bomb-laden F-105s. Olds's Phantom crews deceived the enemy by flying Thunderchief formations, using F-105 radio call signs.

It worked. MiG-21s intercepted the "bombers" and found themselves with a sky full of hungry F-4 crews fully armed with Sparrow and Sidewinder missiles. The "Wolfpack" claimed seven kills, including one by Olds, who had shot down 13 German airplanes in 1944 and 1945. Years later the Vietnamese admitted losing five MiGs in Bolo, although two of the survivors learned the appropriate lesson and became aces against the Americans.

Robin Olds completed his successful tenure at the head of the Wolfpack, running up an unprecedented 3.6 to 1 kill ratio for the wing. His own four MiG kills remained the top American score until 1972. He retired as a brigadier general, commandant of cadets at the Air Force Academy.

AIR-TO-AIR MISSILES

After World War II, the United States began developing a new generation of aviation weapons, including guided and unguided missiles. The latter were briefly deployed but they proved erratic and inaccurate. Although far more difficult to produce, guided missiles offered much greater potential. The first successful version was designated AIM-9 (for air intercept missile), developed by the Navy. Called Sidewinder for its infrared seeker head, the AIM-9 guided on the heat of the target aircraft's engine. Sidewinders were introduced to combat in 1958 when Nationalist Chinese F-86s downed several Communist Chinese MiGs over the Taiwan Strait.

A larger and longer-range missile was the AIM-7 Sparrow, also a Navy project. It used radar guidance from the host fighter to track the enemy aircraft and consequently became known as a "beam rider." Unlike the self-homing Sidewinder, Sparrow and other radar missiles required constant guidance to the target. Both missiles were used extensively in Vietnam, although early results were disappointing. Owing to difficulty in recognizing firing parameters, target evasion, and mechanical complexity, as few as 10 percent of air-to-air missiles scored hits. Consequently, 20mm gun pods were added to Air Force F-4 Phantoms, even though the F-105 Thunderchief already had an internal Gatling gun.

Missile developments in the 1980s led to the advanced medium-range air-to-air missile (AMRAAM, or AIM-120), which combined the best features of heat seekers and beam riders. A radar-guided "launch-and-leave" weapon, AMRAAM does not require constant tracking of the launching fighter to intercept the target.

Apart from occasional MiG kills, when the rules were temporarily relaxed, tactical airmen could and did achieve results. Attacks on North Vietnam's petroleum, transport, and industrial targets yielded satisfying damage on occasion, but the industrious enemy usually had roads, bridges, and facilities operating again in short order. Frequently it was because after the "stick" of air strikes, the "carrot" of a bombing halt was again offered as a means of drawing Hanoi into deeper negotiations.

An inherent contradiction existed in the conduct of the air war. Tactical Air Command (TAC) fighters did nearly all the "strategic" bombing "Up North" until 1972, while SAC's B-52s conducted massive tactical strikes in support of the ground war in the South. The role reversal was uncomfortable for many Air Force officers who worried about erosion of their traditional roles and missions, resulting in concerns about future "turf wars."

Nevertheless, the operational requirements continued dictating mission specifics regardless of the usual semantics and definitions. The controversy would continue well into the post-Vietnam era, when the Air Force consolidated its combat arms into a more unified command.

WILD WEASELS

The emergence of radar-guided SAMs posed a serious threat to Air Force planes over Southeast Asia. The 35-foot SA-2 was a 2-stage missile that homed in on the target aircraft with demonic speed and determination. There were few ways to defeat SAMs, and most U.S. aircraft were poorly equipped to do so. Other than evading them with high-G maneuvers, aircrews had to jam the guidance radar or destroy the launch battery on the ground.

Detecting SAMs was the key to defeating them. Consequently, radar warning receivers were placed in specially equipped fighters such as F-100s and F-105s with crews specifically trained for the mission, a pilot and back seater affectionately called the "dancing bear." Once a SAM site was detected, the Wild Weasel crew would attack it with antiradar missiles, bombs, or gunfire. It was a high-risk operation, especially in the early days, when conditions favored the defenses and losses were heavy. However, by experience and cunning, the Weasels gradually gained the upper hand and lived by the proud motto, "First in, last out" of the target area.

Johnson decided not to run for reelection in 1968, resulting in a four-year bombing halt through most of North Vietnam. Meanwhile, Air Force commanders faced a continuing series of hard decisions, struggling to keep up the pressure on Hanoi while abiding by the self-defeating rules of engagement.

At the conclusion of "round one" in the Vietnam air war, the Air Force took stock of itself. In the air-to-air league, the scoreboard showed the USAF ahead on points (86 MiGs against 43 losses) but only by a 2-to-1 margin. It was unacceptable: Even allowing for normal exaggeration, F-86s had claimed nearly 10 to 1 in Korea. In dollars alone the exchange was prohibitive, because Phantoms and Thuds cost a great deal more than Sabres and Thunderjets. Meanwhile, the Navy had done somewhat better at 2½ to 1, largely on the strength of the single-seat F-8 Crusader, "last of the gunfighters."

One of the most remarkable feats of flying in Southeast Asia occurred in March 1967 during a strike "Up North." An 8th Wing Phantom flown by Captain Earl Aman and Lieutenant Robert Houghton was badly damaged by AA fire and lacked fuel to clear the target area. Although his own F-4 was hit hard, Captain J. R. Pardo had Aman lower his tailhook while Pardo gingerly moved into position. The exhaust of Aman's engines caused excessive turbulence, so Pardo had him shut down—Aman was nearly dry anyway. Finessing the controls, Pardo maneuvered so that that Aman's hook was wedged against the base of his windscreen. Then he added power, pushing the crippled Phantom in a series of linkups. After several minutes they reached a safe bailout point in Laos, where all four fliers ejected and were rescued. Colonel Olds recommended Bob Pardo for a Distinguished Flying Cross (DFC), but his exceptional airmanship drew more criticism than praise. Officialdom declared that similar efforts would lead to unnecessary losses. Never mind that the four pilots survived to fly another 280 missions! Robin Olds was disgusted, if not surprised, and got on with the war. Twenty-two years later, the Air Force tardily awarded Silver Stars upon the retirement of Lieutenant Colonel Pardo and Colonel Stephen A. Wayne, his back seater.

LEADERS, LOSERS, AND POLITICS

The Air Force and the other armed forces were ill served by their most senior leaders during the Vietnam War. Despite continuing losses to no definite purpose other than "not losing," the generals and admirals who ran the U.S. military largely failed in their obligation to the troops. When faced with untenable restrictions leading to unnecessary casualties, the star wearers nearly always favored their political masters rather than their subordinates. As one officer bitterly recalled, "Sometimes the worst thing a soldier can do is salute smartly and say 'Yes sir.'"

One particularly galling aspect of the Rolling Thunder campaign was the ongoing statistical war against the Navy. The Air Force had control of the air war throughout Southeast Asia, but the various services kept a wary eye on one another. The sortie count became the Air Force's equivalent of the Army body count: a skewed method of assessing the service's contribution to the war effort. Given the statistical obsession of Secretary McNamara, perhaps it was not surprising. In any case, airmen grew accustomed to seeing fighters take off with one or two bombs beneath each wing. Naturally, in order to deliver a useful tonnage, extra aircraft were required, which in turn ran up the sortie count, which looked good in Washington. Squadron and wing commanders who protested the additional exposure of more aircrews and unnecessary aircraft flight hours (with attendant increased maintenance) got nowhere. Ultimately, the Air Force won the war against its arch rival: 275,000 sorties over North Vietnam to 253,000 for the Navy and Marines. The Air Force was the clear "winner" in Southeast Asia generally, with two thirds of more than 2,596,000 flights by fixed-wing aircraft. The Army won the "helicopter war" hands down.

SORTIE AND MISSION

Sorties and missions are the numeric yardsticks by which air operations are measured. The media seldom understands the distinction, using the terms interchangeably, but a *sortie* (from the French for "to leave") is one flight by one aircraft; a *mission* might involve 2 sorties or 20. In World War II, a major bombing mission could involve 1,500 sorties: 1,000 bombers and 500 fighters.

Individual airmen usually describe their combat flights as missions, but sorties would be equally accurate. Confusion can arise when military statisticians identify two or more tasks within the course of one flight. For instance, a fighter-bomber pilot might engage in aerial combat en route to the target area and then bomb or strafe enemy ground forces on the way back to base. By some reckoning that flight accounted for two sorties.

The situation become so maddening that some airmen said they could not tell who represented the greater enemy: the Communists in Vietnam or the politicians (uniformed and otherwise) in America. One of the most vocal was Colonel Jack Broughton, an F-105 deputy wing commander who wrote two warts-and-all books: *Thud Ridge*, and *Going Downtown: The Air War Against Hanoi and Washington.* The few leaders who took the professional risk to protect their people frequently came to grief: most notably General John D. Lavelle.

Lavelle assumed command of 7th Air Force in 1971, well acquainted with the growing threat against his tactical aircrews despite the partial bombing halt. Facing an improved Vietnamese air-defense network with better integration of SAMs, MiGs, radar, and communications, he felt the need for more effective action. After trying to get the rules of engagement changed in favor of his men and being rebuffed, he authorized "protective reaction strikes" against enemy air defenses. Between November 1971 and March 1972, 7th Air Force fliers conducted 20 or more such missions (about 150 sorties) among 25,000 sorties flown in that period.

Lavelle's action was reported by a disaffected NCO who contacted liberal Democrats opposed to the war. Lavelle was summarily retired "for personal reasons" on April 7, and then recalled to Washington to testify before Congress. Ultimately, his retirement grade was reduced from general (four stars) to major general (two stars). Appeals on his behalf to General John Ryan, the chief of staff, went nowhere. It was widely felt in TAC that Ryan, a bomber man, wanted to discredit "the fighter mafia." Others felt that Ryan had no choice.

Much of the Lavelle affair turned on alleged misrepresentation in aircrew debriefings. Because ROE required the North Vietnamese to take action against U.S. aircraft before fliers could attack, some airmen were thought to have "exaggerated" the actual threat. Lavelle steadfastly denied any such knowledge on his part, stressing that his actions were based on increased losses shortly after he assumed command. He also noted that no losses occurred during any of the protective reaction missions, which tended to confirm his methods.

In retrospect, Lavelle missed an opportunity to make his point without sacrificing his career. The targets attacked in the few controversial missions were air-defense systems whose destruction would not effect the outcome of the conflict. Lavelle could have ceased operations in high-threat areas until the new Nixon administration took time to change the Johnson regime's ROE, and then stated (accurately) that the growing threat required new methods. Undoubtedly the Joint Chiefs would not have been pleased, but the same goal could have been accomplished. Nevertheless, Jack Lavelle emerged as one of a handful of American generals who, given the opportunity, put their troops ahead of their retirement.

EASTER OFFENSIVE

Ironically, on the heels of Lavelle's departure, Hanoi forced Washington's hand. When North Vietnam launched its 1972 "Easter offensive," Communist logistics and air defenses had reached an all-time high. The spring attack was no guerrilla war writ large as the 1968 Tet offensive had been; this one was a modern *Blitzkrieg* with no air cover but plenty of portable and mobile SAMs, tracked AA guns, and battle tanks. American forces had been substantially reduced during President Nixon's "Vietnamization" program to turn conduct of the war over to the Vietnamese and were hard-pressed to stop the enemy steamroller. In fact, South Vietnam could not have survived without U.S. land- and carrier-based aircraft.

In-country use of air power was never better demonstrated than during the siege of An Loc, beginning April 2. Astride Route 13 leading to Saigon 70 miles south, the city was attacked by NVA forces from the north and west. Strong infantry with armor support threatened to overrun the South Vietnamese garrison, and only allied aircraft could redress the difference. It was a FAC's war, with multiple air and ground controllers working under the direction of an airborne "King FAC."

Repulsed the first time, the Communists tried again two weeks later. They came in greater strength, with artillery, rockets, and increased anti-aircraft coverage. U.S. and VNAF pilots dived into automatic weapons fire, and even 57mm "bursting stuff" was reported. A-37 "Tweets" worked with fighter-bombers and Spooky gunships to beat off repeated enemy assaults. However, captured documents and prisoner interrogations proved again that the enemy most feared the mighty BUFFs. B-52s turned to tactical support, capable of carpet bombing swaths of destruction through jungle foliage concealing enemy troop concentrations.

While the "shooters" kept fully occupied, so did the "haulers." Lockheed C-130s flew constantly in support of An Loc and other besieged garrisons, frequently after the airfields had been overrun or rendered untenable. Helicopters picked up part of the slack but could not deliver the volume of supplies required by the South Vietnamese. Consequently, Hercules crews resorted to the container delivery system (CDS), flying low and slow (only 130 knots) to slide the CDS packages out the ramp. One C-130 could deliver as much as 15 tons, and the NVA knew what that meant, so they tried harder. A Herc was shot down, forcing the airlifters to switch tactics. They changed to a ground radar system that permitted controllers to tell the Herc crew when to jettison the parachute packages. Dropping from 6,000 feet or more, the C-130s were largely immune to enemy small-arms fire.

C-130 HERCULES

If any airplane is the successor to the Douglas DC-3/C-47, it's the mighty "Herc." First flown in 1954, the four-engine turboprop transport appears irreplaceable for longevity and versatility. The Hercules began Lockheed's near monopoly on USAF transport aircraft and has been operated by some 55 nations, probably an all-time record. It can carry 90 infantrymen or 64 paratroopers as well as a wide variety of military equipment, and deliver them to small airfields. With a wingspan of 132 feet and 155,000 pound max takeoff weight, it can cruise economically at 340 knots (390 miles per hour). Aside from its usual transport role, it has been successfully adapted as a gunship, tanker, research, and special operations bird. Since its operational debut in 1956, the type has amassed more than 25 million flight hours with an enviable record for reliability.

Some measure of the bombing effort is proven by the bare statistics: Stratoforts logged more than 2,000 sorties inside South Vietnam per month during May and June. Yet the victory came at a price: 39 USAF planes including 14 FACs, O-2 Skymasters, and OV-10 Broncos.

Lest there was any doubt about the importance of air power in stemming the Easter offensive, no less a source than the head of the North Vietnamese Air Force provided testimony. Years after the war, Lieutenant General Tran Van Minh told American officers that An Loc would have been held without B-52s and C-130s.

LINEBACKER

Faced with no option other than capitulation, Washington finally untethered its airmen and launched Operation Linebacker. Strikes resumed throughout North Vietnam with naval aircraft mining Haiphong Harbor. Frequent air battles occurred that spring and summer, and on occasion Air Force crews had to settle for even odds in the score column. It was a harsh reminder that even in the missile age the dogfight was not dead.

In the second and third rounds of the air war (1969 and 1971 and 1972 and 1973), Air Force fighters claimed 51 MiGs against 28 known losses. It was less than a two-for-one exchange, even worse than the Rolling Thunder record. May was the heaviest month of Linebacker as the Air Force went

11–6 against the MiGs, while the Navy, benefiting from the Top Gun program, scored 16–zip. June 1972 was the Air Force's worst air-to-air month of the war: two MiGs for seven Phantoms. July was somewhat better: a six–six tie.

Not even the most optimistic generals could ignore the mounting losses to MiGs. Finally, in August, the 7th Air Force requested professional help from the Navy. Four Vought Crusaders from the carrier USS *Hancock* flew to Udorn, Thailand, to impart some of the F-8 community's knowledge. The detachment leader was Lieutenant Commander John B. Nichols, a former tactics instructor and 1968 MiG killer. What he found appalled him. Checking the statistics, Nichols learned that a survey of 500 Air Force MiG engagements showed only 70 kills. Frequently the F-4s flew predictable profiles, relying mainly on Sparrow missiles, and ignoring the Phantom's excellent vertical performance.

"We used to know this stuff (dogfighting), but we forgot it," the base commander told the naval aviator. "We believed those days were over." While the Udorn wing already had the best record in 7th Air Force, the Navy men saw room for improvement. They held class daily, flying with and against the "blue suiters" to impart Top Gun doctrine. One Phantom pilot later credited the Navy "finishing school" with his two MiGs. Overall, the 432nd Tactical Fighter Wing turned in the best 1972 performance (a three-to-one kill ratio) but it trained for the air-air mission. Most of the other units got by as best they could.

Meanwhile, tactical aircrews made good use of new weapons. Laser-guided bombs (LGBs) had been tested in Vietnam in 1968 but required "tweaking" to be effective. Once fully developed, they were employed against some of the hardest targets in North Vietnam, especially during the Battle of the Bridges, an interdiction campaign integral to Linebacker I. Most notable was the Thanh Hoa Bridge, a 360-foot structure spanning the Song Ma River. Notoriously difficult to knock out, it was called "the Dragon's Jaw" by the North Vietnamese, who regarded it as a symbol of national power.

However, Phantom crews had the means to slay the dragon. One of them was a pilot named Dick Jonas, a part-time songwriter who became the air-war balladeer. One of his tunes said:

> There's a lot of good planes in the mud of Thanh Hoa Bridge,
> And a lot of parachutes laying out on Thanh Hoa Ridge.
> And the guys that took 'em North can't go nowhere,
> Lord, because of the guns on the ground around Thanh Hoa Bridge.
>
> So we sat ourselves together with a tall sing-hai [drink],
> Tryin' to figure out a way to kill a bridge that didn't really want to die,
> So we tossed it up to the boys with the bombs with the brains,
> And they allowed they could kill the Thanh Hoa Bridge without
> much pain ...

The "bombs with the brains" were usually conventional 2,000 pounders fitted with guidance units that steered the bombs via fins in response to laser designators. The technique required two jets: one with the designator to "illuminate" the target, the other to drop the smart bomb into an aerial "basket" within range of the target. It was not a perfect system, but it afforded a "standoff" capability that put the attackers out of effective reach of most AA guns. The Paveway I introduced a family of precision-guided munitions (PGMs) to the Air Force inventory.

On April 27, the 8th Tactical Fighter Wing led the way with eight Phantoms carrying laser- and television-guided bombs against the Dragon's Jaw. Clouds prevented use of Paveways, but the TV-guided munitions inflicted serious damage.

Three weeks later, on May 13, having already struck the prestigious Paul Doumer Railroad Bridge in Hanoi, F-4Ds of the 8th Wing used 3,000-pound Paveways plus "dumb bombs" to drop a span of Thanh Hoa in the water. It was sweet revenge for tactical aircrews, who had lost 11 planes in nearly 900 sorties against the Dragon's Jaw since 1965. Nevertheless, the dragon proved hard to slay, and follow-up strikes by the Air Force and Navy were needed to close the bridge permanently.

Other "choke points" were struck repeatedly, denying North Vietnam the uninterrupted flow of supplies it needed to sustain the attack. From April to June, the Wolfpack alone attacked 105 bridges supporting enemy logistics.

With the failure of its spring offensive, Hanoi appeared more willing to talk in Paris. But negotiations broke down again and Nixon resorted to his final authority. He sent the Stratoforts north.

Ironically, the B-52 campaign was run by fighter pilots. Three World War II aces stood in the chain of command from General John C. Meyer, Commander in Chief (CinC SAC), to Lieutenant General Gerald W. Johnson (8th Air Force on Guam) and Lieutenant General John W. Vogt (7th Air Force in Saigon). Among them they had shot down nearly 50 enemy aircraft, but the intense bombing campaign against North Vietnam was a whole new experience. Coordination was a key factor, especially with SAC headquarters calling the shots, often at the last minute, and widely dispersed B-52s: some 50 at U-Tapao, Thailand, and 150 more at Andersen AFB, Guam. The latter required grueling 12-hour missions.

Some initial wrangling among commanders in Washington, Hawaii, and Saigon was necessary before things kicked off. Some Air Force leaders wanted to paste the MiG fields, while others insisted that B-52s were better employed against logistic targets such as rail yards and supply depots. The latter argument won out, and relatively few BUFF strikes went after airfields.

Operation Linebacker II, conducted from December 19 to 30, employed nearly 750 B-52 sorties. General Meyer, the SAC commander in Omaha, predicted a ballpark estimate of three percent losses. However, early losses were unexpectedly heavy, largely owing to unimaginative tactics dictated by SAC headquarters. Flying "airline profiles" with predictable routes, altitudes, and even schedules, each three-plane cell was subjected to a barrage of SAMs, which the available jammers could not fully defeat. Bomber crews were frustrated at not being permitted to use their "doomsday" equipment, the most effective electronic countermeasures reserved for nuclear missions into the Soviet Union. Consequently, 15 BUFFs were lost with 66 crewmen killed, missing, or captured, and two more Stratoforts reportedly were written off with heavy damage. Although SAC had no way of knowing it at the time, the Vietnamese air-defense commanders had been planning for Linebacker II since 1969.

After the war, rumors circulated of "mutinies" among B-52 crews. It was an exaggeration (only one crewman refused to fly), but SAC's unimaginative tactics generated a great deal of resentment with attendant drooping morale. Still, there was humor among the chaos. On one night over Hanoi, a BUFF flier blew his coach's whistle over the radio, signaling a "time out" in the proceedings. His squadronmates later swore that the SAMs stopped shooting for a minute and a half!

However, other U.S. aircraft suppressed the air defenses sufficiently to enable the '52s to operate with tolerable losses (the final figure was just over 2 percent), and Hanoi's remaining defenses were hammered into submission. An agreement finally was reached in Paris, with the armistice occurring in January 1973. Air power had won a victory of sorts.

THE HANOI HILTON

Some 660 American military personnel were identified as prisoners of war during the Southeast Asia "conflict." Most were airmen and half were Air Force. They became high-value pawns in an eight-year game: exploited and tortured by the enemy, frequently ignored by their country.

The third American airman captured in North Vietnam was a Danang F-100 pilot, Lieutenant Hayden J. Lockhart of the 613th Fighter Squadron. He was shot down on March 2, 1965, becoming the first of 332 known Air Force POWs in the war.

(Photo courtesy of the USAF via Robert F. Dorr)

The F-100 Super Sabre, which became operational in 1954 and served well into the 1970s.

Even in the extortionist prison environment of Hanoi, the chain of command remained strong because leaders such as Colonel Robinson Risner emerged. Robby Risner, a Korean War ace, became a pillar of the POW community. Shot down attacking enemy trucks in September 1965, the F-105 pilot ruefully recalled, "Those gunners had a better target in their sights than I did." Nevertheless, he carried on the war "by other means" from his cell in the "Hanoi Hilton."

Two POWs received Medals of Honor for their continued resistance: Major George "Bud" Day, a career fighter pilot shot down as a Fast FAC, in 1967, and Captain Lance Sijan, who died rather than submit to his captors. Day survived an incredible two-week epic, escaping his immediate shoot-down captivity in North Vietnam to make his way across the Demilitarized Zone (DMZ) into the south before a heartbreaking recapture two miles from safety. He was the only POW of the war to escape from the North, however briefly.

Treatment of POWs was generally harsh until 1969, shortly after Ho Chi Minh died, although any correlation remains uncertain. An unknown number of prisoners died in Vietnamese hands; some were intentionally murdered (a Cuban interrogator was notorious for his ruthlessness), while others succumbed to disease or neglect. Still, the emphasis was on propaganda value, and those men still unwilling to demonstrate their captors' "lenient" treatment faced solitary confinement and withholding of mail. Most who were offered early release in exchange for propaganda stunts declined the chance for a quick ticket home.

On November 21, 1970, a high-risk commando operation was launched in an effort to retrieve POWs held at Son Tay, west of Hanoi. The main Air Force contribution was two HC-130 tankers plus a "Combat Talon" Hercules to lead five HH-3 helicopters and an HH-1 delivering 53 special forces troopers to the target. Additionally, 5 A-1 Skyraiders followed an HC-130 to the area by a separate route to provide direct air support while 69 Navy planes conducted a diversionary raid from carriers in the Tonkin Gulf.

In a *coup de main*, the HH-1 intentionally crash-landed inside the main prison yard. The Green Berets were only there for five minutes before discerning they'd struck "a dry hole." The POWs were gone. Meanwhile, a spirited firefight broke out nearby; the supporting troops encountered determined resistance and killed as many as 200 of the enemy. All the raiders were safely away in just 29 minutes. Afterward it was learned that the Vietnamese had moved the prisoners only days before.

In the end, the surviving POWs returned in Operation Homecoming in 1973. They stepped off the C-141s with a brisk salute and their heads up. They had accomplished their mission: Return with honor.

Special operations helos were involved in a brief postwar episode in Cambodian waters. In May 1975, the freighter SS *Mayaguez* was seized by hostile forces, prompting a confused confrontation at Koh Tang Island. Unknown to the U.S. military command, the crew was released before the "rescue" forces arrived: Marine infantry in Air Force helicopters. Three of the choppers were destroyed, with 18 U.S. dead or missing and 50 wounded. Nevertheless, the rescue effort was lauded by the public and counted a "success" by the brief Ford administration following Nixon's resignation the year before.

WINNERS AND LOSERS

Unquestionably, the biggest losers included everyone in South Vietnam: those who sided with the Americans and, ironically, the Viet Cong who fought alongside the North Vietnamese. With completion of its conquest in 1975, Hanoi swept aside the VC and placed northerners in every key position. Some former VC even wound up in "re-education" camps.

Hanoi's success seemingly left it the clear winner of the Second Indochina War, but the victory proved fragile. The nation was fractured economically and politically, with thousands of capable individuals fleeing as "boat people." Most of those who made their way to America did extremely well; some arrived as children speaking no English yet graduated with honors from U.S. military academies and civilian colleges. Said one educator, "My best students are almost always Vietnamese. They aren't smarter than anybody else, but they work three times harder." Hanoi's loss was America's gain.

The Vietnam conflict split the United States as no event since the War Between the States. Previously respected institutions such as the military and much of the government came under increasing criticism and scrutiny as the war dragged on, with no end in sight. Confidence in American political institutions also suffered, as did relations between the generations.

Political discord and frequent violence in the streets and on campuses reinforced the rift. The fault lines would take decades to repair, and even then incompletely.

Air Force strength peaked in 1968 with 904,000 personnel, although those serving in Vietnam represented a fraction of the total. America's global concerns ensured that while aircrews fought a "hot" war in Southeast Asia, the Cold War remained an overriding concern with strategic deterrence the service's primary mission.

Nevertheless, the Air Force could claim a major share of whatever success resulted from the war, as B-52s and tactical aircraft forced Hanoi's intransigent negotiators back to the "peace" discussions after the short "Christmas War" of 1972. However, two decades passed before air power's shaky reputation was fully restored in Operation Desert Storm. The junior officers of the 1960s and 70s took hard lessons to heart as colonels and generals in 1990.

From 1962 through 1973, the Air Force lost 2,257 aircraft to all causes in Southeast Asia. Personnel losses were commensurate: 2,118 killed and more than 300 known prisoners or missing. Despite political rhetoric then and since, unknown numbers of U.S. fliers were left in captivity.

Perhaps the ultimate epitaph for the Vietnam air war came from General Curtis LeMay. Looking back, he mused that in 1944 and 1945 the United States dropped 502,000 tons of bombs on Japan and won the war. From 1965 to 1973, American airmen dropped 6,162,000 tons on Southeast Asia and lost. "The difference," LeMay stated, "was that I was calling the targets in Japan, and Lyndon Johnson was calling the targets in Vietnam."

B-1 LANCER

The B-1 has spent its entire career surrounded by controversy, even before its first flight in 1974. Barely had the original North American Rockwell B-1A entered production in 1977 when the program was cancelled by the Carter administration. The follow-up B model, intended for conventional rather than nuclear warfare, appeared in 1985 and later underwent a four-year conversion program but still had serious problems. Eventually the combination of an early operational date, a limited budget, and a government-controlled program involving four prime contractors limited acquisition to 100 airplanes.

Nevertheless, the Lancer remains an impressive airplane, a sleek "swing wing" design measuring 146 feet long and 137 feet with wings spread. The four-man crew operates a versatile bomber powered by four General Electric turbojets with a supersonic top speed. In recent years, B-1s have conducted joint exercises with U.S. Navy units in the maritime control mission. Unit cost is pegged at more than $200 million.

ACTION IN THE 1970S

Post-Vietnam operations were many and varied, including humanitarian and relief efforts around the world. However, undoubtedly the most publicized was a complete failure.

On November 4, 1979, the U.S. Embassy in Tehran was seized by hundreds of Iranian militants opposed to the Shah, a longtime American ally who had left in January. An exiled religious leader, Ayatollah Khomeini, came to power as ruler of a new theocracy. President Jimmy Carter's administration was unable to effect a diplomatic solution to the crisis, and weeks turned into months. The nightly news routinely took note of "America Held Hostage" and counted off the growing number of days. On day 172, something finally happened.

After more than 5 months of ineffective boycott, Carter authorized a military operation to free at least some of the 52 U.S. hostages. The April 24 multiservice mission involved an aircraft carrier, 8 Marine Corps HH-53 helicopters, 15 Hercules tankers and transports, and Army special forces with Air Force combat controllers. The commandos launched from Oman and landed at "Desert One," a remote site 200 miles from Tehran, to refuel and prepare for the assault. However, one helo aborted en route and another landed at the rendezvous with mechanical problems. Then, in the darkness a KC-130 tanker and an H-53 helicopter collided on the ground, resulting in eight fatalities. Deprived of adequate airlift, the operation was cancelled and the raiders withdrew.

The revolutionary government in Tehran had a public relations field day, showing international reporters the burned-out aircraft as well as charred American corpses. The 52 hostages remained in captivity until the eve of Ronald Reagan's election, 444 days after the embassy seizure.

CHAPTER 7

AIR POWER TRIUMPHANT: DESERT STORM AND BEYOND

Following the Vietnam debacle, the Air Force regrouped and re-evaluated its roles and missions. Organizational changes were contemplated, and considerable research and development funding was obtained. The R&D dollars invested from the mid-1970s onward proved well spent, becoming readily apparent during Operation Desert Storm in 1991.

Doctrinal changes also were underway. Analyzing the Vietnam experience as well as the Israeli Air Force's severe casualties in the 1973 Yom Kippur War (35 percent losses in 19 days), the U.S. Air Force concluded that integrated air-defense networks were the long-term challenge. A premium was placed upon electronic combat capability (jamming or destroying enemy communications and sensors) as well as "signature-reduction" measures. Stealth technology, the blackest of all "black" programs, was especially significant, but much improved targeting and ordnance technology also figured prominently. "Smart bombs," tested and proven in Vietnam, were refined and delivered to the squadrons in increasing numbers.

COLONEL JOHN BOYD (1927–1997)

John Boyd was an exceptional fighter pilot who, it was said, "can be on anybody's tail in 40 seconds." After flying F-86s in Korea, Boyd instructed at Nellis Air Force Base, Nevada, where he began developing his revolutionary theories. His advocacy of energy maneuverability rather than a fighter's top speed or ceiling challenged the conventional wisdom, but he began proving his theory with superb flying and higher mathematics. Eventually, Boyd developed the "OODA" sequence for all types of combat, not just dogfighting. Observe, Orient, Decide, and Attack were the phases he identified in any conflict, with fast, accurate decision-making enabling one opponent to get inside the other's time-cycle loop. In hardware terms, Boyd advocated the light, agile F-16 Fighting Falcon, which was purchased despite some congressional and Air Force resentment among those favoring bigger, more complex jets.

Boyd retired as a colonel in 1975 and became a consultant to the defense establishment. However, unlike nearly all his peers, he refused lucrative contracts and insisted upon living on his retirement pay in order to demonstrate his objectivity. He retired fully in 1988, leaving his mark on the way planners and war fighters approach armed conflict.

Among other things, the U.S. armed forces began rethinking the role of women in the military. At least part of the reason was found in serious retention problems with male pilots and aircrews following a decade of sacrifice in Southeast Asia. The Navy led the way with its first female pilot trainees in 1973, followed by the Army in 1974.

Simultaneously, moves were afoot to accept women at the Air Force Academy. The first female "doolies" were admitted in 1976, graduating in the class of 1980.

The Air Force accepted women for pilot training in 1976 with the first 10 receiving their silver wings in 1977. The combat-exclusion clause was dropped in 1993 and female aircrew became eligible for assignments to fighter, bomber, and attack squadrons.

During the Vietnam War, the Air Force gained its first female general officer. Colonel Jeanne M. Holm, a World War II veteran, pinned on her star in 1971. She retired as a major general four years later, handling personnel matters for the Secretary of the Air Force.

(Photo courtesy of the USAF via Robert F. Dorr)

The SR-71 Blackbird, able to fly more than three times the speed of sound, was the United States' premier spy plane for more than two decades.

CULTURAL WARS

Besides women pilots, another difference in the post-Vietnam Air Force was a determined effort to modify the male culture. (In recent years, a female consultant to the government cited the need to change attitudes about aggressiveness, dominance, and independent thinking in war fighting. We are not making this up.)

For as long as there have been wars, they have been fueled to one extent or another by alcohol. Whether from concern for flying safety or political pressure, the mid-1970s brought a series of changes regarding that holiest of Air Force holies, the officer's club.

Circa 1975, some base commanders directed that there could be no more references to "happy hour," dictating that the traditional O-club gathering should be called something else. So at Air Force bases across the fruited plain and around the world, weekend gatherings were posted accordingly: "Come Enjoy Something Else on Friday Evening." The traditional Friday beer and steak night at air bases in Southeast Asia faded into a fond memory for the war fighters who had consumed quantities of both. Alcohol and red meat may have been unhealthy and politically incorrect, but did not prevent consumers from putting ordnance on target.

High spirits were common in all O-clubs, at home or abroad. "Crud," a sort of contact sport around the billiard table, was especially popular. "Crash-landings" on barroom "runways" lubricated with beer and ice cubes also were common. And if you wanted to bring a screeching halt to the proceedings, just holler "Dead bug!" The last man to hit the floor with his arms and feet in the air bought a round for the house. After all, quick reflexes are important in aviation.

What really rankled many fliers was the advent of O-club "finks," officers who sat through happy hour (or "something else") taking note of who ordered more than one or two drinks. In Bob Dylan's nasal tones, the times they were a-changin', and some veteran drink-all-night, fly-all-day throttle jockeys felt it was not for the better. While flying became demonstrably safer, it didn't seem as much fun. A second drunk-driving charge (not necessarily a conviction) can derail a military career, so club attendance plummeted. Today, few bases retain officer's clubs, since diminished use of booze and slot machines forced consolidation into "all-ranks clubs" with limited hours.

However, O-club festivities were enjoyed during deployments north of the border. Canadians have always been a fun-loving bunch, and RCAF Cold Lake, Alberta, was legendary for its free-wheeling atmosphere. The most popular game was "Rodeo," wherein the designated "rider" stood by the bar awaiting appearance of the first unescorted female. If the rider could bite the lady's posterior and hold on for eight seconds, he won a drink from all the other contestants. (We're not making this up, either. Accommodating fillies were seldom lacking.) Eventually, however, even those good times fizzled out.

Fortunately, in partial compensation, new aircraft had been in development for years, and they appeared on flight lines during the 1970s. The two most significant post-Vietnam aircraft were the F-15 Eagle and F-16 Fighting Falcon, deployed in 1975 and 1979, respectively. They afforded Tactical Air Command (TAC) the desired "hi-lo mix" of a sophisticated twin-engine fighter-interceptor and a relatively simple, single-engine fighter-bomber. Both employed fingertip controls and a head-up display (HUD) for the pilot to simplify cockpit chores, permitting him to keep his hands on the stick and throttle(s). Both would prove long-lived, highly exportable products.

HEAD-UP DISPLAY

In air combat, a pilot wants to fly with his head "outside the cockpit" rather than looking down at his instrument panel for vital information. Consequently, modern tactical aircraft have a head-up display (HUD) to simplify the task. The HUD—an inclined plate of glass in front of the pilot's face—is a two-in-one tool, doubling as gun or bombsight and flight-data display. To the layman, the symbols and numbers displayed on the HUD appear a baffling mixture of esoterica, but the military aviator learns them as a second language. Altitude, airspeed, artificial horizon, compass heading, G load, weapon choice, and targeting information all are readily available without dropping one's eyes from the surrounding airspace.

Among the most significant changes occurred in 1982 with establishment of Air Force Space Command. Eventually, the command expanded to control a galaxy of surveillance satellites providing weather, reconnaissance, and navigation information worldwide.

The Air Force lost its outspoken chief of staff on the eve of Desert Shield. In December 1990, General Mike Dugan was interviewed at length in a grounded aircraft and committed the sin of speaking his mind. Asked about likely U.S. intentions in the Middle East, he alienated the Army by insisting that air power was "the only answer available to our country in this circumstance." He further ensured his departure by speaking of

Saddam Hussein: "If and when we choose violence, he ought to be the focus of our efforts." The Bush administration and Secretary of Defense Dick Cheney had no regard for such candor. Dugan departed two days later, having served less than six months. He was succeeded by Merrill "Tony" McPeek, a former Thunderbird.

F-15 EAGLE

The McDonnell Douglas Eagle was the Air Force's first fighter designed with the lessons of Vietnam in mind. First flown in 1972, the twin-engine, twin-tailed, air-superiority fighter combined a gun, Sidewinder and Sparrow missiles, and a powerful radar to engage enemy aircraft from minimum to maximum range. The first F-15As entered squadron service in 1975 and immediately proved successful. In 1987, the first wing of Strike Eagles became operational as two-seat F-15E models were built with an increased offensive capability for long-range attack missions. The rear cockpit accommodates a weapon system operator (WSO) responsible for sensors, navigation, and targeting data.

McDonnell Douglas broke its own record with the F-15 when the Eagle surpassed the F-4 Phantom for the most supersonic fighters delivered to the Air Force. Additionally, the Eagle also is flown by Israel, Saudi Arabia, and Japan. Israeli F-15s scored significant victories over the Bekaa Valley in 1982, and Royal Saudi Air Force Eagles logged combat missions in Operation Desert Storm. Subsequently, McDonnell Douglas was absorbed by Boeing, which is now the F-15 manufacturer.

STORM OVER THE DESERT

In 1990, the Air Force numbered 535,000 personnel, a level comparable to early 1942. Combat and tactical aircraft numbered about 2,800: a mixture of "high-low" technology and an assortment of old and new equipment. It was a force that had remade itself in the two decades since Vietnam, both technically and organizationally.

Air Force Secretary Donald Rice presided over a new doctrinal study, released in June 1990. *Global Reach, Global Power* focused on the five elements of air power and how they could best be used: speed, range, precision, flexibility, and lethality. Those tenets were about to be tested.

The de facto end of the Soviet Union also figured in USAF policy and doctrine as new threats had emerged. The most immediate arose in the desert of Mesopotamia.

Iraqi dictator Saddam Hussein's forces invaded tiny Kuwait on August 2, 1990, seeking to monopolize the region's oil supply. Iraq possessed the fourth largest army in the world, and at the time much was made of its combat experience from eight years of war against Iran. The United States had nominally supported Saddam through the 1980s, but the Bush administration bungled its diplomatic efforts, leaving him the impression that he had a free hand. He guessed wrong.

U.S. Air Force and Navy aircraft rushed to reinforce Saudi Arabia while plans were quickly laid to begin the huge logistics effort to support a war against Iraq. Diplomatic efforts were long and intense but came to nothing: Saddam exhorted his forces to prepare for "the mother of all battles."

Airlift played a huge role in Desert Shield, the buildup to Desert Storm. Air Force and civilian reserve air-fleet transports logged more than 18,000 sorties to the Saudi Arabia area; half by C-141s. In fact, much of the remaining airframe life of the C-141 fleet was used up during 1990 and 1991, but the "trash haulers" kept delivering the goods. While the media almost universally ignored airlift in favor of sexier, pointier machines that could bomb and strafe, the Military Airlift Command (MAC) crews were indispensable. Some were overage in grade majors and lieutenant colonels who remained in the cockpit rather than (in the words of a USAF historian) "filling dance cards in onerous headquarters jobs." The "old goats" with gray hair (or no hair) received most of the "must pump" assignments that kept wing commanders' heads off the professional chopping block.

The airlift contribution cannot be overstated: as of early June more than half a million passengers and nearly 600,000 tons of cargo.

C-5 GALAXY

One of the world's most impressive aircraft, Lockheed's C-5 is a huge machine spanning 223 feet with a length of 247 feet. (The Boeing 747's span is 196 feet and its length 231 feet.) The Galaxy's four General Electric TF39 engines can lift nearly 40 tons including 51,000 gallons of fuel, and it is the only American aircraft capable of carrying any equipment of the U.S. Army. Ease of loading and unloading is much enhanced by the tail-mounted ramp and the "swing up" nose section. Standard crew is six: two pilots, two engineers, and two loadmasters.

> The Galaxy first flew in 1968, but due to early cost overruns it was can-
> celled in 1970, shortly after the C-5A models were delivered to the Military
> Airlift Command. However, the need for an intercontinental heavy lifter
> was such that Lockheed and the government reached an accommodation
> and some 120 were procured.

The Kuwaiti theater of operations (including Iraq) covered an area slightly smaller than Oregon and Idaho: about 175,000 square miles. Most of it was desert, devoid of natural cover and presumably vulnerable to aerial observation. Such was not the case: Haze was frequent in the region, and many operations were conducted in the dark.

Air Force planners, led by Colonel John A. Warden, developed a "peel back" strategy for attacking Iraq's armed forces. Warden's "Checkmate" division postulated an onion of five layers, each with specific targets to be peeled off—not necessarily in succession. The outermost layer was Iraq's military, especially its air-defense system and ground forces in Kuwait. Next were production centers, transport networks, and the general population. The latter was specifically not targeted, although some accidents did occur. Checkmate aimed instead at Iraqi morale, hoping to convince much of the nation that Saddam's rule had brought only misery. The core (undoubtedly rotten!) was national leadership and agencies of government control. Saddam himself was considered semi-inviolate, at least for public consumption. The U.S. had previously foresworn the use of assassination as a means of national policy, however shortsighted it may have proven.

Target "sets" were many and varied, including Iraq's means of producing nuclear energy, chemical-biological production, and "Scud" ballistic missiles. Other targets included the electrical grid and oil production. The Coalition air commander was Lieutenant General Charles A. Horner, a burly fighter pilot who had flown F-105s and well remembered the lessons of Vietnam. There would be little of the tit-for-tat strategy that characterized the Johnson and Nixon regimes: The region was divided into 30-mile-wide "kill boxes" patrolled by Coalition aircraft seeking targets of opportunity. The ongoing "Scud hunts" absorbed nearly 3,000 sorties with little success, as the Iraqis proved adept at dispersal and deception. Nevertheless, the 85 or so intermediate-range missiles that were launched caused relatively little damage.

Horner had his priorities well in mind at the outset; he knew that the air war could only go one way. Consequently, he told his aircrews, "There is nothing in Iraq worth dying for."

The air campaign to oust Saddam Hussein's forces lasted from January 17 to February 28, 1991, involving aircrews from 11 Coalition nations. The campaign had three aims: suppression of enemy air defenses, "preparation" of the upcoming battlefield, and support of the allied ground offensive. More than 800 USAF aircraft of 17 types were directly involved.

Desert Storm was a contradiction: unprecedented levels of technology and applied violence described in the sterile language of the late twentieth century. Targets were not attacked; they were "visited" or "revisited." They were not destroyed; they were "neutralized."

Global positioning satellites (GPS) and precision-guided munitions (PGMs) (smart bombs) were used. The precision bombers or "delivery platforms" were F-111F "Aardvarks," F-117A Nighthawk stealth "fighters" (which in truth are bombers), and F-15E Strike Eagles; a total of about 130 aircraft. The Paveway family of PGMs was widely employed, as were bunker-buster weapons capable of penetrating underground command centers.

The other USAF planes involved in Desert Storm included "dumb" bombers such as F-16 Fighting Falcons and tank-busting A-10 "Warthogs." B-52 Stratofortresses also were heavily committed, largely attacking Iraqi troop concentrations rather than "hard" or strategic targets. Numerically the most important aircraft was the F-16, which represented more than one quarter of the USAF total. However, significant in-theater support was provided by nearly 200 KC-135 tankers and 150 C-130s.

F-16 FIGHTING FALCON

Winner of the lightweight fighter competition in the 1970s, the General Dynamics entry was a small, agile, single-engine design that has become one of the world's most familiar jets. After entering USAF service in 1979, it was quickly adopted as a NATO standard and to date has been flown by nearly 20 other nations, including traditional rivals Greece and Turkey as well as Israel and Egypt. (In contrast, the F-15 Eagle is flown by three other countries, and the F-14 Tomcat by one.) The Israeli air force has used it with considerable success as a fighter and bomber, including the strike against an Iraqi nuclear power plant in 1981.

While the F-16 is officially the Fighting Falcon, it is more often called "Viper" by its pilots and support personnel. Armament includes radar- and heat-seeking missiles, an internal 20mm gun, and a variety of air-to-ground ordnance. Nearly 250 F-16s were committed to Desert Storm—more than any other type of Coalition aircraft. Both single- and two-seat versions are produced. Ironically, considering its origins, the F-16 has seldom engaged in air combat in U.S. service but is more used as a "striker."

OPENING NIGHT

Zero Hour was 3 A.M. local time on January 17; it was the start of a bad night in Baghdad.

The Coalition air campaign opened with many players. Seven B-52s flew all the way from Barksdale AFB, Louisiana, to deliver the first air-launched cruise missiles (ALCMs) in Air Force history—an incredible 14,000-mile round trip. Of 35 ALCMs fired from the Stratoforts, 31 were assessed as hits against electrical power stations and military communications.

Almost simultaneously, U.S. Army Apache helicopters played "knock-knock" with Iraq's forward radar sites. Two teams (Red and White) opened the first paths into enemy airspace, each composed of four AH-64s led by two Air Force MH-53J Pave Low helos with GPS navigation. Once in position, the Army fliers began taking down advanced air-defense stations with Maverick missiles. Warden's "peel back" strategy was taking effect, paring successive layers off the Iraqi onion. Of 14 air-defense sector head-quarters, most were struck or intimidated early on.

Navy ships in the Persian Gulf and Red Sea launched million-dollar Tomahawk cruise missiles against command and control centers. The first jets into Iraqi airspace were EF-111 Ravens, jamming enemy radars. Their Navy counterparts, Grumman EA-6B Prowlers, zapped fighter direction frequencies. Meanwhile, an awesome 160 Coalition tankers had lifted off air bases in the region, en route to refueling tracks to succor hundreds of strikers. They included 19 Strike Eagles that pounced on reported Scud sites in western Iraq.

Meanwhile, 10 F-117s used the openings created by defense suppressors to penetrate to the heart of Baghdad, putting PGMs down elevator shafts and through specific windows of Iraqi army and air force headquarters and sector control centers. The world watched in rapt attention as live television covered the event. The night sky over Baghdad erupted with bursting flak and sparkled with tracers, nearly all of which found empty air. Meanwhile, the lights went out in Saddam Hussein's capital and would largely remain out for six weeks.

SMART BOMBS

Smart bombs differ from "dumb" bombs in their ability to identify and track a target by electro-optical or laser guidance. Whereas "gravity bombs" rely wholly upon the weapon's ballistic characteristics (mainly by the pilot's vision and experience), smart or precision-guided munitions (PGMs) remove most of the guesswork. Guidance methods include television cameras in the nose of the ordnance (tried with moderate success in World War II) or illumination of the desired impact point by a laser. Both types of PGMs were deployed in the Vietnam War, including the Walleye TV guided weapon and the Paveway series of laser-guided bombs (LGBs) with a launching aircraft and a laser designator. The latter were particularly successful in destroying targets such as the notorious Thanh Hoa Bridge, which had resisted repeated attacks up to 1972.

Smart bombs might be powered by rocket motors or they might be adaptations of "dumb" bombs with guidance units affixed to the nose. In either case, PGMs offer significant advantages in that they are more accurate (often with a "which window" option on a target building) and permit the attacking aircraft to launch from a relatively safe distance. The "precision revolution" arrived in the 1990s during air campaigns in the Middle East and the Balkans, with nightly television coverage showing combat footage of uncanny accuracy.

Armed with precision-guided munitions, Nighthawk pilots launched from their Saudi base to strike specific targets in Iraq. Of 60 LGBs carried, 49 were dropped because 11 could not be reliably targeted. Of those dropped, 28 were assessed as striking their aim point, often within ten feet (3 meters) of the desired spot. Because of the potential accuracy of PGMs, a bomb that hits the target still might be scored a "miss" if its impact is beyond the expected CEP.

After the Nighthawks, BQM-74 drones were launched to lure some surviving radar sites into action. The Iraqis were seldom sophisticated in their use of radar, preferring to rely on static sites rather than mobile units that came "up" only when a definite target was established. Consequently, those radars that went active to track the drones exposed themselves to immediate attack by latter-day Wild Weasels, heirs to the legacy dating from Vietnam. F-4G Phantoms and F-16C Fighting Falcons zapped sites with high-speed anti-radiation missiles, aptly known as HARM. They were devastatingly effective: Iraqi radar activity declined nearly 90 percent in the next six days, to almost zero after February 21.

F-117 NIGHTHAWK

The subsonic F-117 "stealth fighter" is no fighter at all. Despite its absurd F designation, the single-seat, twin-engine jet has no air-to-air capability and cannot defend itself against enemy aircraft. Developed under extreme secrecy in the 1980s (the F-19 designation was disinformation), it was designed as a precision attack aircraft capable of penetrating hostile air-defense networks and destroying specific targets with precision-guided munitions (smart bombs). Its airframe with radar-absorbing materials and angled surfaces permits the F-117 to operate well within enemy radar coverage before being detected. First flown in 1981, about 65 production models were delivered from 1982 to 1990 at an average cost of $52,500,000.

The Nighthawk was committed to combat during the Panama operation of 1989 but made its name during Operation Desert Storm. F-117s led the air campaign by striking Iraqi command centers and radar sites in downtown Baghdad on the opening night. Only 36 F-117s were involved (2.5 percent of the Coalition air forces), but they logged one third of the sorties on day one. Nighthawks thus opened the door for other Coalition aircraft to begin dis-mantling Saddam Hussein's defenses. Subsequent combat included the 1999 air offensive in Yugoslavia, where one Nighthawk was shot down.

Owing to its black color and unusual shape, the Nighthawk also is known irreverently as the "Stink Bug." It is built by Lockheed, which produced so many other revolutionary aircraft from the Burbank, California, "Skunk Works."

Behind the first wave came a seemingly endless procession of Coalition aircraft: Royal Air Force Tornados and Jaguars; Saudi Eagles; Kuwaiti Skyhawks; French and Arab Mirages. Aerial tankers were essential to keeping up the pressure on Iraq. They flew around the clock, sometimes with only 500 feet of altitude separation on designated tracks. It seemed as if there were not enough ramp space in Arabia to accommodate all the air power.

Air superiority was quickly achieved; U.S. fighters shot down eight Iraqi jets on January 17, including five by F-15s. Outright air supremacy came in days. Meanwhile, much of the Iraqi air force fled to Iran: 115 combat aircraft and more than 30 commercial planes. Those figures were more than three times the number shot down in air combat.

Iraq's potentially effective Mirages, Sukhois, and MiGs often were destroyed on the ground. Czech-designed aircraft shelters—10 feet (3 meters) of hardened steel and sand—were nevertheless penetrated repeatedly by specially conceived ordnance. Bunker-buster bombs did their work on Iraqi airfields throughout the campaign.

Nevertheless, a few of the defenders proved resilient and capable. After the cease-fire, Coalition airmen spoke in respectful tones of the surface-to-air missile (SAM) battery in central Iraq that downed three allied aircraft "and we never laid a glove on him." That shooter, however, was decidedly in the minority.

Critical to the conduct of both the air and ground campaigns were E-3 AWACS and JSTARS aerial command centers possessing a "God's eye view" of the theater. They monitored the status of Coalition and enemy forces, provided warning of Scud launches, and directed fighters to intercept Iraqi jets. Never in warfare had such complete information been available; in some cases it was too much data. Around-the-clock coverage was especially important given the frequency of night operations and reduced visibility from burning oil wells.

AWACS AND JSTARS

Computer technology has provided the basis for an awesome surveillance capability. Consequently, a family of battle-management aircraft emerged after Vietnam, the most familiar being the Airborne Warning and Control System (AWACS). Based on the Boeing 707 airliner, the E-3 Sentry provides extensive radar coverage to a range of more than 250 miles. A rotating antenna 30 feet wide and 6 feet thick mounted atop the fuselage is the Sentry's most distinguishing feature. The type entered service in 1977 and has been upgraded frequently.

Like the AWACS, the E-8 Joint Surveillance Target Attack Radar System (a.k.a. Joint STARS) is a modified Boeing 707. However, with improved computer technology it features a 26-foot-long gondola beneath the fuselage. The "canoe" houses a powerful, sophisticated radar that provides a photographic overall view of the battle area with data link to ground stations as well. The two original E-8As were deployed to Desert Storm and logged nearly 50 missions. Subsequent upgrades include the current E-8C.

The Navy's AWACS is the Grumman E-2 Hawkeye, optimized for overwater surveillance and, of course, carrier capable.

Upon their withdrawal, Iraqi forces set fire to Kuwaiti oil wells, causing severe pollution and reduced visibility. Pilots reported the eerie sensation of flying in blackened skies lit by the garish orange glow of burning well-heads.

Airmen had allowed themselves to hope that Iraq might provide the long-awaited military millennium: a pure air victory. They knew that the enormous amount of Coalition air power could destroy or cripple most of Saddam's military and industrial base, with the possibility that Iraq would cuts its losses and pull out of Kuwait. It did not happen. After 41 days of relentless bombardment, Saddam ordered his forces to remain in place, absorbing heavy losses from Coalition aircraft. All manner of ordnance was employed, including massive quantities of cluster bombs that were effective against exposed forces and "soft" targets.

CLUSTER BOMBS

Cluster bombs are the shotguns of military aviation. A cluster bomb unit (CBU) contains small munitions that are ejected from the main canister at a desired height above the ground. Rather than a single projectile such as a conventional bomb, the cluster unit strews scores or hundreds of sub-munitions over a wide pattern, increasing the prospects of destroying or damaging enemy targets. Different types of ordnance may be deployed in CBUs, but typically they are used against "soft" targets such as vehicles owing to the relatively small size of the submunitions.

Cluster bombs were widely used in Operation Desert Storm, where Iraqi forces were vulnerable to air attack in the wide-open spaces of the desert. With sophisticated antiaircraft weapons such as SAMs, attacking jets are placed at greater risk if they have to make a second or third pass at a target. CBUs saturate the target area on the first pass, reducing or even eliminating the need for a follow-up attack.

Denied the air victory, General Norman Schwarzkopf, the overall Coalition commander, ordered the ground offensive to roll on February 28.

One hundred hours later, the Bush administration reined in the tanks and declared victory. General Colin Powell, chairman of the Joint Chiefs, later stated that further punishment of the enemy forces would have been "unchivalrous."

Saddam's most potent units, the Republican Guard divisions, were badly mauled in the short war but some escaped. Air power was relentless in its pursuit of armored units in particular, and "tank plinking" became almost a sport for some A-10 pilots.

A-10 THUNDERBOLT II

Like the F-16 Fighting Falcon, Fairchild's A-10 is seldom called by its official name. "Thunderbolt II" was a salute to the Republic P-47 of World War II fame, as Fairchild absorbed the company in the 1960s. However, owing to its decidedly nonstreamlined shape, the A-10 became universally known as the Warthog, presumably because it's so ugly.

The A-10 was first flown in 1972 and became operational five years later. When production ended in 1984, 715 had been delivered at an average cost of $13 million.

Whatever its aesthetics, the A-10 is a potent weapon. As the A designation indicates, it is an attack aircraft specializing in ground-support missions. With two engines in pods away from the fuselage to minimize battle damage, it can destroy enemy tanks with an awesome variety of weapons, including a huge 30mm Gatling gun that weighs nearly as much as a Volkswagen. The Warthog pilot also can engage targets with nearly eight tons of conventional bombs and precision munitions, while his rugged airframe can survive heavy damage.

The A-10's main combat occurred in Desert Storm, where it flew 8,100 combat sorties to claim destruction of 987 Iraqi tanks and 1,800 other vehicles. However, A-10s proved effective in additional roles; two pilots even bagged enemy helicopters. Day and night observation as well as rescue coverage were all part of the Thunderbolt II's repertoire.

The Warthog also was adapted to the "fast FAC" mission as a low-level forward air controller. In that mission the designation became OA-10, with the pilot observing battlefield developments and directing other jets to lucrative targets much as Cessna "bird dogs" had done over Vietnam 30 years before.

The most celebrated antitank action of the war occurred on February 25, when two A-10 pilots claimed 23 armor kills and 10 tanks damaged.

Flying three missions, Captain Eric "Fish" Salomonson and First Lieutenant John "Karl" Marks of the 23rd Tactical Fighter Wing began their record-making day at dawn, claiming four tanks destroyed with Maverick missiles. In two subsequent missions, they used Mavericks and their 30mm cannon to destroy 19 more tanks.

Salomonson said that he had been hunting Iraqi armor since the war began, but had had little luck. Then, acting on reports of OA-10s the night before, he and Marks got to the "hot" area shortly after sunup. "There's nothing like it," he told reporters. "It's the biggest Fourth of July show you've ever seen, and to see those tanks just 'boom' ... and stuff just keeps spewing out of them, and shells flying out to the ground, they become white hot. It's wonderful."

Some fliers were relieved at the fast, relatively bloodless conclusion. Others were frustrated, believing (rightly, it was proven) that as long as Saddam remained in power he would continue causing problems in the region and the world.

The air war consumed nearly 110,000 sorties, 59 percent flown by the U.S. Air Force. The coalition lost 75 aircraft, including about 15 USAF planes in combat (not all losses were fully known). Twenty Air Force personnel were killed in action and half a dozen died in accidents. Total U.S. combat casualties were 148 dead and 467 wounded.

Some 40 Iraqi planes or helicopters were shot down; 35 by USAF Eagles (two by a Saudi F-15), and two by A-10s. No fourth-generation American aces emerged from Desert Storm, although two Eagle drivers each notched three kills.

Friendly fire incidents accounted for about 17 percent of total Coalition combat casualties, including two episodes wherein A-10s hit British forces owing to confusion of the reported target's locale. However, the proportion was small: 9 air-to-ground incidents among 28 total "blue-on-blue" episodes.

NO-FLY ZONES

In the aftermath of the cease-fire, a "no-fly" zone was established to protect Kurdish tribesmen in the northern part of Iraq. Unfortunately, General Schwarzkopf erred in permitting Iraqi forces to continue flying helicopters on liaison and administrative flights since many of Iraq's bridges were destroyed. But the Coalition commander neglected to prohibit armed helicopters from flying, and Saddam immediately sent his gunships to attack the Kurds, who had rebelled against their oppressors while expecting support from the Bush administration, which had implied that it would be given. The most the Air Force was permitted to do was to conduct humanitarian flights to the region, delivering food and supplies.

Occasionally Iraqi jets penetrated the no-fly zone with predictable results. In late March, two Eagle drivers added kills to their Desert Storm victories as Captain Thomas "Vegas" Dietz and First Lieutenant Robert "Gigs" Heheman ran their scores to three. Occasional Iraqi intrusions into prohibited airspace resulted in two F-16 victories during 1992 and 1993.

However, tragedy ensued during prolonged patrolling over northern Iraq. In April 1994, F-15 pilots shot down two U.S. Army Black Hawk helicopters carrying Coalition representatives on an inspection flight. The jets somehow misidentified the H-60s as Russian-built Mi-24 Hinds and killed all 26 passengers and crew. The jets were led by a senior officer, and although a junior AWACS controller was investigated, no one was held responsible.

WINNERS AND LOSERS

A decade afterward it could be argued who won and who lost in Desert Storm. The Coalition achieved its goal of ejecting Iraq from Kuwait, but Saddam Hussein proved that he could outlast the victors. In less than a year, President George H. W. Bush and British prime minister Margaret Thatcher were out of office while the Baghdad despot retained a firm grip on power. He prevented UN inspectors from completing their search for his weapons of mass destruction and generally demonstrated the resilience for which he has long been known.

Perhaps the biggest winner was American air power, which staged a stunning comeback after Vietnam. The situation was ironic, since aviation achieved most of what it was permitted to do in Southeast Asia—most notably forcing Hanoi to accept a temporary lapse in its eventual conquest of Saigon.

Although the Air Force and Navy seldom paused very long to avoid sniping at one another, the relative contributions were clear enough. The aircraft carrier USS *Independence* was the first significant U.S. presence in the region, and Air Force partisans ruefully claimed that CNN stood for Carrier News Network. However, rapid Air Force deployment to Saudi Arabia soon redressed the balance.

The American public grew fascinated with strike footage during and after the war. Precision delivery of aviation ordnance became a regular feature of news reports and documentaries, with video clips providing a missile's-eye view from launch to impact. This was late-twentieth-century warfare mated to twentieth-century reporting: immediate, graphic, and comprehensible.

It was also simplistic, but the resolution would have to wait until some-time in the next millennium. The second President Bush would declare Saddam a threat to world peace who had to be removed. The forty-third president was backed by his father's defense secretary and Joint Chiefs chairman, now vice president and secretary of state, respectively. The irony was apparent to Gulf War veterans who asked the obvious question: If Saddam Hussein was already "the modern Hitler" in 1991, how was he any more of a threat a dozen years later?

AFTER THE STORM

Despite the overwhelming if self-limited success of Desert Storm, the Air Force examined itself and decided on some changes. Under the Chief of Staff, General Merrill "Tony" McPeak, the service underwent a major restructuring in June 1992 with consolidation or elimination of traditional forces. The Strategic Air Command (SAC) completed its 44-year deterrent mission and slipped into history, a victim of the Cold War that it had helped prevent from turning white hot. Meanwhile, MAC evolved into Air Mobility Command (AMC) while TAC, with new assets, became Air Combat Command (ACC). Special Operations Command (SOC) also emerged as a separate entity within the Air Force hierarchy.

There was plenty of work for the AMC airlifters that year. In 1992, the Air Force flew extensive humanitarian missions: Operation Provide Hope lifted supplies to former Soviet republics, Provide Promise aided

Yugoslavian refugees, and Miami hurricane relief flights also were logged. The following year, AMC was involved in aid to Midwest cities overtaken by heavy floods.

However optimistic some people may have been about the end of the Cold War, other challenges arose to fill the void. The Air Force soon found itself committed to more overseas deployments, not less, and some of them involved shooting.

B-2 SPIRIT

Resembling the comic strip *Bat Plane,* the Northrop B-2 is more popularly known as the stealth bomber. Its "flying wing" configuration harkens back to Northrop designs of the post–World War II era, a "low observable" concept that is extremely hard to see from front, back, or sides. Combined with sophisticated composite materials and its rounded airframe, which deflects or absorbs rather than reflects radar beams, the B-2 appears far smaller on radar than its 172-foot wingspan indicates.

The Spirit was first flown in 1989 to counter the Soviet threat but entered service in 1993, too late for the Cold War, which effectively ended two years before. Flown by a pilot and mission commander, the subsonic B-2 is powered by four GE F118 engines and is capable of more than 5,000 miles of unrefueled flight. Weapons include nuclear, conventional, and precision ordnance.

Because of its staggering cost (at least $2.2 billion each) the Spirit has been built in small numbers: about 20, typically with 6 or 8 operational at a given moment. Combat use is extremely limited but includes the 1999 campaign against Yugoslavia and the early part of the war against terrorism in Afghanistan.

DENY FLIGHT, DELIBERATE FORCE, AND ALLIED FORCE

In 1914, a British politician is reputed to have dismissed the start of World War I as "some damned thing in the Balkans." Eight decades later, the wheel had come full circle, although thankfully without the same extent of bloodshed. What did occur in the 1990s was bad enough.

In 1992, Yugoslavia, the most gerrymandered of all European nations, was coming apart at the seams. The collapse of communism resulted in eruption of ethnic rivalries that had simmered since the country was established after World War I. Slovenia and Croatia broke with the federal government, leading to inevitable conflict with Serbia. Yet another conflict arose in Bosnia, with Muslims subjected to "ethnic cleansing" by the hard-line Belgrade government. UN troops assigned as peacekeepers proved woefully inadequate owing to military and political constraints.

In order to limit Yugoslav action against the ethnic enclaves, NATO commenced Operation Deny Flight in April 1993. It was intended to prevent the Serbian-dominated air force from bombing with impunity, and generally succeeded.

On February 28, 1994, a flight of F-16Cs from the 86th Tactical Fighter Wing intercepted six Yugoslavian Soko jets in the prohibited zone over Bosnia. An E-3 AWACS detected their takeoff from Banja Luka and, despite warnings, the Serbians reportedly attacked a hospital and a depot at Bugojno. Next they bombed a factory at Novi Travnik.

Black Section of the 526th Fighter Squadron was vectored to the scene and acquired the intruders visually. The leader, Captain Robert "Wilbur" Wright, requested permission to fire before the Super Galebs escaped and received a "weapons hot" reply. He downed three in succession with Advanced Medium Range Air-to-Air Missiles (AMRAAM) and Sidewinders, while his wingman took a Sidewinder shot against a hard-turning target at low level. There were reports that the intended victim may have crashed while evading the AIM-9M. In any event, Black Section was running short of fuel and disengaged.

Meanwhile, Captain Stephen L. Allen's Knight section was ordered to attack and he bagged another Super Galeb. Lieutenant Scott "Zulu" O'Grady missed a Sidewinder shot as the remaining Serbs escaped into prohibited airspace. From detection to the fourth "splash," the episode lasted 17 minutes, the engagement merely 5 minutes.

Fourteen months later, O'Grady was shot down by a Yugoslavian missile battery and was rescued after six days on the ground.

Deny Flight ended in December 1995 after 100,000 NATO sorties during 983 days of operations. However, conflict continued elsewhere in the region. Following the collapse of Bosnian safe areas in 1995, NATO launched Operation Deliberate Force on August 30 in response to Serbian attacks on Sarajevo. Some 3,500 sorties were flown by the U.S. Air Force and 7 other nations.

That year the Serbs and Croatians reached an accord providing for separate entities within Bosnia. Internal violence erupted four years later, resulting in further air action. Operation Allied Force was authorized in March 1999.

Following 11 months of planning, Allied Force was executed in a 78-day air campaign. Air Force planes mainly operated from Aviano Air Base in northern Italy, within reasonable reach of their operating areas. The goal was to protect the Albanian majority population of Kosovo in southern Serbia. Some 30,000 sorties were flown without one NATO combat death, although a French aircrew was shot down and captured.

Again there was limited air combat. On March 26, Captain Jeff "Claw" Hwang of the 493rd Expeditionary Fighter Squadron downed two MiG-29s while squadronmates bagged two more. A fifth MiG was claimed May 4.

But the air war was not wholly one-sided. On the fourth night of the campaign, March 27, Captain Ken Dwelle's Nighthawk was bagged by a Serbian SA-3 missile about 40 miles from Belgrade. After seven hours on the ground, Dwelle was scooped up by an airborne rescue team and returned to safety. His Nighthawk remained the only U.S. aircraft lost in the campaign. It was also the first F-117 combat loss; eight had been destroyed previously with three pilots killed.

In addition to the SAM battery, Yugoslavian MiG-29 pilots also claimed Dwelle's F-117, and perhaps the contradictions cannot be resolved. "Yugo" Fulcrums also claimed four F-16s and an F-15 during the short war, but no convincing evidence has been forthcoming.

The operation ended in June, although not as many airmen would have preferred. Some aviation incidents were thoroughly scrutinized by the world's media, most notably when a Strike Eagle bombed a bridge with a train upon it, leading to heavy loss of civilian life. One Air Force officer described Kosovo as "rolling thunder with PGMs," noting that the highly political nature of the endeavor recalled the 1960s era of Washington control with 1990s technology.

Some interservice feuding followed the Kosovo operation when the Air Force announced presentation of 115 Bronze Star Medals to personnel elsewhere in Europe and the United States. Because at that time the Army (with more personnel in-theater than the Air Force) had presented few medals, resentment was palpable. However, the Department of the Air Force insisted that regulations permitted presentation of medals for "combat support" functions in Allied Force. Clearly, however, medal inflation was endemic and not about to be cured. One Air Force sergeant with six rows of ribbons confessed that he had never been stationed outside the continental United States.

KHOBAR TOWERS

On the night of June 25, 1996, a truck bomb detonated with immense force at Khobar Towers near Dhaharan, Saudi Arabia. Nineteen Air Force personnel were killed and 370 people injured in the nocturnal attack by Hezbollah terrorists. The Chief of Staff, General Ron Fogleman, launched two investigations that absolved Brigadier General Terry Schwalier, the Southwest Asia area commander, of culpability. Fogleman felt that Schwalier had not been provided adequate information on the capability of truck bombs, especially since the Khobar Towers explosion was far larger than any anticipated. However, a Department of Defense investigation concluded that Schwalier was negligent in security measures.

General Fogleman felt so strongly about Schwalier's situation that the chief took early retirement in protest. Fogleman, who had previously demonstrated both support of subordinates and a willingness to fire lax generals, became one of a handful of senior officers to take a stand on principle. He felt that Khobar Towers could not have been prevented with the level of intelligence available at the time, and stood by Schwalier.

SEXUAL POLITICS

A perennial topic during the 1990s was sexual politics in the armed forces. The Navy's miserable handling of the 1991 Tailhook scandal ruined a generation of aviators while the Bush administration sought to destroy the innocent civilian organization that had sponsored the professional symposium for 35 years. In the ensuing race to put women in combat aircraft, the Navy "won" at the expense of at least one life lost. A decade later, the service still had not recovered, and hundreds of officers who had done no wrong were still tainted.

In 1993, the "combat-exclusion clause" was lifted, permitting women to be assigned as shooters in a variety of roles—except aboard submarines. The admirals who insisted on integrating naval aviation drew the line at submarines. Aviators noted that many of the senior admirals were submariners.

The process continued to the end of the twentieth century. A female member of the first Bush administration advocated "changing the military culture" and "weeding out the white male as the norm." The Clinton administration pushed "gender norming" (factoring women's physical requirements against males') while adopting the "Don't ask, don't tell" policy toward homosexuals.

Meanwhile, the Air Force—to its credit—took a more measured approach. Women were phased into combat aircraft more slowly and methodically than in the Navy, and the process seemed to be going well. However, things came unraveled in 1997 when Lieutenant Kelly Flinn of Minot AFB, North Dakota, received a general discharge following at least two affairs (one with an enlisted man, the other with the husband of a female airman).

Two years previously, Flinn, a Colorado Springs graduate, had become the first woman B-52 pilot and seemed destined for success. Her cause was immediately picked up by women's rights activists who failed to understand (or did not care) that adultery is not direct cause for dismissal under the Uniform Code of Military Justice. Flinn's discharge (which attached no formal blame) was based on violation of the nonfraternization policy and disobedience of a direct order to end one of her affairs.

"Gender" politics was heightened only days later when General Joseph W. Ralston's career was derailed. As vice chairman of the Joint Chiefs, he was considered a logical choice for chairman. But Ralston, a Vietnam War F-105 Wild Weasel, removed himself from contention when it was learned that he had conducted an adulterous relationship 13 years previously.

Meanwhile, other women got on with their careers that year. At the time there were 14 female fighter pilots in the Air Force, including Captain Amy Svoboda who was killed in a night training flight when her A-10 Warthog struck the ground in Arizona. Svoboda, a 29-year-old Academy graduate, had previously been an instructor pilot and was remembered by squadronmate Martha McSally who said, "Amy … was a breath of fresh air for me. I'm really going to miss my sister." Captain Svoboda was the service's first woman fighter pilot to die in the line of duty.

She was not the last.

AFGHANISTAN FLASHPOINT

On September 11, 2001, Islamic extremists hijacked four U.S. airliners in American airspace and flew three of them into high-visibility targets: both towers of New York's World Trade Center and the Pentagon in Washington, D.C. The fourth plane crashed in Pennsylvania, apparently the result of passengers resisting the hijackers. The world was stunned. Brilliantly conceived and well executed, the terrorists' plan met with unprecedented success despite heightened U.S. government security measures. "You have to hand it to them," said one airline pilot. "They didn't have an air force so they used ours."

September 11 was immediately compared to Pearl Harbor as a surprise attack on American soil producing heavy casualties. In all, 3,025 U.S. and foreign citizens were killed with four stolen airliners; in 1941, the Japanese needed 350 carrier aircraft to kill 2,400 Americans. The national airline and private aviation industries were temporarily shut down, and the new Bush administration, concerned about appearing lax, resorted to absurd measures. When airliners began flying again, nail clippers and plastic razors were declared "contraband." Embittered travelers noted that because federal security had failed, four "Saturday-night specials" would have saved thousands of lives.

The Air Force immediately was mobilized, including the Guard and Reserves. F-15s and F-16s began flying "combat air patrols" over metropolitan areas, while AWACS aircraft scanned the skies for unreported private planes or airliners off their routes. Fighters were armed and briefed to shoot down any suspicious airplanes, regardless of how many passengers might be aboard. Some travelers welcomed the visible evidence of aerial guardians; others recognized the reality. That fall, on a Boeing 737 approaching Portland, Oregon, a lady looked outside to find a Falcon cruising nearby. "Oh, I'm glad to see him," she opined. "I feel safer now."

Seated behind the woman, a "dead-heading" pilot hitching a ride on the flight muttered to himself, "Geez, lady, don't you know he's there to *kill* you?"

Before long, two radical Islamic movements were identified as perpetrators of September 11. The al Qaeda terrorists and Taliban militia of renegade Saudi Osama bin Laden were known operating in Afghanistan, and soon American forces were on the ground, tracking suspects in the rarified mountain atmosphere as high as 10,000 feet. Air Force special operations personnel were involved almost from the start.

Air Force squadrons deployed to Southwest Asia in growing numbers. B-1s, B-52s, F-16s, and A-10s all contributed, but perhaps the most useful were KC-135 tankers. In addition to refueling Air Force and coalition planes in the crowded skies above Pakistan and Afghanistan, the Stratotankers enabled U.S. Navy carrier-based jets to conduct long-range operations.

In the first year after the airliner attacks, the largest engagement in Afghanistan occurred during Operation Anaconda in March 2002. Air Force personnel were heavily engaged on the ground as well as in the air, and two men were recommended for posthumous Air Force Crosses. On March 4, near Takur Gar Mountain, an Army MH-47 helicopter (call sign Razor 3) with SEALs aboard was struck by rocket-propelled grenades from the nearby ridge. One SEAL fell from the Chinook, which force-landed farther up the valley. The SEAL became the object of a frantic search, although he was already dead.

Aboard the rescue choppers were Senior Airman Jason Cunningham, a medic riding Razor 1, and Technical Sergeant John Chapman, a combat controller on Razor 4. Arriving at the ridge, "Dash Four" offloaded its operators, including Chapman, and then returned to base. Chapman continued calling in close air support until he became separated from the SEALs he assisted.

Next, Razor 1 was shot down by automatic weapons and Rocket Propelled Grenades (RPGs). Although repeatedly wounded, Cunningham ignored his own severe wounds to continue treating other special forces troopers. He was credited with saving as many as 10 lives before he died. In all, 7 Americans and as many as 40 al Qaeda were killed.

And the war continues.

AIR FORCE SPECIAL OPERATIONS COMMAND

Air commandos have been part of the Air Force since World War II, perhaps best known to the public in the *Terry and the Pirates* comic strip. Today, AFSOC is based at Hurlburt Field, Florida, with a variety of highly trained aircrews and other experts operating specially modified aircraft.

Combat search and rescue is a big part of AFSOC's mission, with pararescue men trained in airborne operations, scuba swimming, field medicine, and infantry skills. Still known as PJs for the old parajumper designation, their dedication to lifesaving is legendary, harking back to the "Jolly Green Giant" helicopters of the Vietnam War.

Combat control teams (CCTs) direct air traffic in combat zones while tactical air control parties (TACPs) supervise close air support, mostly working with Army Green Berets. Similarly organized combat weather teams (CWTs) are airborne meteorologists providing climatic information that could affect flight operations in battle zones.

The standard aircraft of SOC is the Lockheed C-130 Hercules in several iterations. AC-130 "Spooky" gunships can bring awesome fire support to friendly forces, while EC-130s provide airborne command and control capability to survey and oversee a combat operation. MC-130 "Combat Talon" aircraft deliver SOC operators and can provide fast resupply of deployed teams. The Combat Shadow version is primarily an aerial tanker for long-range missions but also retains a limited combat delivery capability.

SOC flies two helicopters, the MH-53 "Pave Low" and MH-60 "Pave Hawk," special variants of the Sikorski Jolly Green and Black Hawk, respectively. The MH-53 can deliver as many as 38 troops, while the smaller MH-60 is capable of 11 passengers.

Additional special operations airlift is possible with a limited number of C-141s and C-5s equipped with minimum SOC capabilities such as night-vision goggles.

CHAPTER 8

PEACETIME DUTY

The peacetime mission of the U.S. Air Force is to be prepared for war. That was the SAC credo ("Peace is our profession") based on nuclear deterrence, but since the end of the Cold War the Air Force has been committed to more overseas deployments without significant increases in personnel. It's a typical military cycle: inadequate budgets, a crisis leading to exceptional buildups and funding, resolution of the crisis, and a return to inadequate budgets before the next crisis.

HUMANITARIAN OPERATIONS

The Air Force's global ability to respond to natural and man-made disasters has been demonstrated hundreds of times since 1947. The process began immediately upon the service's independence with delivery of cholera vaccine to Egypt in October 1947. Only eight months later, the Berlin Airlift began and continued for nearly a year.

During the late 1940s and early 1950s, the Military Air Transport Service provided a variety of humanitarian aid and disaster relief: locust-plagued areas in India; yellow fever outbreaks in Central America; earthquake-damaged areas of Japan; floods in Italy and the Netherlands; volcanic eruptions in the Philippines; and hurricane damage in the Pacific. Similarly, Air Rescue Service helicopters and amphibians saved crew members of sinking ships and downed aircraft.

ATC, MATS, MAC, AND AMC

The alphabetic jungle of military airlift causes confusion among many who venture into the thicket of acronyms. Here's the short version:

Air Transport Command (ATC). Evolving out of the prewar AAF Ferrying Command, ATC was established in February 1942 as a quasi-independent organization. In fact, it relied heavily upon commercial airline crews and aircraft to provide the airlift necessary to support a truly global war. ATC was separate from Troop Carrier Command, which had a direct combat role such as delivering paratroops and gliders.

Military Air Transport Service (MATS). Establishment of the Department of Defense (DoD) in 1947 brought most military airlift capabilities under the MATS aegis on June 1, 1948. By merging ATC and Naval Air Transport Service, MATS supported DoD operations generally, administered by the Air Force with naval assets remaining available to their parent service. MATS's greatest achievement was the Berlin Airlift of 1948 and 1949.

Military Airlift Command (MAC). On New Year's Day 1966, MATS was redesignated Military Airlift Command, resulting in Air Force wings becoming military airlift units. The change from MATS was largely administrative, although some organizational distinctions were changed between strategic and tactical roles.

Airmobility Command (AMC). Following Operation Desert Storm in 1991, the Air Force absorbed the lessons learned in fighting Iraq. No longer a multiservice or "joint" organization, AMC is the Air Force's dedicated airlift component with C-130s, C-141s, C-5s, and C-17s.

The Regular Air Force, Reserves, and Air National Guard also provide direct assistance at home. One of the largest domestic operations was Hayride, with 200 sorties delivering food, supplies, and equipment to eight western states during the blizzard of 1949. Earthquakes in Anchorage, Alaska, in 1964 brought more than 100 airplanes and helicopters with 1,850 tons of supplies. Floods and forest fires from California to North Carolina have engaged airlifters in response to natural disasters within the continental United States.

Additionally, military transport aircraft are frequently deployed during times of political crisis. In Operation Safe Haven, 10,000 Hungarian refugees who had fled their Communist government were brought to the

United States from West Germany and Austria during 1956 and 1957. During the Iranian crisis of 1978 through 1979, Military Airlift Command evacuated 5,800 American citizens from the country.

Airlifters also repatriated American and Allied POWs at the end of the Korean War and delivered Americans from Vietnamese captivity during Operation Homecoming in 1973.

Immediately following the end of Desert Storm in 1991, MAC launched Operation Provide Comfort to support thousands of Kurds in northern Iraq. It was a daunting task, conducted over rugged terrain to prevent more deaths among a fiercely independent people caught between Saddam Hussein's army and the traditionally hostile Turkey.

RECRUITING AND TRAINING

Military flight training is a complex, expensive process. Applicants must meet extraordinary mental, physical, and emotional standards just to be accepted, and even then the "washout" rate is fairly high. Similar standards exist for aircrew such as navigators, and the most strenuous program in the Air Force is not for pilots at all: Special Operations personnel such as medics and combat-control teams can spend longer periods in training than jet pilots, and the physical requirements are more demanding.

Of course, pilot training is hard enough. Just a sampling of the subjects to be mastered include theory of flight, engines, meteorology, aviation physiology, navigation, and communications. That's before the students touch a jet airplane, although they are already rated private pilots. Beginning with T-37s or other basic trainers, aspiring pilots are provided familiarization flights to learn the aircraft and procedures. From then on they rehearse basic flight maneuvers plus takeoffs and landings before progressing to aerobatics and formation flying.

The pace is fast, the pressure unrelenting. Students are frequently tired; they often describe the curriculum as "force-feeding with a firehose." It is not unusual to see aspiring pilots asleep in their seats during speeches or programs not directly related to flying. However, the Air Force retains the demanding curriculum for a reason. Each student is a prospective combat airman, and history demonstrates that only a portion of the pilots in frontline units are fully productive. Therefore, the logic is impeccable: A student who can't "hack" the strain of training is a poor candidate for wartime, whether he (or she) flies a fighter, attack plane, transport, or helicopter. The ideal is "every man a tiger," but some tigers are hunters and others are prey.

(Photo courtesy of the USAF via Robert F. Dorr)

The new design and improved stealth capabilities of the B-2 bomber heralded a new age in aircraft technology.

RED FLAG AND ALL THAT

In the mid-1970s, the Red Flag concept was born, pitting tactical squadrons against a sophisticated array of "enemy" forces including dedicated aggressor squadrons. The adversaries were specially trained in the methods and tactics of Soviet Bloc pilots, flying a variety of U.S. aircraft that matched the performance of many Russian types. Additionally, Warsaw Pact radar, SAMs, and AAA were duplicated to the extent possible.

THUNDERBIRDS

The U.S. Air Force Air Demonstration Squadron was formed at Luke Air Force Base, Arizona in 1953, seven years after the Navy's Blue Angels. The Thunderbirds' primary mission is recruiting and public relations, which includes representing the United States at international events. Since its formation, the team has flown a succession of jets as diverse as the huge F-105 and the diminutive T-38 trainer. The "T-Birds" transitioned to F-16 Fighting Falcons in 1982.

Typical squadron composition is 8 pilots (6 flying slots) and more than 130 maintenance and administration personnel. Pilots usually fly with the T-Birds for two years with half the team rotating out annually, while most nonflying personnel are assigned for three or four years. Competition for any position in the Thunderbirds is keen, and maintenance assignments are as coveted as cockpit seats. Pilot applicants must have completed a tour in tactical aircraft with a minimum amount of jet flight time, and be selected by current squadron members.

A Thunderbirds performance is a memorable sight and sound experience, with close-formation flying, vertical and ground-level maneuvers, and afterburner noise—"the sound of freedom." However, squadron announcers typically exaggerate by insisting that all maneuvers are derived from combat tactics. Experienced pilots and other knowledgeable observers question the wartime application of the *fleur de lis* break or the "diamond dirty roll," a formation stunt with wheels and flaps down!

The annual airshow schedule calls for 80 to 90 appearances in the United States and abroad, deploying from home base at Nellis Air Force Base, Nevada. In a half-century of flying, the Thunderbirds have performed 3,500 airshows in 57 nations before an estimated 280 million people.

Since the post–Cold War "right sizing," budgeteers and others have questioned whether the DoD needs two flight-demonstration teams. However, as long as the Air Force and Navy are separate services, it is likely that the Birds and the Blues will retain their individual identities.

Some of the most demanding—and most satisfying—training occurs at Nellis AFB, Nevada. Evaluation of Vietnam air operations revealed that combat pilots were most vulnerable during their first 7 to 10 missions, with a disproportionately high ratio of losses in that period. Consequently, the Air Force determined to provide the most realistic training possible for its aircrews and those of friendly nations. Red Flag also afforded use of live ordnance (except air-to-air weapons) on the Nellis ranges—an increasingly rare asset in the PC era of environmentalism. Said one disgusted pilot of the Gila Bend, Arizona, range, "You can bomb and strafe this place but you can't ride a motorcycle on it."

The result was dramatic. From 1975 onward the "visiting teams" learned from every Red Flag deployment, bringing their combat readiness to unprecedented levels of competence. As the program grew, more and more nations sent delegations, including Britain, West Germany, France, the Netherlands, and Italy. The U.S. Navy and Marine Corps, as well as Australia and Singapore, also participate. Each Red Flag typically lasts six weeks, divided into three-week segments for different "players."

Other exercises evolved from Red Flag, including Maple Flag (Canadian operations), Blue Flag (command and control of a theaterwide exercise at Hurlburt Field, Florida), and Green Flag (an electronic warfare exercise eventually incorporated into Red Flag). With the end of the Cold War, NATO aircrews became accustomed to the once-chilling sight of MiG-29s now in a familiar setting on the Nellis flight line, bearing the Iron Cross emblem of a reunified Germany.

Smaller Air Warrior exercises usually are interspersed between Red Flags, permitting continuing training for other units including the Guard and Reserve. Foreign deployments have included such far-flung operations as Amalgam Chief in Canada, Bright Star in Egypt, Team Spirit in South Korea, and more recently the global Millennium Challenge exercise.

AIR FORCE ONE

Although several presidential aircraft are maintained by the 89th Airlift Wing at Andrews Air Force Base, Maryland, any aircraft carrying the president is "*Air Force One.*" Andrews is only 20 miles southeast of the White House, easily accessible by helicopter.

Since 1990, the Presidential Maintenance Branch of the 89th Wing has operated two Boeing VC-25A jumbo jets, deluxe versions of the 747-200. (The "V" prefix denotes "very important people" aboard.) The Boeings are equipped with extensive communications gear and capable of in-flight refueling with an unrefueled range of 7,800 statute miles. Maximum rated takeoff weight is 833,000 pounds.

In addition to a lavish executive suite (thank you, Mr. and Mrs. Taxpayer), *Air Force One* boasts an office, conference room, and two galleys capable of providing 100 meals at once. For staff and the inevitable reporters, there are six lavatories in addition to those reserved for the First Family.

The term "Air Force One" was informally used at least from 1947 but was formalized after a confusing episode in 1953. The president's aircraft was Air Force 8610, which became confused with Eastern Air Lines 8610. Thereafter, *Air Force One* was used almost exclusively.

Previous presidential aircraft included the following:

VC-54 (Douglas DC-4), 1944–1947, *Sacred Cow,* Roosevelt, Truman

VC-118 (Douglas DC-6), 1947–1953, *Independence,* Truman

VC-121 (Lockheed 749), 1953–1960, *Columbine,* Eisenhower

VC-118 (Douglas DC-6), 1961–1962, *Air Force One*, Kennedy

VC-137 (Boeing 707), 1962–1990, *Air Force One,* Kennedy, Johnson, Nixon, Ford, Carter, Reagan

VC-25 (Boeing 747), 1990–, *Air Force One,* Bush, Clinton, Bush

In 1962, John F. Kennedy became the first president with an executive jet when a Boeing 707 (designated VC-137) replaced the C-118 he was using. During its brief service, the plane was named for his young daughter. Harry Truman's plane was named for his Missouri hometown, while the Eisenhowers' two *Columbines* honored the Colorado state flower favored by Mamie.

The Sacred Cow, Independence, Columbine III, and the first VC-137 are displayed at the Air Force Museum near Dayton, Ohio. A backup VC-137 is on view at the Seattle Museum of Flight while Eisenhower's *Columbine II* is preserved at the Pima Air Museum near Tucson, Arizona, as is Kennedy's VC-118. His privately owned Convair 240, named for his daughter Caroline, is held by the National Air and Space Museum in Washington, D.C.

Presidential helicopter support usually is provided by the Marine Corps. When the commander in chief is aboard, the chopper is *Marine One*. The vice president's aircraft is *Air Force Two* or *Marine Two*.

CHAPTER 9

THE U.S. AIR FORCE OF TOMORROW

The Air Force, like any organization, is always in transition. The trick is to anticipate future challenges and requirements, with the long lead time always a factor. Typically a major new weapon system needs 15 years of design, development, and maturation. Desert Storm was an example: Stealth technology and precision-guided munitions (PGMs) underwent development from the mid-1970s onward.

In the 1960s, record-setting test pilot Scott Crossfield was asked about prospects for unmanned aircraft in war and space. The noted X-15 pilot wryly observed that pilots are in no danger of being replaced by machines because no other guidance system can be produced so cheaply by unskilled labor!

Nevertheless, "uninhabited air vehicles" (un*manned* is un-PC) definitely have a place in today's Air Force, and tomorrow's. They include reconnaissance platforms such as the Predator drone, which can linger at high altitude in a threat area without risking a human life. In some cases, doctrine specifies, "Don't send a man (or woman) where you can send a machine."

(Photo courtesy of the USAF via Robert F. Dorr)

The F-117A Nightbird stealth "fighter" is the world's first operational aircraft to exploit low observable stealth technology. It is designed to penetrate dense threat environments and attack targets with pinpoint accuracy.

Regardless of the numbers, there will be more women in flying billets. In 2001, the Air Force had some 300 female pilots, 100 navigators, and about 600 enlisted aircrew.

Consistent with the man-versus-machine philosophy, the Air Force will increasingly use more standoff weapons. Air-to-surface ordnance such as JDAM, the Joint Direct Attack Missile, permits strike aircraft to launch precision weapons from beyond the most effective range of current anti-aircraft weapons.

Knowledge definitely is power, and the Air Force will place more emphasis on information warfare and technology. Today's high school hackers may well become tomorrow's cyberwarriors, devising means of infiltrating hostile (and even friendly) computer networks either to absorb the contents or to plant viruses—or both.

Future operations will involve greater "interconnectivity" among ground, airborne, and space-based sensors. Information sharing within the Air Force and with the other services and allied nations certainly will be a feature of twenty-first-century warfare. Although some bureaucratic hurdles undoubtedly will remain, the natural tendency to protect one's own turf has been reduced by requirements for "joint" tours among most career officers. Sending fighter pilots to serve with a tank division or airlift navigators to stand watch with naval officers does a great deal of good for all concerned, leading to greater appreciation for those on the other side of the military hill.

POSSIBLE FUTURE CONFLICTS

The United States' military planners live in perennial fear of "conference-call warfare," wherein two enemies can decide on short notice to open hostilities jointly, possibly on opposite sides of the planet. For decades, American military doctrine held that the armed forces would be capable of fighting two regional wars simultaneously, but post–Cold War reductions rendered that prospect unlikely.

In the period following collapse of the Soviet Union, the Air Force was reduced by 45 percent but was expected to conduct 450 percent more operations. The situation persisted until declining retention rates forced the professional optimists in the Pentagon to admit what even Congress already knew: The U.S. military was far overextended. The much-heralded "peace dividend" was a myth.

"Hypersonics" will become a more familiar term in the decades ahead. The end of the Soviet Union has by no means ended the nuclear threat, and the prospect of rogue governments or even quasi-independent movements acquiring nukes cannot be discounted. Controversial as the 1980s "Star Wars" program was, something similar to the Strategic Defense Initiative probably will be deployed to meet the diminished volume but perhaps greater probability of inbound missiles.

In order to respond to an ICBM attack, the United States must have almost immediate knowledge of the launch and its likely trajectory. Therefore, increased satellite surveillance is essential to meet the typical 15-minute window of opportunity to intercept and destroy the target "vehicle." Space-based weapons capable of generating extremely fast particle beams or other media will be necessary to destroy such threats outside Earth's atmosphere. Research and development has been underway for years; continued funding is up to Congress.

THE NEXT WAR

Let's briefly consider a possible earthbound scenario:

The histories tell us that early in the second decade of the new millennium, a brief conflict was fought in the remote People's Republic of Stankistan (PRS) near the borders of India, China, and Afghanistan. Ethnic rivalry, common to the region, has boiled over and manifested itself in the seizure of several Western embassies in the capital, Odiossa. The Revolutionary Council demands billions of dollars in "reparations" for their release.

American options are limited. The Chinese, who profess neutrality, are known to be funding the main dissident group in hopes of making inroads against neighboring Kazakhstan, a former Soviet republic.

Also professing neutrality, India refuses basing rights for the United States and other Western nations whose diplomats are being held for ransom. Again, the public posturing is disingenuous, because New Delhi is suspicious of Stankistan's Muslim plurality and its natural affinity for Pakistan. That leaves Afghanistan and Kazakhstan as the likely bases for allied forces in the region.

The main air power for the alliance reposes in the 3570th Expeditionary Wing, a composite organization with fighter, attack, tanker, AWACS, and special operations units. Heavy metal is available via B-52s flying long-range missions from Egypt and Saudi Arabia, a one-way trip of some 2,000 miles. A Navy battle group in the Indian Ocean can launch 1,000-mile strikes only with Air Force tanker support.

While diplomats attempt to settle the hostage crisis, planning continues in northern Afghanistan. The government, increasingly stable in recent years, welcomes the American presence with its attendant increased foreign aid. The 3570th's commander, Brigadier General Jason "Rough" Reddy, coordinates his staff's work with other forces. They know that a hostage-rescue mission is not an option, since the Stankistanis have distributed the embassy personnel throughout Odiossa, and likely will execute them in event of a raid. Therefore, the best bet is to "take down" the nation's infrastructure in a short, sharp campaign calculated to make the Revolutionary Council resented by the population. The Western nations issue a joint declaration stating that if any hostages are harmed, retribution will be swift and terrible. In fact, the operation is called "Swift Sword." Beijing calculates that its interest in Stankistan is marginal, and takes no active role—at least not publicly.

Stankistan possesses a relatively small but capable air-defense network. A combination of Russian, French, and Israeli systems are well integrated with hardened command and control centers and reasonably secure communications. Radar-guided, electro-optical, and passive Surface-to-Air Missiles (SAMs) are deployed with a large number of antiaircraft guns. Two fighter regiments provide a limited air-to-air threat with late-model Sukhois and upgraded Mirage 2000s. Allied intelligence knows that Chinese and Iraqi advisors are de facto commanders of the air-defense network, with a few freelance Russians and Westerners.

While aircrews practice and politicians pontificate, the war against Stankistan is already underway. Working in extreme secrecy within the bowels of the Pentagon, a cell of hard-core computer geeks has spent weeks hacking into the PRS computer network. The "Black Hole" crew fights its desperately quiet war with surprising harmony for so disparate an organization. Air Force, Navy, and Department of Defense personnel combine their efforts with the single-mindedness that only true believers can muster. Working tirelessly, without hope of Air Medal or pride of DFC, they access many of Stankistan's secret files and plant viruses set to go active at H Hour on S Day.

At 2:20 on the morning of October 9, Revolution Day in Stankistan, Rough Reddy's aircrews go to work. Nearly three months of planning and rehearsal have gone into the carefully choreographed operation, with Royal Air Force (RAF) Tornados and French Mirages, plus Russian MiGs and Sukhois all playing their roles: striking air-defense targets, engaging Stankistan Air Force interceptors, and providing cover for the tankers and AWACSs. Six B-52s release a wave of Air Launched Cruise Missiles (ALCMs) with a variety of warheads to destroy hostile radars and SAM sites, opening a narrow path for the fighter-bombers. Simultaneously, some key radar sites and telephone exchanges mysteriously fall offline as the Black Hole's viruses emerge from recent implantation. Meanwhile, many PRS e-mail programs turn to hash. The defenders realize they've been had.

With retirement of the last EF-111 Ravens in 1998, the Air Force finds itself without a tactical jamming aircraft of its own. Consequently, four Navy EA-6B squadrons have been designated expeditionary units, as are all four Marine Corps Prowler squadrons. Because carrier air wings are increasingly dependent upon Air Force tankers for deep-strike missions, a symbiotic relationship has grown up between the blue suiters and the tailhookers. After years of lip service, "jointness" has become reality.

Among the first attackers on station are F-15 Strike Eagles of the 362nd Tactical Fighter Squadron. They launch AGM-154 Joint Stand Off Weapons (JSOWs) from 15 to 40 miles range, depending on release altitude. Using GPS navigation with a 1,000-pound warhead or greater, the JSOWs impact with eerie accuracy on regional command and communication centers. Meanwhile, F-22 Raptor stealth fighters of the 363rd Squadron engage two flights of Sukhois near Odiossa and destroy four with AMRAAM missiles. The surviving PRS pilots reply with a volley of radar- and heat-seeking missiles, but only one finds its mark. The Raptor is damaged and limps back to base.

By dawn the Stankistani air-defense network is badly degraded. Some areas are electronically blind and others are limited to low-altitude coverage. However, the enemy proves innovative and activates a data-link contingency plan that affords roving coverage of the affected areas. The defenders know that a second wave is bound to follow the first.

While RAF Tornados and Russian Sukhois restrike the sector stations that survived the initial wave, more 3570th planes are inbound. Directed by AWACS and Joint STARS controllers, Reddy's aircrews raise their sights to northern Stankistan's target complex. Again Strike Eagles and Raptors penetrate the outer edge of the radar network, supported by Marine Corps EA-6 Prowlers providing electronic jamming. Two U.S. planes are shot down with one crew killed and the other evading capture. Special Operations troops deploy immediately and scoop up the downed airmen in two hours. AA fire downs one HH-53, but two of the crew survive.

By late afternoon, the PRS fighter force is nearly extinct. French Mirages have finished off the remnants of the second regiment, both in the air and on the ground. With SAM radars largely destroyed or jammed, the second night permits attacks by the 364th Squadron's aging F-16s. The Vipers carry both smart and dumb bombs, including the AGM-158 Joint Air to Surface Standoff Missile (JASSM). It flies a low-level, perhaps circuitous, route, to the target much as a cruise missile. With GPS guidance it is highly accurate. Terminal guidance is via thermal imaging, matching a programmed description of the target. One JASSM pinwheels the meeting room of the Revolutionary Council, which regrettably was delayed in getting to the conference. Nevertheless, the message is not lost on the council members.

Next the "new kids" arrive. In its first combat, an independent squadron of F-35 Joint Strike Fighters executes follow-up attacks on previously struck targets, or those less well defended. Their primary weapon is the Joint Direct Attack Munition (JDAM). More an "overhead" than a standoff weapon, JDAM is highly accurate against small or mobile targets. Again with jamming support and excellent coverage by Joint STARS, the JSF pilots begin disrupting Stankistan's way of life. Bridges, railroads, and power-generating stations all are targeted.

Inevitably there is a public-relations problem. An F-35 pilot, evading one of the few SAMs fired at her, places the electronic cursor on the wrong target. The JDAM spears a nondescript building near a military warehouse and 18 civilians—women and children—are killed. The Stankistanis howl in outrage, bringing in members of the international media to film the carnage. The U.S. president and secretary of state issue regretful statements, pledging greater vigilance. Rough Reddy receives a quiet reprimand from Washington but refuses to pass it to the pilot, who continues flying. The next day, she and her wingman destroy one sixth of Stankistan's remaining diesel-fuel stocks.

By dawn of day three, the PRS is reeling. A nation barely as large as Minnesota and Wisconsin has borne the brunt of more than 1,000 offensive sorties by the Air Force, Navy, and three other air arms. Transportation and communications are badly mauled, and cyberwarriors have degraded more of the PRC computer systems. One third of the country is without electrical power, including most of the capital.

The allies have thus far spared Stankistan's petroleum industry, but Odiossa is informed that unless all hostages are released by noon, the first two refineries go up at 12:01. The Revolutionary Council meets in a hotel basement to discuss the situation and decides that it's time to cut its losses.

Operation Swift Sword is concluded after 82 hours. The hostages are released to an international commission amid much bluster and rhetoric, but the crisis is passed. As after Desert Storm, there is no popular uprising against the PRS government, but the region returns to its usual tenuous peace.

While the usual heroic treatment is accorded the returning hostages, the war fighters look inward. General Reddy leads the 3570th Expeditionary Wing back to the United States, where debriefs are conducted and summaries are compiled. Eventually medals are awarded, fitness reports are filed, and the wing begins refitting and retraining. For next time.

In the Black Hole, a few commendations are handed out, and the computer geeks pause briefly to exchange high fives. Then one day the Black Hole is visited by the commanding officer of the Strike Eagle squadron that first penetrated PRS airspace. She presents the cyberwarriors their most valued accolade of all: a charred piece of the inactive radar dish that went offline seconds before the F-15s ingressed. Mounted on a suitable plaque, the trophy declares the airmen's gratitude to their silent comrades who fought the war not in the sky, but far underground.

CHAPTER 10

THE AIR FORCE IN MOVIES, BOOKS, AND SONGS

In 1986, when the Tom Cruise hit *Top Gun* appeared, some U.S. Air Force recruiters set up booths in movie theaters, hoping to capitalize on the military aviation craze. By any objective measure, naval aviation has gained more air time than the USAF, and the reason is unclear. Perhaps it's the glamour of aircraft carriers, which have fascinated the public since Wallace Beery and Clark Gable appeared in *Helldivers* in 1930. At any rate, since Vietnam, the blue suiters have taken a back seat to the "squids" in the entertainment media.

TEN AIR FORCE MOVIES

Here's a list of 10 Air Force movies worth seeing. They're presented in chronological order of the story line. Seven of them deal largely or entirely with bombers, one with fighters, and one with politics and one with training. Gary Merrill, Robert Mitchum, and Van Johnson all appear in two titles. Colonel Beirne Lay Jr., a World War II bomber pilot, co-authored two of the screenplays.

The Court Martial of Billy Mitchell (1955). Directed by Otto Preminger; script by Emmet Lavery and Milton Sperling (Oscar for Best Writing). Gary Cooper stars as the maverick air-power crusader in this bio-pic 19 years after Mitchell's death. Essentially a courtroom drama, the excellent cast includes Ralph Bellamy, Charles Bickford, and Rod Steiger. In truth, Mitchell's predictions proved wrong as often as right, but his courageous battle with bureaucracy deserves tribute. Genuine DH-4s and other vintage flying machines add to the attraction.

I Wanted Wings (1941). Directed by Mitchell Leisen; script by Eleanore Griffin and Sig Herzig. Army flying cadets William Holden, Ray Milland, and Wayne Morris (a future Navy ace) make their way through Randolph Field in vintage trainers, struggling to win their gold bars and silver wings. The standard plot is made all the more alluring by a lithe Veronica Lake with that peekaboo hairdo. Mm-*hmm*. Sign us up. The film deservedly won an Oscar for Effects.

Air Force (1943). Directed by Howard Hawks; script by Dudley Nichols. Although full of the World War II conventions (the tough guy, the old timer, and the kid), this offering has stood the test of time. The crew of the B-17D *Mary Ann* makes its perilous way from California to Pearl Harbor to Wake Island, the Philippines, and ultimately Island X to deliver the knockout blow. With a solid cast (John Garfield, Harry Carey, and George Tobias) and engaging script, *Air Force* remains a far better combat film than most of those that followed. It received four Oscar nominations, including Best Original Screenplay, and won for Film Editing.

Thirty Seconds over Tokyo (1943). Directed by Mervyn Leroy; script by Robert Considine (from his book with Ted Lawson) and Dalton Trumbo. An uncommonly good wartime film, with excellent production values, this is a credible telling of the 1942 Doolittle Raid. Full cooperation of the Army Air Force ensured plenty of B-25s, and Oscar-winning special effects duplicated the rain-swept flight deck of the aircraft carrier *Hornet*. Spencer Tracy delivers a subdued, convincing performance as Jimmy Doolittle in vivid contrast to Alec Baldwin's obnoxious, profane role in the dreadful 2001 offering, *Pearl Harbor.* The cast includes Van Johnson, Phyllis Thaxter, and Robert Mitchum.

Twelve O'Clock High (1949). Directed by Henry King; script by Sy Bartlett and Beirne Lay Jr. from their novel. Gregory Peck received an Oscar nomination for his portrayal of the complex Brigadier General Frank Savage, sent down from 8th Air Force Headquarters to command the hard-luck "918th Bomb Group." The solid cast includes Dean Jagger (Oscar for Best Supporting Actor), Gary Merrill, Hugh Marlowe, and Van Johnson. Filmed only four years after the war, the producers had ample B-17s and combat footage. The movie is reportedly shown at the U.S. Air Force Noncommissioned Officers' Academy as a leadership example.

Winged Victory (1944). Directed by George Cukor; script by Moss Hart from his stage play. The story of a B-24 crew from stateside training to the Pacific theater, told in top-notch fashion by an excellent director and screenwriter. The female parts, rather than merely providing sex appeal, contribute to the film's sense of time and place. Edmond O'Brien, Don Taylor, and Gary Merrill are among the liberator fliers "loaned" back to Hollywood from active duty. The '24 never gets enough PR, and this solid film helps plug some of the gap for the most produced American aircraft in history.

The Memphis Belle (1990). Directed by Michael Caton-Jones; script by Monte Merrick. Basically, this is *Air Force* with less depth but higher production values. Another B-17 crew (minus the regional stereotypes) fights the Nazis instead of the Japanese but does so in color. Approximately based on the story of the first 8th Air Force crew to complete a 25-mission tour, the film was produced by Katherine Wyler, daughter of the director who filmed the wartime documentary of the same name. A combination of real aircraft with computer graphics makes memorable viewing. Matthew Modine leads his crew to completion of its combat tour, including Billy Zane, Eric Stoltz, and D. B. Sweeney.

The Hunters (1955). Directed by William Powell; script by Peter Hyams. The Korean War spawned a variety of aviation films, most of which remain forgettable. The best was *The Bridges at Toko-Ri*, about carrier aviators. *The Hunters* isn't that good but contains plenty of air combat action, F-86s and MiG-15s (a.k.a. F-84s), plus a box office cast with Robert Mitchum, Robert Wagner, and Richard Egan. Mitchum's quiet, forceful competence is probably the best depiction of a professional fighter pilot yet filmed, while

Wagner's brash egotism captures the other side of the coin. Based on the novel by F-86 pilot James Salter.

Strategic Air Command (1955). Directed by Anthony Mann; script by Valentine Davies and Beirne Lay Jr. (Oscar-nominated for Best Screenplay). The Cold War. Nuclear deterrence. B-36s, B-47s, and a cigar-chomping Curt LeMay lookalike. Jimmy Stewart is miscast as a big league pitcher recalled to active duty, but does his patriotic chore in this typical 1950s public relations film. However, the airplanes are nostalgic, June Allyson is sweet, and the aerial photography is downright gorgeous. Don't worry about the lightweight plot: *SAC* appears frequently on cable TV and should not be missed—especially the stunning shots of B-36s streaming contrails into a setting sun. Or maybe it's rising; it doesn't matter because it's all beautiful.

Dr. Strangelove: Or How I Learned to Stop Worrying and Love the Bomb (1964). Directed by Stanley Kubrick; script by Peter George (from his novel), Kubrick, and Terry Southern. Kubrick's dark comedy portrays the U.S. Air Force (and the rest of the human race) with tongue firmly in cheek. Peter Sellers's triple performance as the bumbling American president, a stereotyped Royal Air Force officer, and the Kissingeresque title character remains a landmark. But the film is stolen in deadpan earnestness by perennial hayseed Slim Pickens as Colonel Kong, the dedicated B-52 pilot. The excellent cast also includes Sterling Hayden, George C. Scott, and Keenan Wynn. The ultimate Cold War farce received Oscar nominations for Best Picture, Director, Actor, and Screenplay.

THE AIR FORCE ON TELEVISION

Air Force topics have featured on the small screen as well as in theatrical releases. The following is a short compilation of TV series as well as movies made for television.

Call to Glory (1984–1985) was a well-regarded series dealing with a 1960s Air Force family starring Craig T. Nelson and Cindy Pickett. Among other things, Nelson (Colonel Raynor Sarnac) flew U-2s and supported the Civil Rights movement. Uh-*huh*.

While *Call to Glory* was the only post-Vietnam series in an Air Force setting, the naval services were found in a half-dozen venues. Two stinkers included *Baa Baa Black Sheep* (1976–1977), allegedly based on "Pappy" Boyington's exploits, watchable only for the airplanes. The equally egregious *Super Carrier* (1988) deservedly flopped after a couple of months.

Tom Selleck's enjoyable *Magnum PI* (1980–1988) had a strong naval content, while the glamorous *Emerald Point NAS* (1983–1984) featured Dennis Weaver and knockout Sela Ward. More recently, the long-lived *JAG* (1995–) focuses on Tomcat pilot turned Navy lawyer, Commander Harmon Raab (David James Elliott). *Pensacola: Wings of Gold* (1997–1999) with James Brolin as a Marine Corps squadron commander proved a potboiler.

Although there have been no big-screen Air Force movies since *The Memphis Belle* (the 1997 hit *Air Force One* was not about the service), several were made for broadcast TV or cable, including the following:

Red Flag: The Ultimate Game (1981). Barry Bostwick and William Devane are professional rivals at Nellis Air Force Base.

Enola Gay: The Men, the Mission, the Atomic Bomb (1982). Patrick Duffy, transplanted from *Dallas*, as Colonel Paul Tibbets.

Call to Glory (1984). Based on the series with Craig T. Nelson and Cindy Pickett.

By Dawn's Early Light (1990). The intense Powers Boothe and sexpot Rebecca DeMornay as B-52 pilots on a doomsday mission.

Flight of Black Angel (1991). William O'Leary plays a religiously devout F-16 pilot who decides to cure the evils of Las Vegas with a nuke.

Afterburn (1992). Laura Dern portrays Janet Harduvel's campaign to clear her husband's name after his death in an F-16 accident. Not the Air Force's finest hour.

The Tuskegee Airmen (1996). About the 332nd Fighter Group's battles with racism and the *Luftwaffe*, with Laurence Fishburne and Cuba Gooding Jr. Poor history.

MISSABLE AIR FORCE MOVIES SINCE VIETNAM

… And here's a few you can definitely afford to skip:

Hannover Street (1979). Harrison Ford as an 8th Air Force B-25 pilot involved with a married English woman. (That's right: 8th Air Force B-25s. *Catch 22* made a lot more sense.) But Leslie Ann Down is gorgeous.

Iron Eagle I through *IV* (1986–1995). Air Force brats save the world, or somebody, four times. One reviewer's assessment of "Not boring, just stupid" aptly describes the series.

Pearl Harbor (2001). Despite superb production values, this potboiler remains one of the worst "historic" films of all time. Essentially a romantic triangle in the AAF with Ben Affleck, Josh Hartnett, and Kate Beckinsale. Get the video of *Tora! Tora! Tora!* instead.

THE AIR FORCE FUNNIES

The Air Force featured heavily in two of the most popular comic strips of the 1940s through the 1980s. Such was Milton Caniff's ability and stature that he had no sooner ended *Terry and the Pirates* over a contract dispute than he began *Steve Canyon* and received an industry award before the latter even appeared. The first strip (1934–1947) featured young Terry Lee, an adventuresome lad growing up in Asia who became an Army Air Force pilot fighting the Japanese. There was plenty of intrigue along the way, including the mysterious Dragon Lady.

Steve Canyon emerged as a pilot for hire in 1947, running Horizons Unlimited—an anytime, anywhere outfit involved in often risky government projects. Canyon was recalled to active duty for Korea and remained in uniform through most of the Cold War, but he died with his creator in 1988. There was also a three-year TV series (1958–1960) plus comic books and a series of novels. Square-jawed, blond, and blue-eyed, Colonel Canyon was a recruiting poster Air Force officer for two generations of readers.

Zack Mosley's *Smilin' Jack* (1933–1973) did not focus on the Air Force to the extent that Caniff did, but some crossover was inevitable. In fact, Mosley was a co-founder of the Civil Air Patrol and logged 300 flights searching for enemy submarines during World War II. His strip was beloved by aviation enthusiasts for the immense variety of aircraft depicted, often without relation to the story line. Although Mosley spent most of the war in Florida, the tale is told that federal agents knocked on Mosley's door in Los Angeles, demanding to know how he learned of the secret Northrop P-61 fighter depicted in his strip. At that moment, a Black Widow growled overhead on a test flight. Mosley merely unzipped a *Smilin' Jack* grin. (And if he didn't, he should have.)

LITERATE AIRMEN

The educational requirements for an Air Force career lend themselves to a literate population, and there is no shortage of U.S. Air Force authors, many who became best-sellers. They include no less than Lieutenant Colonel (later General of the Air Force) Henry H. Arnold, who penned the Bill Bruce series of boys' books. The six volumes were released in 1928, including installments of young Bill as a flying cadet, becoming an ace, flying forest patrol, and racing cross-country.

Among the most influential books on the subject was *Victory Through Airpower* by former Russian ace Alexander de Seversky. A devoted friend and disciple of Billy Mitchell, Seversky postulated the supremacy of aviation early in World War II and, despite some notable errors, generally got it right. His 1942 treatise became a widely quoted source during and after the war.

Genuine wartime exploits produced many more titles, several of which became motion pictures. Among the first was Captain Ted Lawson's *Thirty Seconds over Tokyo*, covering his service with the Doolittle Raiders. Elsewhere in Asia, Colonel (later Brigadier General) Robert L. Scott's highly successful *God Is My Copilot* described his tenure as General Chennault's fighter commander in China. It was made into a movie in 1945. Subsequently Scott wrote a dozen other books on flying, big-game hunting, and exotic travel.

Colonel Beirne Lay Jr. co-authored *Twelve O'Clock High*, based on his experience flying B-17s in Britain. Lay also wrote the screenplay for *Strategic Air Command*.

Undoubtedly the most successful book ever written by an Air Force veteran remains Brigadier General Chuck Yeager's autobiography, *Yeager*, followed by *Press On!* His lifelong friend and flying partner, Colonel C. E. "Bud" Anderson, penned another readable memoir, *To Fly and Fight*.

(Anderson's son Jim, also a former fighter pilot, maintains an excellent website on the subject at www.cebudanderson.com.)

The service's most decorated officer, Colonel George Day, related his career and years of imprisonment in Hanoi in *Return with Honor*. The top surviving Air Force ace, Colonel Francis Gabreski, described his World War II and Korean War combat in *Gabby*. He died in 2001.

Colonel Walter Boyne, former director of the National Air and Space Museum, has been a familiar figure in books and television. He has the distinction of placing fiction and nonfiction books on *The New York Times* bestseller list, and he frequently appears as a commentator on TV documentaries.

BIBLIOGRAPHY

The literature of the U.S. Air Force is extensive, and growing constantly. Official and unofficial sources consulted for this volume include the following:

Freeman, Roger A. *The Mighty Eighth: A History of the U.S. 8th Army Air Force.* Garden City, NY: Doubleday, 1970.

Friedman, Norman. *Desert Victory: The War for Kuwait.* Annapolis, MD: Naval Institute Press, 1991.

Futrell, Robert F. *The U.S. Air Force in Korea 1950–1953.* Revised edition. Washington, DC: Air Force History Office, 1982.

Hallion, Richard P. *Strike from the Sky: History of Battlefield Air Attack.* Washington, DC: Smithsonian Institution Press, 1989.

Olynyk, Dr. Frank. *Stars and Bars: A Tribute to the American Fighter Ace 1920–1973.* United Kingdom: Grub Street, 1995.

Rust, Kenn C. *The 9th Air Force in World War II.* Fallbrook, CA: Aero Publishers, 1967.

———. *The 12th Air Force Story.* Temple City, CA: Historical Aviation Album, 1975.

Seversky, Alexander P. *Victory Through Air Power.* New York: Simon & Schuster, 1942.

Swanborough, F. G., and Peter M. Bowers. *United States Military Aircraft Since 1909*. New York: Putnam, 1963.

Thompson, Wayne. *To Hanoi and Back: The U.S. Air Force and North Vietnam, 1966–1973*. Washington, DC: Smithsonian Institution Press, 2000.

Tillman, Barrett. *Above and Beyond: The Aviation Medals of Honor*. Washington, DC: Smithsonian Institution Press, 2002.

TWENTY AIR FORCE CELEBRITIES

Thousands of people in public life have served in the Air Force or its antecedents. Here's a small list of veterans from the worlds of politics and entertainment:

Gene Autry. Immensely successful as the singing cowboy, Autry earned a private pilot's license before entering the Army Air Force. As a C-46 pilot, he flew hundreds of trips across "the Hump" from India into China.

Lloyd Bentsen. A future treasury secretary, Texas senator, and failed vice presidential candidate, Bentsen commanded a B-24 squadron in the 15th Air Force's 449th Bomb Group.

George W. Bush. In 1968, the future forty-third president received a direct commission in the Texas Air National Guard. He completed pilot training and flew F-102 interceptors from 1970 to 1972. Following removal from flight status, he received early separation from the service in 1973.

Jackie Coogan. The child star of silent films and talkies became a flight officer in the Army Air Force (AAF) and was trained as a glider pilot. During 1943 and 1944, he delivered supplies to British forces in the China-Burma-India theater.

Robert K. Dornan. Known in Congress as "B-1 Bob," Dornan was a former F-86, F-100, and F-104 pilot (two ejections, one dead-stick landing) who championed defense spending during the Cold War. He represented his California district from 1977 to 1997 and became a popular radio commentator.

Clark Gable. After his wife, Carol Lombard, was killed in a 1942 plane crash, Gable entered the AAF. As a captain he flew five missions with the 8th Air Force, supervising cameramen for *Combat America*. He left active duty in 1944.

George Gobel. Deadpan "Lonesome George" of early TV fame was an AAF flight instructor for much of World War II. He boasted that he allowed no Japanese aircraft anywhere east of Tulsa.

Barry Goldwater. The Arizona senator and unsuccessful 1964 presidential candidate was a fighter gunnery instructor and ferry pilot during World War II. He became a major general in the Air Force Reserve.

Charlton Heston. Staff Sergeant Heston was a B-25 radio operator with the 11th Air Force in the Aleutians during World War II. He typically played heroic figures in more than 100 feature films and won the Best Actor Oscar for *Ben Hur* in 1959.

Tim Holt. A Western actor best known for his role in *Treasure of the Sierra Madre*, Holt left Hollywood in 1943 to become a B-29 bombardier in the 39th Bomb Group. He mysteriously disappeared from Guam in 1945, turning up in the United States to resume his film career.

Fiorello LaGuardia. The colorful mayor of New York City (1934–1945) returned to his ancestral roots in World War I. As an Air Service captain, he flew Caproni bombers in Italy while still a member of Congress. A lifelong aviation booster, he helped establish the Civil Air Patrol in 1941.

Tom Landry. As a 21-year-old co-pilot, the future Dallas Cowboys coach flew B-17s in the 493rd Bomb Group, logging 30 missions including a crash-landing in Belgium. He followed his older brother into the 8th Air Force; Robert Landry was killed ferrying a Fortress to Britain.

Walter Matthau. A radio cryptographer, Staff Sergeant Matthau served in the 453rd Bomb Group with Lieutenant Colonel Jimmy Stewart. Among his 87 films, Matthau's performance in *The Fortune Cookie* won the Oscar for Best Actor in 1966.

APPENDIX A: TWENTY AIR FORCE CELEBRITIES

George McGovern. Perhaps ironically, considering his later antiwar politics, McGovern was a B-24 pilot in the 455th Bomb Group, 15th Air Force. As a senator from South Dakota, he lost in his bid for the presidency to former Navy man Richard Nixon in the landslide election of 1972.

Glenn Miller. Perhaps the ultimate big-band leader, Miller formed the Army Air Forces Band early in World War II, keeping the troops in touch with music from home. He disappeared on a flight over the English Channel in December 1944.

Jack Palance. Oscar-winner Palance (*City Slickers*, 1991) sustained serious injuries as a B-24 pilot in training when his Liberator crashed on take-off. Alan Ladd, his costar and archrival in *Shane* (1953), briefly served in the AAF as well.

Ronald Reagan. Originally a cavalryman, Reagan entered the Army Reserve in 1937 but transferred to the AAF in 1942. He served in production of information and training films and in 1945 was recommended for promotion to major. Although he remained a captain, in 1980 he became commander in chief as the fortieth president of the United States.

George Reeves. Television's *Superman* hero (1953–1958) was drafted into the Army in 1943 and served in the AAF's Special Theatrical Unit.

Gene Roddenberry. Creator of the *Star Trek* television series, Roddenberry flew 89 missions as a B-17 pilot in the Solomon Islands and subsequently entered commercial aviation.

Jimmy Stewart. A no-kidding combat flier, Stewart was a prewar civilian pilot. He flew with two 8th Air Force B-24 groups and retired as a reserve brigadier general.

AIR FORCE MILESTONES

January 18, 1905	The Wright brothers open negotiations with the government for procurement of one airplane.
February 8, 1908	Three bids for the Army's first plane are approved by the Secretary of War.
January 19, 1910	Three two-pound sandbags are dropped in the first simulated bomb drop experiment.
January 16, 1911	The first photo reconnaissance flight is unable to locate troops from the air.
January 21, 1911	The Army makes the first radio-telephonic transmission from an aircraft.
March 3, 1911	The first aviation appropriation of $125,000 is authorized for the Army.
March 17, 1911	The first Curtiss airplane is bought by the Army Signal Corps.
April 11, 1911	Lieutenants T. D. Milling and Henry H. Arnold are ordered to Dayton, Ohio, for flying instructions.
May 10, 1911	Lieutenant G. E. M. Kelly becomes the second Army officer killed in an airplane.

October 20, 1911	The original Wright Army plane is delivered to the Smithsonian Institution.
February 17, 1912	The first pilot physical examination requirements are published by the Army.
February 23, 1912	The War Department first officially recognizes the Military Aviator rating.
May 6, 1912	Three Army planes make the first group cross-country flight.
June 7, 1912	The first machine gun is fired from an airplane in the United States.
June 14, 1912	Corporal Vernon Burge becomes the Army's first enlisted pilot.
September 28, 1912	Corporal Frank S. Scott becomes the first enlisted fatality in Signal Corps Aviation.
February 11, 1913	The first bill to establish a separate Aviation Corps fails to pass.
May 27, 1913	General Order No. 39 provides that Army officers qualified as Military Aviators receive a Military Aviator's certificate and badge—24 qualified.
February 5, 1914	Lieutenant J. C. Morrow becomes the last flier to qualify as a Military Aviator.
July 18, 1914	Congress creates the Aviation Section of the Signal Corps.
July 12, 1915	Aviation mechanic examination requirements are adopted.
March 15, 1916	The 1st Aero Squadron, commanded by Captain B. D. Foulois, begins operations into Mexico.
March 16, 1916	The first military aerial reconnaissance flight is made over Mexican territory.
September 6, 1916	The first fragmentation bomb is tested.
March 13, 1917	The Army Air Intelligence Subdivision Office is approved.
January 20, 1918	The Air Service's 1st Army Corps headquarters is organized at Neufchateau, France.

January 23, 1918	The Allied Expeditionary Force makes the first American military balloon ascension.
February 7, 1918	Instrument standardization in Army and Navy planes is established.
February 18, 1918	The 103rd Pursuit Squadron is formed with members of the Lafayette Escadrille.
March 14, 1918	The first aerial patrol by the 1st Pursuit Group is flown in France.
March 19, 1918	The 94th Squadron, 1st Pursuit Group, flies the first operations across the lines in France.
April 14, 1918	The American Expeditionary Force shoots down the first two enemy aircraft.
April 29, 1918	Lieutenant Edward V. Rickenbacker downs his first enemy aircraft.
May 11, 1918	The Allied Expeditionary Force receives a DH-4, its first American-made airplane.
May 15, 1918	The government's first permanent airmail route is inaugurated by Army pilots.
September 12, 1918	Lieutenant Frank Luke shoots down his first enemy balloon.
November 11, 1918	The last patrol is flown by the American Air Service over enemy lines.
December 23, 1918	Major General C. T. Menoher is appointed Director of the Air Service.
May 17, 1919	The War Department orders use of national star insignia on all planes.
May 19, 1919	Master Sergeant R. W. Bottriell makes the first free back-type parachute jump.
September 24, 1919	An altitude record of 30,900 feet is set for an airplane carrying a passenger.
February 27, 1920	An official world altitude record of 33,113 feet set at McCook Field.
May 26, 1920	A GAX twin-engine triplane armed with eight machine guns and 37mm cannon is tested.

June 5, 1920	An appropriation bill limits the Air Service to land bases.
March 23, 1921	Lieutenant A. G. Hamilton descends 23,700 feet by parachute at Chanute Field, Illinois.
July 13, 1921	Army-Navy bombing tests sink three captured German ships.
September 4, 1922	The first U.S. transcontinental air crossing is made within a single day.
October 5, 1922	Lieutenants J. A. Macready and O. G. Kelly set a world endurance record of 35 hours, 18 minutes, 30 seconds.
October 20, 1922	Lieutenant Harold R. Harris makes the first emergency parachute jump.
March 29, 1923	Lieutenant Russell Maughan sets a world speed record of 236.587 miles per hour in a Curtiss R-6.
May 2, 1923	The first nonstop transcontinental flight from New York to San Diego begins.
June 20, 1923	The Army's first all-metal airplane, the CO-1, makes its first flight.
August 22, 1923	The Barling Bomber makes its initial flight.
August 28, 1923	A new world refueled flight duration record of 37 hours, 15 minutes, 4.8 seconds is set.
September 5, 1923	Two condemned naval vessels are sunk by Army bombing tests.
April 6, 1924	Air Service officers begin the first around-the-world air tour.
September 28, 1924	Two Douglas World Cruisers complete the first successful around-the-world flight.
October 28, 1924	Army planes break up a cloud formation with electrified sand.
September 15, 1925	The first semi-rigid helium airship constructed in the United States is completed.

October 15, 1925	Lieutenant Cyrus Bettis wins the 1925 Pulitzer race in a specially built Curtiss R3C-1 racer and establishes a new speed record of 248.9 miles per hour.
July 2, 1926	Congress establishes the Distinguished Flying Cross and makes the award retroactive to April 6, 1917.
May 25, 1927	Lieutenant James H. Doolittle performs the first known successful outside loop.
October 12, 1927	Wright Field replaces McCook Field as the Air Service test site.
December 14, 1927	Major General J. E. Fechet becomes Chief of the Air Corps.
February 3, 1928	Lieutenant H. A. Sutton receives the Mackay Trophy for spin tests made at Wright Field.
October 19, 1928	An American six-man machine gun team parachutes from a six-plane formation.
June 21, 1930	Randolph Field at San Antonio, Texas, is dedicated.
November 6, 1930	Captain Eddie Rickenbacker is awarded the Medal of Honor for his action in World War I.
August 31, 1932	Air Corps pilots fly five miles above the earth's surface to photograph an eclipse of the sun.
February 9, 1934	All domestic airmail contracts are canceled, and the Army is ordered to fly mail.
May 22, 1934	The Mackay Trophy is awarded to Captain W. T. Larson for developing instrument takeoff and landing procedures.
February 19, 1936	Brigadier General William "Billy" Mitchell dies in New York City.
December 27, 1935	U.S. Army planes divert a Hawaiian lava flow by aerial bombardment.
August 23, 1937	The first wholly automatic landing in history is accomplished.
January 27, 1939	The XP-38 makes its first flight.

January 12, 1939	President Roosevelt asks Congress for a revision of the authorization for Army aircraft.
February 14, 1939	The XB-15 flies a mercy mission from Virginia to Chile in 29 hours, 53 minutes.
April 27, 1939	The U.S. Army Air Corps orders the P-38.
February 26, 1940	The Air Defense Command is created to integrate U.S. Army Air Force defenses against an air attack.
May 31, 1941	Major General George H. Brett is appointed Chief of the U.S. Army Air Corps.
July 31, 1941	The U.S. Army Air Force officially establishes Tuskegee Army Air Field.
December 1, 1941	The Civil Air Patrol is created.
December 7, 1941	The Japanese attack Pearl Harbor.
December 8, 1941	The United States declares war on Japan.
December 11, 1941	Germany and Italy declare war on the United States.
January 2, 1942	General H. H. Arnold directs the establishment of a new numbered Air Force, later designated the 8th Air Force.
January 13, 1942	The XR-4, the Army Air Force's first helicopter, makes its initial flight.
March 7, 1942	The first class of Tuskegee Airmen graduate from U.S. Army Air Force Tuskegee Army Air Field.
April 18, 1942	In the early morning hours, 16 B-25B Mitchell bombers, led by Lieutenant Colonel James Doolittle, strike Tokyo, Kobe, Nagoya, and Yokohama. "Doolittle's Raid" inflicts little physical damage to Japan but gives a needed lift to morale in the United States. In Japan, the psychological damage of the attack is more important and causes the Japanese to extend its defensive perimeter.
June 24, 1943	Lieutenant Colonel W. R. Lovelace makes a record parachute jump from 42,200 feet.

July 8, 1943	Colonel M. G. Grow, 8th Air Force surgeon, receives the Legion of Merit for developing the flak vest.
January 1, 1944	U.S. Strategic Air Forces in Europe is activated.
January 6, 1944	Major General James Doolittle assumes command of the 8th Air Force.
May 8, 1945	Germany surrenders unconditionally.
August 6, 1945	The B-29 *Enola Gay* drops an atomic bomb on Hiroshima, Japan.
August 9, 1945	The second atomic bomb is dropped on Nagasaki, Japan, by B-29 *Bock's Car.*
December 3, 1945	The P-80 becomes the U.S. Army Air Force's first jet fighter.
January 10, 1946	An Army R-5 sets an unofficial world helicopter record of 21,000 feet.
January 24, 1946	General Carl Spaatz is named the first Chief of Staff of the Army Air Forces.
January 26, 1946	Colonel W. Council, flying a P-80, sets a new cross-country record of 4 hours, 13 minutes, 23 seconds.
March 1, 1946	General Carl Spaatz is designated Commander, Army Air Forces.
March 21, 1946	The Strategic Air Command, Tactical Air Command, and Air Defense Command are created.
February 28, 1947	An F-82B sets a record by flying nonstop from Hawaii to New York in 14 hours, 33 minutes.
July 26, 1947	President Harry S Truman approves the National Security Act of 1947. He also issues Executive Order 9877, which, by presidential directive, out-lines the duties of the three services. Each is responsible for the area in which it operates—ground, sea, and air, although the Navy retains an air arm and the Marine Corps.

September 17, 1947	The new National Military Establishment, including the Office of Secretary of Defense and the departments of the Army, Navy, and Air Force, comes into being as new Secretary of Defense James Forrestal is sworn in.
September 18, 1947	W. Stuart Symington is sworn in as the first Secretary of the Air Force. The transfer of air activities from the Army to the new Department of the Air Force takes effect.
September 25, 1947	General Carl Spaatz is appointed the first U.S. Air Force Chief of Staff.
October 14, 1947	Captain Charles E. Yeager, at Muroc Air Base, California, makes the first faster-than-sound flight in a rocket-powered research plane, the Bell XS-1 rocket ship. Captain Yeager wins the Mackay Trophy for the most meritorious flight of the year.
February 20, 1948	The Strategic Air Command receives its first B-50 Superfortress bomber. Equipped for in-flight refueling, the B-50 is an improved version of the B-29, with larger engines and a taller tail fin and rudder.
April 26, 1948	The U.S. Air Force becomes the first service to plan for racial integration, anticipating President Truman's executive order to be issued in July.
June 12, 1948	Congress passes the Women's Armed Service Integration Act, establishing Women in the Air Force.
June 26, 1948	The Berlin Airlift (Operation Vittles) begins as a response to a ground blockade imposed by the Soviet Union on Berlin.
January 7, 1949	The X-1 climbs to 23,000 at a record rate of 13,000 feet per minute.
January 25, 1949	The U.S. Air Force adopts a slate-blue uniform.
March 2, 1949	*Lucky Lady II* lands at Carswell Air Force Base, Texas. The B-50 Superfortress completes the first nonstop, around-the-world flight in history, covering 23,452 miles in 94 hours, 1 minute.

April 16, 1949	The Berlin Airlift delivers a record 12,940 tons in a 24-hour period.
June 2, 1949	General Henry H. Arnold is given the permanent rank of General of the Air Force.
June 29, 1949	The U.S. Air Force becomes the first service to announce an end to racial segregation in its ranks.
September 30, 1949	The Berlin Airlift, gradually reduced since May 12, officially ends. Allied aircraft carry 2,343,301.5 tons of supplies on 277,264 flights. U.S. planes carry 1,783,826 tons.
January 15, 1950	General of the Air Force Henry H. Arnold dies of a heart ailment in Sonoma, California.
March 15, 1950	The U.S. Air Force takes responsibility for all strategic guided missiles.
June 27, 1950	President Truman announces that he has ordered the U.S. Air Force to aid South Korea, which North Korean Communist forces had invaded two days previously.
June 30, 1950	President Truman authorizes General Douglas MacArthur to dispatch air forces against targets in North Korea.
August 5, 1950	Major Louis J. Sebille is killed in action flying a severely damaged F-51 Mustang against an enemy force concentration in Korea. Major Sebille is the first member of the recently created U.S. Air Force to be awarded the Medal of Honor.
November 8, 1950	In history's first battle between jet aircraft, a U.S. Air Force F-80 Shooting Star, piloted by Lieutenant Russell J. Brown, downs a North Korean MiG-15.
March 1, 1951	The Air Force establishes its northernmost operational base, Thule Air Base, Greenland, 690 miles north of the Arctic Circle.

April 18, 1951	An Aerobee research rocket flies the first primate, a monkey, into space from Holloman Air Force Base, New Mexico.
May 20, 1951	Captain James Jabara becomes the world's first jet ace, shooting down his fifth and sixth MiGs in the Korean War.
July 6, 1951	An Air Materiel Command KB-29M tanker, operated by a Strategic Air Command crew assigned to the 43rd Air Refueling Squadron, conducts the first air refueling over enemy territory under combat conditions.
January 7, 1952	The Air Force announces plans to increase its effective combat strength by 50 percent and personnel by 20 percent. The result will be a full 143-wing, 1,273,200-person Air Force.
April 15, 1952	The YB-52, eight-jet Stratofortress prototype, the first all-jet intercontinental heavy bomber, makes its first flight.
May 3, 1952	A ski-and-wheel-equipped U.S. Air Force C-47 Skytrain makes the world's first successful North Pole landing.
July 29, 1952	An RB-45 assigned to the 91st Strategic Reconnaissance Wing flies from Elmendorf Air Force Base, Alaska, to Yokota Air Base, Japan, making the first nonstop transpacific flight by a jet aircraft.
February 8, 1953	The American Medical Association recognizes Aviation Medicine as a medical specialty, the first to evolve from military practice and research.
June 8, 1953	At Luke Air Force Base, Arizona, the U.S. Air Force Thunderbirds, officially designated the 3600th Air Demonstration Flight, perform for the first time.
September 1, 1953	The U.S. Air Force announces the first instance of aerial refueling of jet-powered aircraft by jet-powered aircraft, in which a standard B-47 Stratojet received fuel in the air from a KB-47B Stratojet.

September 11, 1953	The Sidewinder infrared-guided air-to-air missile makes the first successful interception, sending an F-6F drone down in flames.
March 1, 1954	The United States explodes the first hydrogen bomb in the Marshall Islands.
April 1, 1954	President Eisenhower signs into law a bill creating the U.S. Air Force Academy.
December 10, 1954	In a rocket-propelled sled run, Colonel (Dr.) John P. Stapp goes 632 miles per hour and sustains greater G-force than ever endured in recorded deceleration tests. The test determines that humans can survive ejection from aircraft at supersonic speeds.
May 16, 1955	U.S. Air Force marking is approved for use on aircraft wings.
June 29, 1955	The first Boeing B-52 Stratofortress to enter operational service is delivered to the 93rd Bombardment Wing, Castle Air Force Base, California.
October 22, 1955	The Republic F-105A Thunderchief fighter-bomber, designed to carry nuclear weapons and support field armies, exceeds the speed of sound on its initial flight at Edwards Air Force Base, California.
September 15, 1956	The 701st Tactical Missile Wing, scheduled to be equipped with the Matador cruise missile, activates under the 12th Air Force at Hahn Air Base, Germany. This is the first U.S. Air Force tactical missile wing.
December 9, 1956	The 463rd Troop Carrier Wing receives the Air Force's first C-130 Hercules tactical cargo and troop carrier. This four-engine turboprop airlifter has an unrefueled range of more than 2,500 miles. It can take off and land in about 3,600 feet.
January 27, 1957	The last operational P-51 fighter is retired to the Air Force museum.

June 11, 1957	Assigned to the 4080th Strategic Reconnaissance Wing, the first U-2 high-altitude, long-range reconnaissance aircraft arrives at Laughlin Air Force Base, Texas. The U-2 can fly 10-hour missions at exceptionally high altitudes at a top speed of 600 miles per hour.
June 28, 1957	Assigned to the 93rd Air Refueling Squadron, the first KC-135 Stratotanker arrives at Castle Air Force Base, California. The jet tanker can cruise at the same speed as jet bombers while refueling.
July 19, 1957	The U.S. Air Force fires the first air-to-air nuclear defense rocket, the Douglas MB-1 Genie, from an F-89J over Yucca Flat, Nevada.
August 1, 1957	The North American Air Defense Command, a joint United States–Canadian command with an air-defense mission, is informally established.
August 15, 1957	General Nathan F. Twining becomes the first U.S. Air Force officer to serve as chairman of the Joint Chiefs of Staff.
October 4, 1957	The Soviet Union launches *Sputnik*, the world's first artificial space satellite.
January 31, 1958	*Explorer I*, the first U.S. satellite to go into orbit, is launched by a Jupiter C rocket from Cape Canaveral, Florida.
February 27, 1958	Missile Director William M. Holaday approves the U.S. Air Force's Minuteman Project, a program for building 5,000-mile-range solid-fuel ballistic missiles launched from underground installations.
April 28, 1958	After an in-flight explosion, 1st Lieutenant James Obenauf notices an unconscious crewmember. Instead of ejecting, Obenauf pilots the B-47 to a safe landing at Dyess Air Force Base, Texas. He later receives the Distinguished Flying Cross for his heroism.

December 18, 1958	The U.S. Air Force places in orbit the first artificial communications satellite using the four-ton Atlas launcher. The next day, the satellite broadcasts a taped recording of President Dwight D. Eisenhower's Christmas message.
January 7, 1959	A 1959 U.S. Air Force study of UFOs reveals fewer than 1 percent could be classified as unknown.
February 6, 1959	The U.S. Air Force successfully launches the first Titan I ICBM. With a range of 5,500 nautical miles, the two-stage liquid-fueled missile will be deployed in underground silos but has to be raised to the surface before launch.
February 12, 1959	Strategic Air Command retires its last B-36 Peacemaker to become an all-jet bomber force.
March 20, 1959	The site in Cheyenne Mountain, Colorado, is approved as the location for NORAD.
May 28, 1959	Monkeys Able and Baker are recovered alive from the Atlantic Ocean near Antigua Island after a flight to an altitude of 300 miles in the nose cone of a Jupiter missile launched from Cape Canaveral.
June 3, 1959	The U.S. Air Force Academy graduates the first class of 207 graduates; 205 receive commissions as regular officers in the U.S. Air Force.
February 2, 1960	The Air Force Titan Missile enters the advanced flight phase.
April 13, 1960	Major R. M. White becomes the first U.S. Air Force pilot to fly the X-15 rocket research aircraft.
August 1, 1960	Strategic Air Command's 43rd Bombardment Wing at Carswell Air Force Base, Texas, accepts the first operational B-58 Hustler medium bomber. The first supersonic bomber, the delta-wing aircraft, flies at twice the speed of sound and can be refueled in-flight.
August 16, 1960	Captain Joseph W. Kittinger Jr. parachutes from 102,000 feet—a world record.

August 19, 1960	Piloting a C-119, Captain Harold F. Mitchell retrieves the Discoverer XIV reentry capsule in midair. This is the first successful aerial recovery of a returning space capsule.
August 30, 1960	The first Atlas intercontinental ballistic missile squadron becomes fully operational.
	With six Atlas missiles ready to launch, the 564th Strategic Missile Squadron at F. E. Warren Air Force Base, Wyoming, becomes the first fully operational ICBM squadron.
November 4, 1960	The U.S. Air Force reveals the use of a converted C-97 as an airborne command post.
January 31, 1961	A Redstone booster carrying Ham, a chimpanzee, in a Mercury space capsule launches from Cape Canaveral, Florida, on an 18-minute, 420-mile flight. Ham performs well during the flight, apparently suffering no ill-effects.
February 1, 1961	A Minuteman ICBM launches for the first time at Cape Canaveral in a major test. Under full guidance, the solid-fueled missile travels 4,600 miles, hitting the target area.
February 3, 1961	Strategic Air Command initiates the Looking Glass airborne command post. Maintaining continuous 24-hour coverage in shifts, Looking Glass aircraft are equipped to communicate with the Joint Chiefs of Staff, any Strategic Air Command base, or any Strategic Air Command aircraft.
May 26, 1961	A B-58 Hustler supersonic bomber from the 43rd Bombardment Wing sets a record, flying from New York to Paris in 3 hours, 19 minutes, 41 seconds at an average speed of 1,302 miles per hour.
June 9, 1961	Delivery of the first C-135 Stratolifter jet cargo aircraft marks the beginning of modernization of Military Air Transport Service's former all-propeller-driven fleet.

July 1, 1961	The North American Air Defense Command begins operation of a space detection and tracking system designed to provide electronic cataloging of man-made space objects.
July 15, 1961	The first Minuteman I missile wing is activated at Malmstrom Air Force Base, Montana.
July 21, 1961	America's second Project Mercury astronaut, Captain Virgil I. Grissom, attains an altitude of 118 miles and flies 5,310 miles per hour in a 303-mile suborbital space flight from Cape Canaveral in the *Liberty Bell* 7 capsule.
November 9, 1961	Major Robert M. White attains a top speed of 4,093 miles per hour in an X-15 hypersonic rocket plane while flying at full throttle at an altitude of 101,600 feet.
November 17, 1961	The U.S. Air Force successfully launches the first Minuteman intercontinental missile from an underground silo at Cape Canaveral, Florida. It flies 3,000 miles down the Atlantic Missile Range.
December 1, 1961	The first Minuteman Missile Squadron, the 10th Strategic Missile Squadron, is activated at Malmstrom Air Force Base, Montana.
March 5, 1962	The crew of a B-58 Hustler assigned to the 43rd Bombardment Wing sets three speed records in a round-trip flight between New York City and Los Angeles, California. The bomber makes the trip in 4 hours, 41 minutes, 15 seconds, averaging 1,044.46 miles per hour.
April 18, 1962	At Lowry Air Force Base, Colorado, Strategic Air Command declares operational the U.S. Air Force's first Titan I squadron, the 724th Strategic Missile Squadron, equipped with nine missiles, the first placed in hardened, underground installations.
August 7, 1963	The Lockheed YF-12 makes its maiden flight.

November 20, 1963	The U.S. Air Force accepts the first two F-4C jet fighters.
December 17, 1963	The U.S. Air Force's new C-141A Starlifter jet cargo transport flies for the first time at Dobbins Air Force Base, Georgia. Capable of crossing any ocean nonstop at more than 500 miles per hour, the Starlifter can transport 154 troops. It can carry a 70,000-pound payload.
May 11, 1964	The XB-70 Valkyrie, built by North American Aviation, rolls out at Palmdale, California. Designed to fly at three times the speed of sound and at altitudes above 70,000 feet, the 275-ton aircraft measures 185 feet in length and 105 feet in wingspan.
September 21, 1964	The XB-70 experimental aircraft makes its first flight. At Palmdale, California, the B-70A Valkyrie flies for the first time.
December 15, 1964	The first U.S. Air Force gunship, the AC-47, enters combat in Vietnam.
December 21, 1964	An F-111A (later named Aardvark) variable-sweep-wing fighter makes a successful maiden flight at Carswell Air Force Base, Texas.
December 22, 1964	The new U.S. Air Force strategic reconnaissance plane, the SR-71 "Blackbird," in its first flight at Palmdale, exceeds an altitude of 45,000 feet and a speed of 1,000 miles per hour. The U.S. Air Force team that tested the SR-71 will receive the Mackay Trophy.
January 1, 1965	The U.S. Air Force's first SR-71 unit, the 4200th Strategic Reconnaissance Wing, activates at Beale Air Force Base, California.
February 8, 1965	The U.S. Air Force performs its first retaliatory air strike in North Vietnam. A North American F-100 Super Sabre flies cover for attacking South Vietnamese fighter aircraft, suppressing ground fire in the target area.

APPENDIX C: AIR FORCE MILESTONES

March 2, 1965	Operation Rolling Thunder begins over North Vietnam.
March 5, 1965	The U.S. Air Force's F-111 completes its first supersonic flight at Fort Worth, Texas.
April 23, 1965	The first operational Lockheed C-141 Starlifter aircraft is delivered to Travis Air Force Base, California.
June 18, 1965	Strategic Air Command B-52s are used for the first time in Vietnam when 28 aircraft, flying from Guam, strike Vietcong targets near Saigon.
July 10, 1965	Scoring the first U.S. Air Force air-to-air combat victory in Southeast Asia, two F-4C aircrews of the 45th Tactical Fighter Squadron down two Communist MiG-17 jet fighters over North Vietnam.
January 1, 1966	Military Air Transport Service is redesignated Military Airlift Command. Air Rescue Service becomes Aerospace Rescue and Recovery Service. Air Photographic and Charting Service is renamed Aerospace Audio-Visual Service.
July 9, 1966	The F-111 Aardvark variable-sweep-wing fighter-bomber flies for the first time at Mach 2.5—about 1,800 miles per hour. Officials call the performance the highlight of the F-111 flight-test development program.
August 25, 1966	The first class of German air force student pilots enters training at Sheppard Air Force Base, Texas. The school will provide 212 pilots per year with training similar to that received by U.S. Air Force pilots.
October 7, 1966	The U.S. Air Force selects the University of Colorado to conduct independent investigations into unidentified flying object reports.
February 6, 1967	The North American Aerospace Defense Command's Space Defense Center moves into Cheyenne Mountain, Colorado, completing the movement of all units into the hardened, underground facility.

March 15, 1967	The Sikorsky HH-53B, the largest and fastest helicopter in U.S. Air Force inventory, makes its first flight. It is slated for Aerospace Rescue and Recovery operations in Southeast Asia.
April 3, 1967	Paul W. Airey becomes the first chief master sergeant of the U.S. Air Force.
February 28, 1968	The last of 284 C-141 Starlifter cargo aircraft purchased by the U.S. Air Force is delivered to Tinker Air Force Base, Oklahoma.
June 17, 1968	The first C-9 Nightingale aeromedical evacuation aircraft ordered by Military Airlift Command for airlift of patients within the United States is rolled out at McDonnell Douglas Corporation, Long Beach, California.
June 30, 1968	The Lockheed C-5 Galaxy, the U.S. Air Force's newest and largest aircraft, makes its first flight.
February 24, 1969	An enemy mortar shell strikes an AC-47 gunship on which Airman 1st Class John L. Levitow serves. Although seriously wounded, he ejects a smoking flare and becomes the first enlisted airman to win the Medal of Honor in Vietnam.
June 4, 1969	The Thunderbirds, the U.S. Air Force Air Demonstration Squadron, hold their first exhibition using the F-4 Phantom aircraft.
December 17, 1969	The U.S. Air Force concludes the UFO reporting and investigating project designated "Blue Book."
December 23, 1969	McDonnell Douglas is named prime contractor for the U.S. Air Force's F-15 Eagle air-superiority fighter. With a top speed of 920 miles per hour, the heavily armed fighter will have a ferry range of 3,450 nautical miles.
May 5, 1970	Air Force Reserve Officer Training Corps expands to include women after test programs at Ohio State, Drake, East Carolina, and Auburn universities prove successful.

June 2, 1970	The U.S. Air Force Southern Command begins massive disaster relief operations for victims of a devastating earthquake in Peru that killed 70,000 and left 800,000 homeless. Crews airlift 1.5 million pounds of cargo and 2,827 passengers.
June 19, 1970	Minuteman III missiles become operational.
October 21, 1970	The X-24A aerospace vehicle makes its first supersonic flight.
October 27, 1970	Doctors at Wilford Hall U.S. Air Force Medical Center, Lackland Air Force Base, Texas, develop a new device to save infants who are suffocating. Costing only about $1,000 and built from various standard hospital components, the device helps newborn babies breathe.
February 27, 1971	The U.S. Air Force launches Operation Haylift in response to urgent pleas from farmers in blizzard-swept Kansas and drops 35,000 bales (nearly 1 million pounds) of hay for 275,000 cattle stranded in deep snow.
March 2, 1971	The U.S. Air Force introduces a policy permitting women who become pregnant to remain on active duty or to be discharged and return to duty within 12 months of discharge.
March 17, 1971	Jane Leslie Holley becomes the first woman commissioned through the Air Force Reserve Officer Training Corps program. She graduated from Auburn University, Alabama.
March 18, 1971	Captain Marcelite C. Jordon becomes the first woman aircraft maintenance officer after completing the Aircraft Maintenance Officer School.
April 7, 1971	Second Lieutenant Susanne M. Ocobock becomes the first woman civil engineer in the Air Force and is assigned to Kelly Air Force Base, Texas.

July 1, 1971	The Aerospace Defense Command turns over Selfridge Air Force Base, Michigan, to the Air National Guard. It is the first major active U.S. Air Force base to come under control of the Air Guard.
July 16, 1971	Jeanne M. Holm, director of Women in the Air Force, becomes the first woman promoted to brigadier general.
September 3, 1971	President Richard M. Nixon dedicates the new Air Force Museum.
April 1, 1972	Air Training Command activates the Community College of the Air Force at Randolph Air Force Base, Texas.
May 10, 1972	Operation Linebacker begins during the Vietnam War.
July 11, 1972	The U.S. Air Force launches a giant 962-foot-tall balloon system in support of NASA's Viking Project for landing an unmanned spacecraft on Mars in 1976.
October 13, 1972	Captain Jeffrey S. Feinstein achieves ace status by shooting down his fifth MiG-21.
December 18, 1972	President Nixon directs the resumption of full-scale bombing and mining in North Vietnam, in an operation known as Linebacker II.
February 12, 1973	A U.S. Air Force C-141 lands in Hanoi to pick up the first returning POWs.
February 2, 1974	The YF-16 makes its first official flight.
December 23, 1974	The first flight of a B-1 Lancer aircraft is made from Palmdale, California, to Edwards Air Force Base, California.
January 13, 1975	The Secretary of the Air Force, Dr. John L. McLucas, selects the General Dynamics YF-16 prototype as the U.S. Air Force's air combat fighter, a low-cost, lightweight, highly maneuverable fighter aircraft.

April 10, 1975	The B-1 Lancer aircraft attains supersonic flight speed for the first time.
September 1, 1975	General Daniel "Chappie" James Jr. becomes the first African American officer to achieve four-star rank in the U.S. military.
January 9, 1976	The U.S. Air Force's first operational F-15 Eagle, the new air superiority fighter aircraft, arrives at 1st Tactical Fighter Wing, Langley Air Force Base, Virginia.
March 10, 1976	The first woman navigator candidates report to Mather Air Force Base, California, to begin undergraduate navigator training.
March 22, 1976	The first A-10 Thunderbolt is delivered to Davis-Monthan Air Force Base, Arizona, for operational test and evaluation.
June 28, 1976	The U.S. Air Force Academy becomes the first of the big three service academies to admit women cadets when it admits Joan Olsen.
July 27, 1976	An SR-71 flies at a speed of 2,092.29 miles per hour over a 1,000-kilometer course over Edwards Air Force Base, California. This flight sets three closed-circuit records: world absolute speed, world jet speed with 1,000-kilogram payload, and world jet speed without payload.
September 29, 1976	The first of two groups of 10 women pilot candidates enters undergraduate pilot training at Williams Air Force Base, Arizona—the first time since World War II that women could train to become pilots of military aircraft.
January 8, 1977	The first YC-141B (stretched C-141A Starlifter) rolls out of the Lockheed-Georgia Marietta plant. It is 23.3 feet longer than the original C-141A and capable of in-flight refueling.
May 2, 1977	First Lieutenant Christine E. Schott becomes the first woman undergraduate pilot training student to solo in the T-38 Talon.

August 3, 1977	Cadet First Class Edward A. Rice Jr. of Yellow Springs, Ohio, becomes the first African American commander of the Cadet Wing at the U.S. Air Force Academy.
September 2, 1977	The first class of women pilots graduates at Williams Air Force Base, Arizona.
October 12, 1977	The first class of five U.S. Air Force women navigators graduates, with three of the five assigned to Military Airlift Command aircrews.
March 23, 1978	Captain Sandra M. Scott, a KC-135 Stratotanker pilot, becomes the first woman tanker commander to perform alert duty for Strategic Air Command.
April 6, 1980	The stretched C-141B flies its first operational mission. An aircrew from the 443rd Military Airlift Wing flies it nonstop from Beale Air Force Base, California, to RAF Mildenhall, England, in 11 hours, 12 minutes, with only one aerial refueling.
May 2, 1980	Second Lieutenant Mary L. Wittick is the first woman to enter the Air Force undergraduate helicopter pilot training program in Class 81-05.
May 28, 1980	For the first time, 97 women are among those receiving commissions as second lieutenants in graduation ceremonies at the U.S. Air Force Academy.
June 18, 1981	The first flight of the F-117A Nighthawk occurs at Edwards Air Force Base, California.
August 30, 1982	The F-5G (later renamed the F-20) Tigershark makes its first flight at Edwards Air Force Base, California.
September 21, 1982	A B-52 Stratofortress of the 416th Bombardment Wing, Griffiss Air Force Base, New York, conducts the first air-launched cruise missile operational test.
December 3, 1983	The National Transonic Tunnel, a wind tunnel to test ultra-fast aircraft, is dedicated at Langley Air Force Base, Virginia.

January 28, 1984	The first F-16 Fighting Falcon is accepted by the U.S. Air Force Reserve at Hill Air Force Base, Utah.
May 25, 1984	A Military Airlift Command C-141 Starlifter transports the body of the Unknown Soldier of the Vietnam War for interment at Arlington National Cemetery.
December 1, 1984	The C-5A Galaxy enters service with the U.S. Air Force Reserve at Kelly Air Force Base, Texas.
January 4, 1985	Major Patricia M. Young becomes the first woman commander of an Air Force Space Command unit—Detachment 1, 20th Missile Warning Squadron.
July 7, 1985	The first operational B-1B Lancer is accepted by Strategic Air Command and the 96th Bombardment Wing at Dyess Air Force Base, Texas.
January 8, 1986	Military Airlift Command accepts delivery of its first C-5B Galaxy at Altus Air Force Base, Oklahoma.
March 25, 1986	For the first time, an all-woman crew, assigned to the 351st Strategic Missile Wing, Whiteman Air Force Base, Montana, stands Minuteman missile alert.
April 14, 1986	The U.S. forces launch Operation Eldorado Canyon, a retaliatory bombing raid in response to terrorist activities supported by Libyan leader Muammar Qadhafi.
September 24, 1987	The first-ever Thunderbirds show in Beijing, China, attracts an audience in excess of 20,000.
November 10, 1988	The U.S. Air Force reveals the F-117A Stealth fighter to the public for the first time. Manufactured by Lockheed, using radar-absorbent materials and a radical new design, the F-117A can evade radar detection.

June 10, 1989	Captain Jacqueline S. Parker becomes the first female pilot to graduate from the U.S. Air Force Test Pilot School.
July 6, 1989	President Bush presents the Presidential Medal of Freedom, the nation's highest civilian award, to General James H. Doolittle, U.S. Air Force, retired, at the White House. General Doolittle led the famous World War II raid on Tokyo.
July 17, 1989	The first flight of the B-2.
October 1, 1989	General Hansford T. Johnson, U.S. Air Force, becomes the first Air Force Academy graduate to become a four-star general.
December 14, 1989	For the first time, Military Airlift Command allows women to serve as crew members on C-130 and C-141 airdrop missions. This marks the entry of women into combat crew roles.
December 20, 1989	During Operation Just Cause, Military Airlift Command units transport 9,500 airborne troops from Pope Air Force Base, North Carolina, to Panama in fewer than 36 hours, making it the largest night-combat airdrop since the Normandy invasion of 1944.
January 31, 1990	After more than 11 years, the Air National Guard's rotational deployments to defend the Panama Canal, known as Operation Coronet Cove, closes. The Air National Guard flew more than 13,000 sorties, totaling 16,959 hours, since the operation began in 1979.
April 4, 1990	The U.S. Air Force adds to its inventory the last of 60 official KC-10A Extender tanker/cargo aircraft built by McDonnell Douglas.
July 12, 1990	The U.S. Air Force accepts delivery of the last of 59 Lockheed F-117A Stealth fighter-bombers.

August to December 1990	Air Force Space Command establishes the first space system infrastructure to directly support a military conflict. The satellite systems will relay communications, provide meteorological data, and detect short-range missile launches.
August 7, 1990	Operation Desert Shield begins in response to Iraq's August 2 invasion of Kuwait. The operation's immediate objective is to protect Saudi Arabia from Iraqi aggression and build allied military strength.
August 9, 1990	The Alaskan Air Command is redesignated as the 11th Air Force and assigned to Pacific Air Forces.
August 17, 1990	President Bush activates the Civil Reserve Air Fleet for the first time since it was authorized in 1952. The activation increases airlift availability for the Middle East.
August 23, 1990	The 89th Military Airlift Wing receives the first of two Boeing VC-25A presidential transport aircraft at Andrews Air Force Base, Maryland. The VC-25A is a modified 747-200B commercial transport that replaces the VC-137C Air Force One.
August 29, 1990	An Air Force C-5, carrying supplies destined for the Gulf theater, crashes on take-off from Ramstein Air Base, Germany. Thirteen persons are killed and four are injured.
January 17, 1991	Strikes by B-52Gs and F-117As open the Gulf War. B-52G Stratofortress crews from the 2nd Bomb Wing of the 8th Air Force fly from Barksdale Air Force Base, Louisiana, to Iraq; launch 35 cruise missiles; and return to Barksdale. This event marks the longest bombing mission in history. Constituting less than 2.5 percent of all coalition aircraft, F-117A Stealth fighter-bomber crews attack more than 31 percent of Iraqi strategic targets during the first day of the Gulf War.

Captain Jon K. "J. B." Kelk, a 58th Tactical Fighter Squadron F-15C pilot assigned to the 33d Tactical Fighter Wing (Provisional), shoots down a MiG-29 with an AIM-7 missile at 0310L in the vicinity of Mudaysis, Iraq.

January 17 to February 28, 1991	In 42 days of combat, 16 U.S. Air Force Reserve C-130s fly more than 3,200 combat sorties against Iraq. Air Force Reserve A-10s fly more than 1,000 combat sorties against enemy targets.
January 27, 1991	Coalition aircraft attain air supremacy in the Gulf War after 10 days of aerial combat.
February 6, 1991	Reserve Captain Robert R. Swain of the 706th Tactical Fighter Squadron scores the first-ever A-10 Warthog air-to-air kill by shooting down an Iraqi helicopter.
February 28, 1991	The Gulf War ends at 8 A.M. with a coalition-declared cease-fire. Overall, during the entire Gulf air war, the F-117A Stealth fighter-bombers have flown only 2 percent of the combat sorties but have attacked 40 percent of Iraqi strategic targets.
March 8, 1991	The first Martin Marietta Titan IV propelled by a heavy-lift space booster is launched from Vandenberg Air Force Base, California. Augmenting the space shuttle, the Titan IV has two upper-stage options that enable it to carry several critical military payloads.
April 18, 1991	The U.S. Air Force completes the first successful flight test of the Martin Marietta/Boeing ICBM (small version). The flight trajectory is 4,000 miles from Vandenberg Air Force Base, California, to the Pacific Island target area at the Kwajalein Missile Range.
September 15, 1991	A C-17A makes its first flight from Long Beach, California, to Edwards Air Force Base, California. Capable of delivering outsized cargo in a tactical

environment, the Globemaster III can operate from the same austere airfields as the C-130.

November 26, 1991 The lowering of the American flag at Clark Air Base, Philippines, signals the closing of the largest overseas U.S. Air Force base in the world as well as the end of more than 90 years of U.S. presence there.

January 17, 1992 In a move to modernize its fleet of training aircraft, the Air Force accepts the first production model T-1A Jayhawk.

January 30, 1992 U.S. Air Force Space Command assumes control of Defense Department satellites and the operation and management of the Air Force Satellite Control Network.

February 10 to 26, 1992 Provide Hope I, a humanitarian airlift operation, delivers thousands of tons of food and medical supplies to the Commonwealth of Independent States, former republics of the USSR. The U.S. Air Force flies 65 missions in support of the operation.

February 29, 1992 Operation Provide Hope II begins. Like Provide Hope I, it transports American food and medical supplies to the former USSR. The U.S. Air Force flies in supplies, while the U.S. Navy and U.S. Army transport more cargo by sea and land.

March 24, 1992 The last U.S. Air Force fighter aircraft to be stationed in Spain departs, ending a 26-year span of service in that country.

June 1, 1992 The U.S. Air Force inactivates Strategic Air Command, Tactical Air Command, and Military Airlift Command. It also activates Air Combat Command and Air Mobility Command, comprising most of the resources of the inactivated commands.

July 1, 1992 Continuing reorganization, the U.S. Air Force inactivates Air Force Logistics Command and Air Force Systems Command, replacing them with the Air Force Materiel Command.

July 3, 1992	The U.S. European Command launches Operation Provide Promise to provide relief flights to Bosnia-Herzegovina. Eventually, the U.S. Air Force delivers tens of thousands of tons of food, medical supplies, and other humanitarian cargo to Bosnia.
December 15, 1992	England Air Force Base, Louisiana; Eaker Air Force Base, Arkansas; and George Air Force Base, California, close.
January 13, 1993	U.S. Air Force Major Susan Helms, a member of the space shuttle *Endeavour* crew, becomes the first U.S. military woman in space.
February 19, 1993	The 64th Flying Training Wing launches the first student sortie in the new T-1A Jayhawk trainer aircraft.
February 28, 1993	The 435th Airlift Wing begins the first Provide Promise airdrop missions over parts of eastern Bosnia, a haven for refugees who had fled their villages in the face of advancing Serb forces.
March 31, 1993	Myrtle Beach Air Force Base, South Carolina, closes, and flying operations cease at MacDill Air Force Base, Florida.
June 17, 1993	Lieutenant Colonel Patricia Fornes assumes command of the 740th Missile Squadron at Minot Air Force Base, North Dakota. She is the first woman commander of a combat missile squadron.
June 30, 1993	Wurtsmith Air Force Base, Michigan, closes after being an active military installation since 1924.
July 1, 1993	The 20th Air Force, which is responsible for day-to-day operation of the nation's ICBM force, transfers from Air Combat Command to Air Force Space Command. Air Training Command is redesignated the Air Education and Training Command, to which Air University, now ceasing to be a major command, is assigned. Air Combat Command transfers Vandenberg Air Force Base, California,

	to U.S. Air Force Space Command, which activates the 14th Air Force to perform missile warning, space surveillance, and launch and satellite control.
August 6, 1993	Dr. Sheila E. Widnall is sworn in as Secretary of the Air Force, becoming the first woman armed services secretary.
September 27, 1993	General James H. Doolittle, who led the first air raid on Tokyo and commanded the 8th Air Force during World War II, dies at the age of 96.
September 30, 1993	Chanute Air Force Base, Illinois; Mather Air Force Base, California; Williams Air Force Base, Arizona; Bergstrom and Carswell Air Force Bases, Texas, close. Additionally, U.S. Air Forces in Europe turn over RAF Bentwaters to the British.
October 8, 1993	Operation Provide Promise, the airlift of humanitarian relief supplies to Bosnia, surpasses in duration (but not in tonnage or missions) the Berlin Airlift, becoming the longest sustained relief operation in U.S. Air Force history.
December 17, 1993	The first B-2 Spirit bomber arrives at Whiteman Air Force Base, Montana. The B-2 is the first "stealth" heavy bomber.
January 4, 1994	A C-130 Hercules aircraft squadron composed of Air Force Reserve and Air National Guard personnel joins Operation Provide Promise to deliver relief supplies to Bosnia. It is called "Delta Squadron" and operates from Rhein-Main Air Base, Germany.
January 13, 1994	The final F-15 Eagle of the 32nd Fighter Group departs Soesterberg Air Base, ending 40 years of U.S. Air Force operations in the Netherlands.
January 30, 1994	The U.S. Air Force inactivates the 717th Air Base Squadron and closes Ankara Air Base, Turkey.

February 10, 1994	Lieutenant Jeannie Flynn, the first woman selected for U.S. Air Force combat pilot training, completes training in an F-15E Eagle.
May 6, 1994	First Lieutenant Leslie DeAnn Crosby graduates from the Air National Guard's F-16 Fighting Falcon training course in Tucson, Arizona, becoming the first U.S. Air Force Reserve woman fighter pilot.
June 30, 1994	U.S. Air Forces in Europe ends its presence in Berlin, 46 years after the beginning of the Berlin Airlift, with the inactivation of Detachment 1, 435th Airlift Wing.
September 29 and 30, 1994	U.S. Air Forces in Europe vacates Soesterberg Air Base, the Netherlands, and RAF Upper Heyford, United Kingdom, marking further reduction of American air bases in Europe after the Cold War.
September 30, 1994	Grissom Air Force Base, Indiana; Loring Air Force Base, Maine; Lowry Air Force Base, Colorado; Richards-Gebaur Air Force Base, Montana; and Rickenbacker Air National Guard Base, Ohio, close.
January 17, 1995	Air Mobility Command declares the 17th Airlift Squadron the first operational C-17 Globemaster III squadron. Simultaneously, General Robert L. Rutherford, commander of AMC, approves use of the new C-17 Globemaster III for routine missions.
February 3, 1995	U.S. Air Force Lieutenant Colonel Eileen M. Collins becomes the first woman space shuttle pilot.
June 27, 1995	Lockheed Martin begins assembling the first production model of the F-22—a stealthy, advanced tactical fighter that will eventually replace the F-15 Eagle.
September 1, 1995	The SR-71 Blackbird, the fastest aircraft in the world, returns to active service. It was removed from the U.S. Air Force inventory in 1990 when planners assumed that satellites could perform the strategic reconnaissance mission.

APPENDIX C: AIR FORCE MILESTONES

September 22, 1995   After 53 years of operation, Griffiss Air Force Base, New York, closes.

September 30, 1995   The 93rd Bomb Wing, the first B-52 wing in Strategic Air Command, inactivates after 47 years of continuous service. Its home base at Castle Air Force Base, California, also closes. Also closing after 41 years is Plattsburgh Air Force Base, New York.

November 1, 1995   Wright-Patterson Air Force Base, Ohio, hosts the presidents of Bosnia, Croatia, and Serbia for peace talks designed to end the war in the former Yugoslavia.

January 4, 1996   Operation Provide Promise, the longest sustained humanitarian airlift in history, officially ends, after delivering 160,536 metric tons of relief cargo since July 1992. The U.S. Air Force flew 4,597 of the 12,895 sorties.

February 14, 1996   The joint surveillance and target attack radar system E-8A flies its 50th mission in support of Operation Joint Endeavor. This surpasses the JSTARS record of 49 missions during Operation Desert Storm.

March 1996   The last F-4 Phantom aircraft in the active-duty Air Force goes into storage at Davis-Monthan Air Force Base, Arizona. The F-4 has served the Air Force for more than 30 years.

May 1, 1996   A German officer assumes command of a German tactical training center at Holloman Air Force Base, New Mexico. This is the first time a foreigner has commanded a unit at an Air Force base within the United States.

June 25, 1996   Terrorists bomb the Khobar Towers near King Abdul-Aziz Air Base in Saudi Arabia, killing 19 Air Force personnel and injuring some 300 other Americans.

September 3, 1996	The 11th Reconnaissance Squadron becomes the first Air Force unit to operate the Predator, an unmanned aerial vehicle designed for aerial surveillance and reconnaissance.
April 9, 1997	The Lockheed-Martin-Boeing F-22 Raptor stealth air superiority fighter, designed to secure air dominance for the United States in the twenty-first century, rolls out.
March 24, 1999	Operation Allied Force begins in Kosovo. The USAF portion is code-named Noble Anvil. The air war begins with 250 U.S. aircraft committed. Some 720 U.S. aircraft are eventually deployed, including 517 USAF types—40 A-10, 18 F-15C, 32 F-15E, 35 F-16CG, 64 F-16CJ, 25 F-117, 11 B-52, 5 B-1, 6 B-2, 151 KC-135, 24 KC-10, 25 various ISR, 38 Special Operations/CSAR/other, and 43 transports.
	The first shots of Allied Force were AGM-86C CALCM launches from six B-52s. There were 400 sorties flown the first night. Two MiG-29s are shot down by F-15Cs of the 493rd FS, 48th FW, RAF Lakenheath, England, and another MiG-29 is shot down by a Dutch F-16.
March 24 to June 9, 1999	The B-2 makes its combat debut during Operation Noble Anvil. Eventually, 49 B-2 combat sorties are launched from Whiteman Air Force Base, Montana. Of these, 45 sorties reach their target and 652 joint direct attack munitions and 4 GBU-37s are dropped. The round-trip missions last 28 to 32 hours; however, only 6 of the 9 available B-2s are used.
March 27, 1999	A combat search-and-rescue team rescues an F-117 Nighthawk pilot shot down during Operation Allied Force.

April 3, 1999	During Operation Allied Force, NATO missiles strike central Belgrade for the first time and destroy the Yugoslav and Serbian interior ministries.
May 4, 1999	An F-16CJ pilot of the 78th EFS scores the first F-16CJ victory of Allied Force when he shoots down a MiG-29.
May 23, 1999	NATO begins a bombing campaign of the Yugoslav electricity grid, creating a major disruption of power affecting many military-related activities and water supplies.
June 9, 1999	Operation Allied Force ends. More than 800 SAMs were fired at NATO aircraft, but only 1 F-117 and 1 F-16 were downed. Another F-117 suffered minor damage from an SA-3 that exploded nearby and two A-10s were damaged by anti-aircraft artillery fire. During the campaign, 35,219 sorties were flown, 16,587 nonprecision guided missiles and 6,728 precision guided missiles (23,315) were dropped.

Reprinted from the Office of the Secretary of Air Force (Public Affairs) and the Defense Technical Information Center.

INDEX

INDEX

H

"Halpro" (Halvorsen Project) mission, 77
Halvorsen, Colonel Harry, World War II, 50, 77
Hanes, Colonel Horace A.
  speed record, 50
  test pilot, 162
Hanover Street, 250
Hanoi Hilton, Vietnam War, 198-200
Hansell, Major Haywood S., World War II, 62
Harduvel, Janet, 249
Harmon, Lieutenant General Hubert R., first superintendent AFA, 7, 173
Harris, Lieutenant Harold, 41-43
Hartsfield, Major Henry W. (astronaut), 172
head-up display (HUD), 207
Hegenberger, Lieutenant Albert F.
  first blind flight, 48
  flight to Honolulu, 48
Heheman, First Lieutenant Robert, Desert Storm, 219
Helldivers, 245
Hennon, Captain Bill, World War II, 69
Herzig, Sig, *I Wanted Wings*, 246
Heyser, Major Richard S., Cuban missile crisis, 175
High Seas Fleet, U-boats, 26
Hiroshima, 133-135
Hitler, Adolf, 56
Ho Chi Minh Trail, 179
Holm, Colonel Jeanne M., first female general officer, 204
Hooe, Sergeant Ray, 50
Horner, Lieutenant General Charles A., Desert Storm, 210
hostage crisis, Iran, 202
Houghton, Lieutenant Robert, Vietnam War, 189
Hound Dog cruise missile, 165

HUD (head-up display), 207
Hudson, Lieutenant William G., Korean War, 155
humanitarian operations, 229-231
Humphreys, Brigadier General Frederick E., first certified pilot, 17-18
Hunter, Commander Frank O'Driscoll, World War II, 79
The Hunters, 247
Hussein, Saddam, Kuwait invasion, 209
Hwang, Captain Jeff, Bosnia, 223
hypersonics, 239

I

I Wanted Wings, 246
ICBM (intercontinental ballistic missile), 166-169
in-country war, Vietnam, 178-183
Independence, presidential plane, 235
intercontinental ballistic missile (ICBM), 166-169
intermediate-range Thor, 168
Iran, hostage crisis, 202
Iraq, Desert Storm, 208-212
  bombing campaign, 212-218
  end of war, 219-220
  no-fly zones, 218-219
Iron Eagle, 250
Irwin, Captain W. W., speed record, 50
Irwin, Major James B. (astronaut), 172

J

Jabara, Major James, 37
  Korean War ace, 157-158
JAG, 249
Jagdstaffeln (German aircraft), 35
Jagdwaffe, 101
James, Colonel Daniel "Chappie" Jr., Vietnam War, 181

X–Y–Z